JULIE H. HANSON

FIRE AND LIGHT

A Method of Painting for Artists Who Love Color

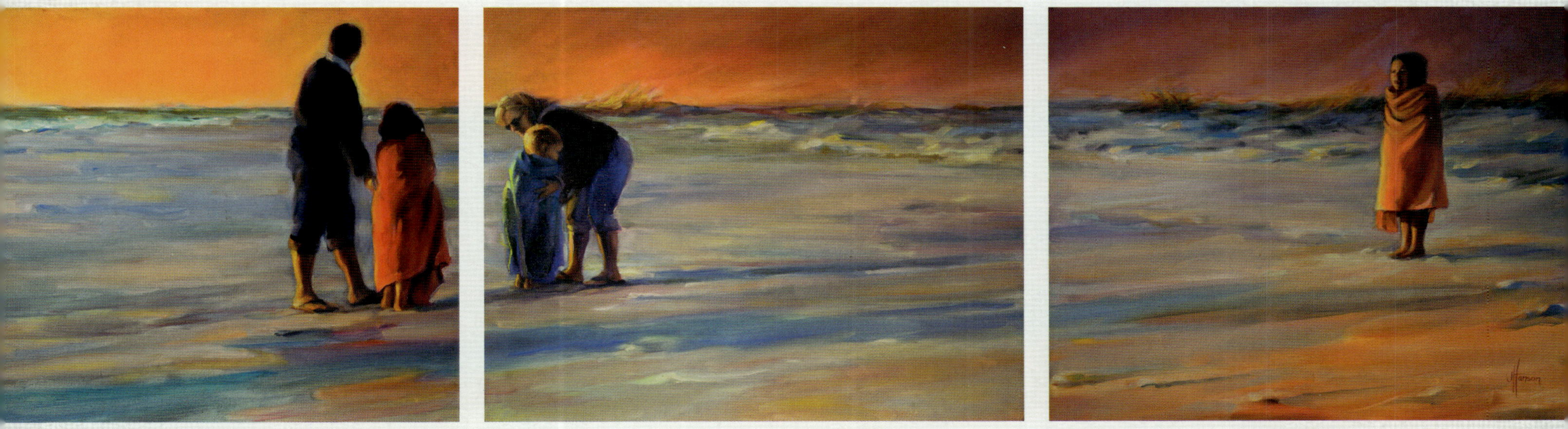

Schiffer Publishing Ltd

4880 Lower Valley Road · Atglen, PA 19310

Library of Congress Control Number: 2016952255

Cover artwork by Julie H. Hanson
Paintings by Julie H. Hanson unless otherwise noted.
Type set in Coronet/Garamond/Gothic
ISBN: 978-0-7643-5217-1
Printed in China
5 4 3 2

Published by Schiffer Publishing, Ltd.
4880 Lower Valley Road
Atglen, PA 19310
Phone: (610) 593-1777; Fax: (610) 593-2002
E-mail: Info@schifferbooks.com
Web: www.schifferbooks.com

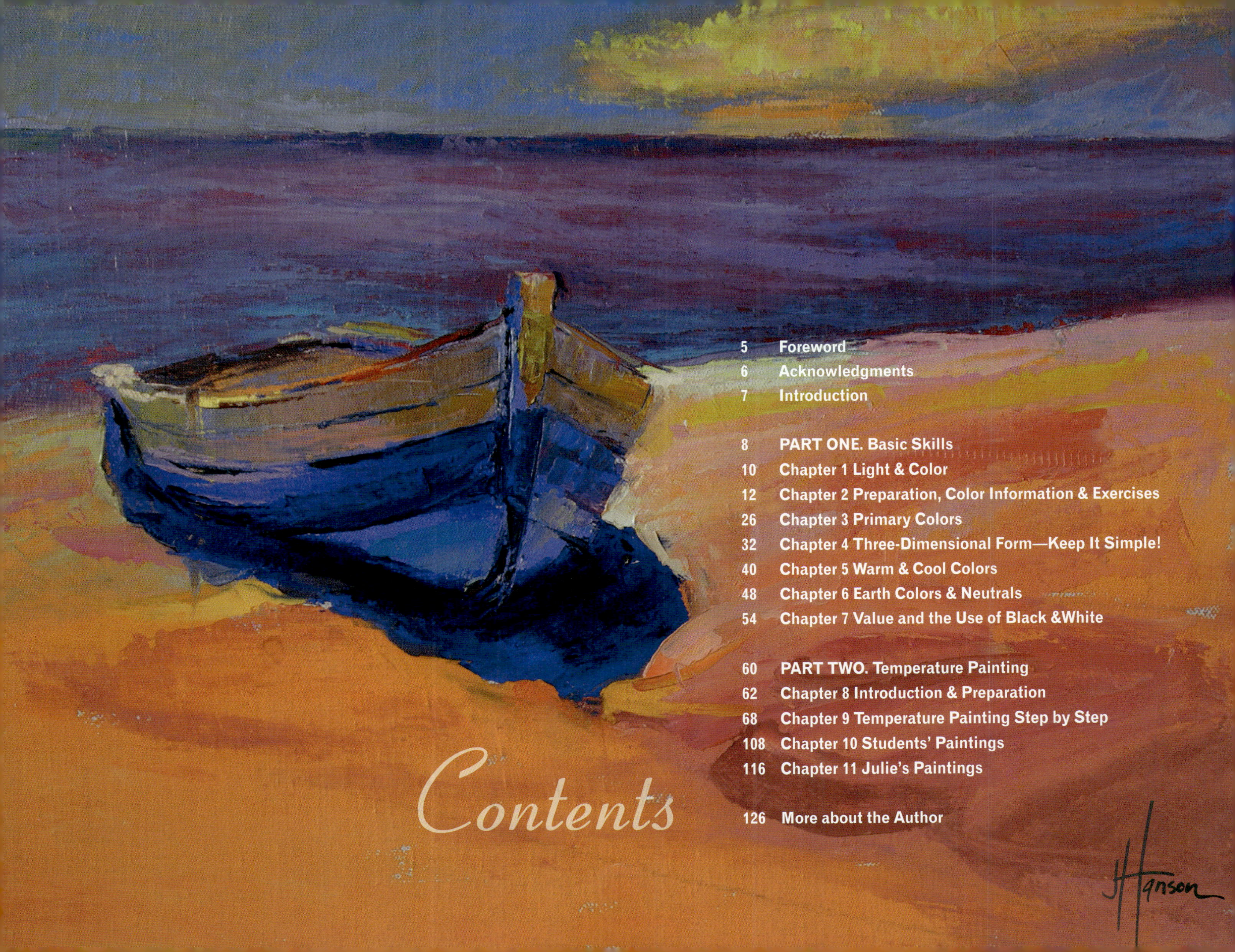

Contents

This book is dedicated to those artists and students looking to find their own unique voice. I am grateful, especially to my family and my husband, Bob, for supporting mine.

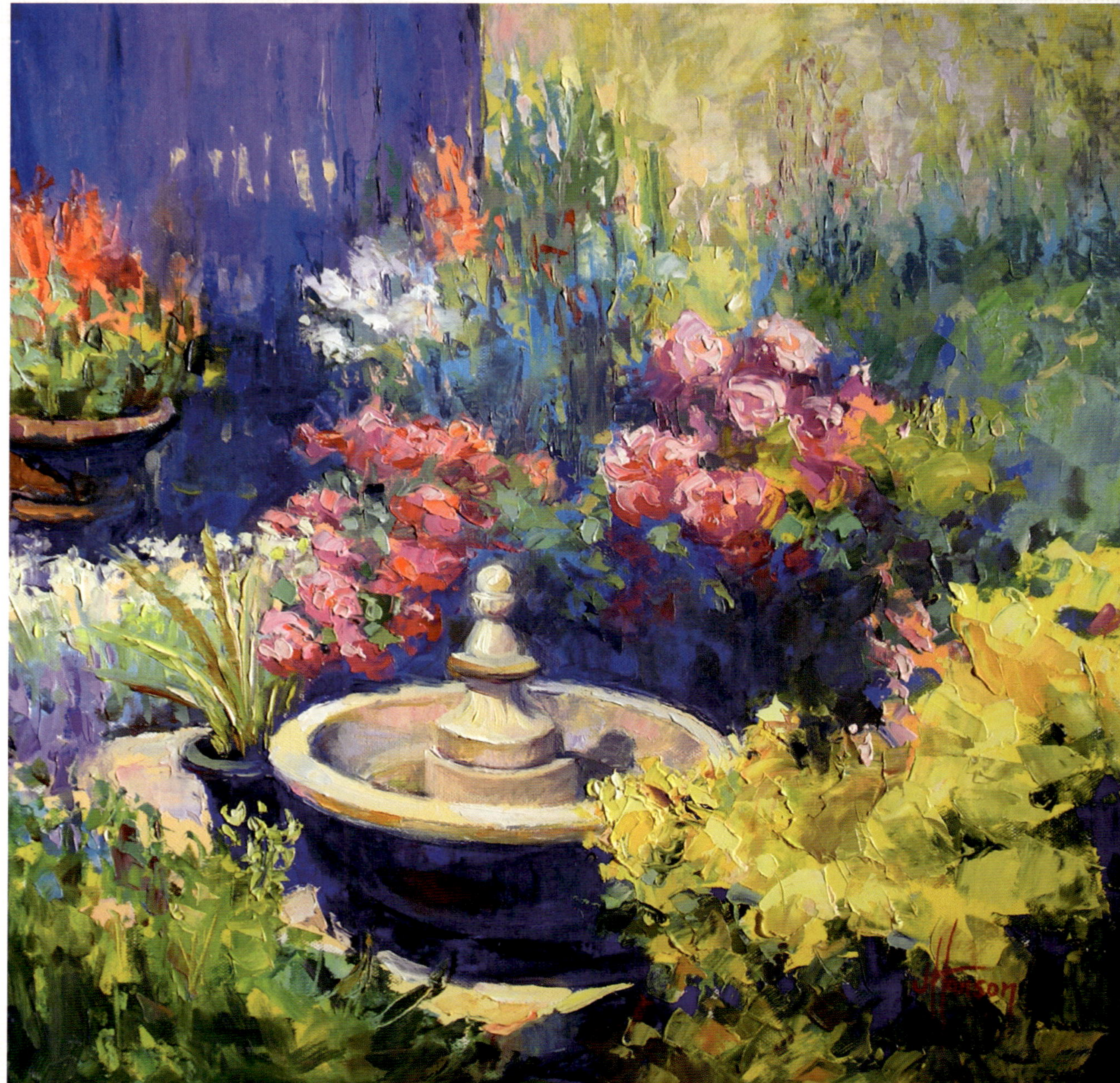

Garden Fountain by Julie Hanson, 2013.
Oil on canvas: 18" × 18".

Foreword

When I first came to Florida after retiring from teaching high school art, and after a long and successful career as a three-dimensional artist, I decided to try my hand at oil painting, a lifelong dream. As I believe it is important for a beginning painter to find a mentor who is an established artist and will give constructive criticism, I frequented local art galleries and art associations in search of painting that would speak to me. I had been painting on my own for a while, mostly self-taught through many books on the oil painting medium. When I finally came upon work by Julie Hanson, I knew I had found my mentor.

Her magic use of color with its glowing nuances appealed to me immediately. Somehow, that joyful, childlike quality we all are born with, but which becomes stifled as we grow up, survived in her work.

There are professional artists who are teachers and there are teachers who paint. Julie is extremely gifted at both, and one of her greatest strengths is her ability to communicate and share these skills with her students. She uses a creative approach in her teaching yet does not ignore the underlying principles of composition, value, and color. She has developed a unique method of working that can easily be utilized by the beginning and advanced student alike.

Through her classes and workshops, students from various parts of the country are improving their skills and becoming better artists. Proof of her success lies in the fact that many of her students have gone on to become successful artists themselves by learning from her style.

Someone once said that if you were ever to paint the perfect painting and were completely satisfied with it, you would never paint again. Artists at all levels of ability always seek to improve, as vision usually exceeds ability. Even famous artists struggled with this and looked to the masters for guidance.

Julie's technique will put you on a path to higher and higher achievement and satisfaction in your painting experience if you are willing to persevere with hard work, joy, enthusiasm, and love for your work. This book allows you to sit alongside an exceptionally talented painter as she unfolds the secrets of her unique and successful technique.

—Shirley Charron is an artist and the author of *Modern Pewter*, Van Nostrand-Reinhold, 1973.

Acknowledgments

I have so much gratitude for the wonderful people in my life who helped make this book a reality—from the early support from my parents, Len and Helen, who encouraged my choice to go to art school and follow wherever that would lead, to my students, years later, who encouraged me too. Thank you. I especially want to thank Jim Karell, whose contributions as the "idea guy" were invaluable, not to mention his skill with the camera, computer, and organization. He and Mary Sturz made the entire painting and book building process more fun than I ever imagined it could be! Thanks, guys, for your great sense of humor! Thank you, Mary, for your enthusiasm and willingness to do your homework! Thank you, Donna McIntyre, Dorothy Nichols, and Janice and Roger Koehn for letting me work on this book at your houses. It is hard to paint and write at home when you run a nonprofit cat rescue from there as well! Elizabeth Goodwill, I so appreciate your "can do" attitude. And thanks to so many of my students who have become my friends and who contributed their artwork for this book. There are too many of you to mention. Thank you, Jeanne Guertin-Potoff, for helping me proofread this book and giving me multiple English lessons in the process. Thank you, Shirley Charron, Ruth Colby, and Nancy Donnellan for your encouragement and support. As my husband Bob said, "We can do this," and we did.

Introduction

I have written this book because my students wanted to learn more about my method of painting and use of color. Early in my career, after studying sculpture, it was important for me to understand how color could best express three-dimensional form. That led to the realization that each color has a job to do, and so I started to look for the simplest and most effective way to use color to build form. I couldn't write this book without a section devoted to seeing and working with color in this way. After my first impressions in art school of trying to use a realist's palette of earth colors and practicing a tonal underpainting in the traditional way, I realized that I wanted color to be the most important feature of my paintings, not secondary to a value study in earth tones. This search is what has led to this book. In all of my many years of teaching, I see so many others looking to use color in a more contemporary and immediate way as well. This book is for you.

Part One describes the basics of using color to build form. Part Two introduces my method, which I call "temperature painting."

Downtown by Julie Hanson, 2010.
Oil on canvas: 12" × 16".

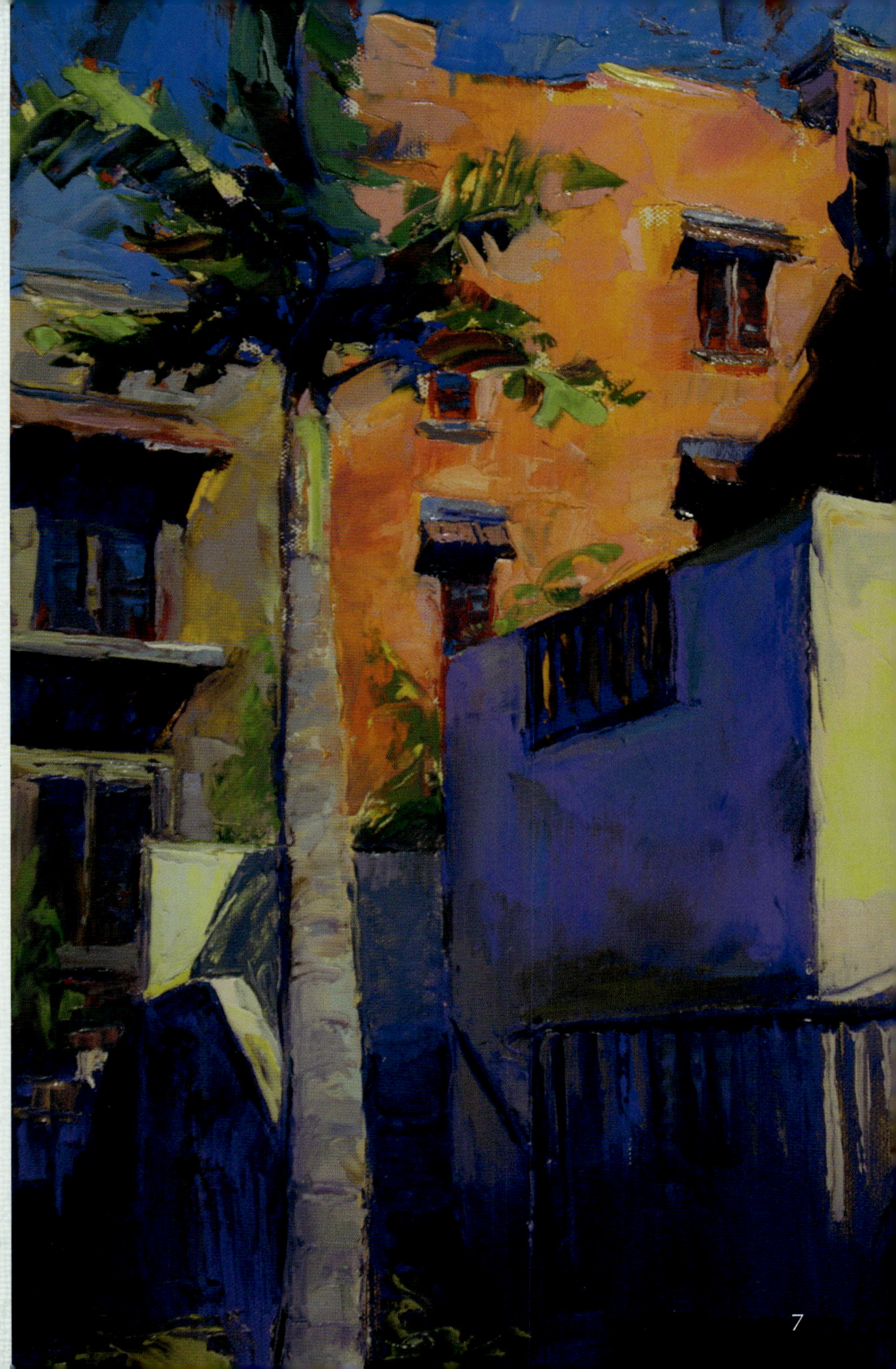

Part One

BASIC SKILLS

Part One covers supplies, basic skills, and exercises for the painter. It also provides background knowledge and training for artists in preparation for "temperature painting" as described in Part Two.

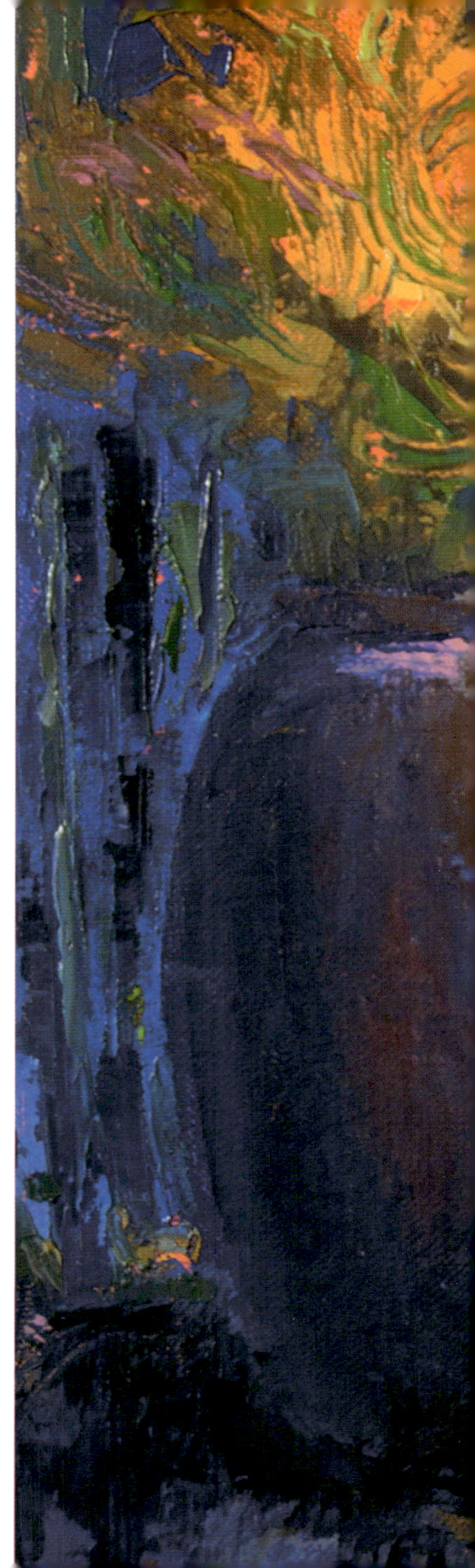

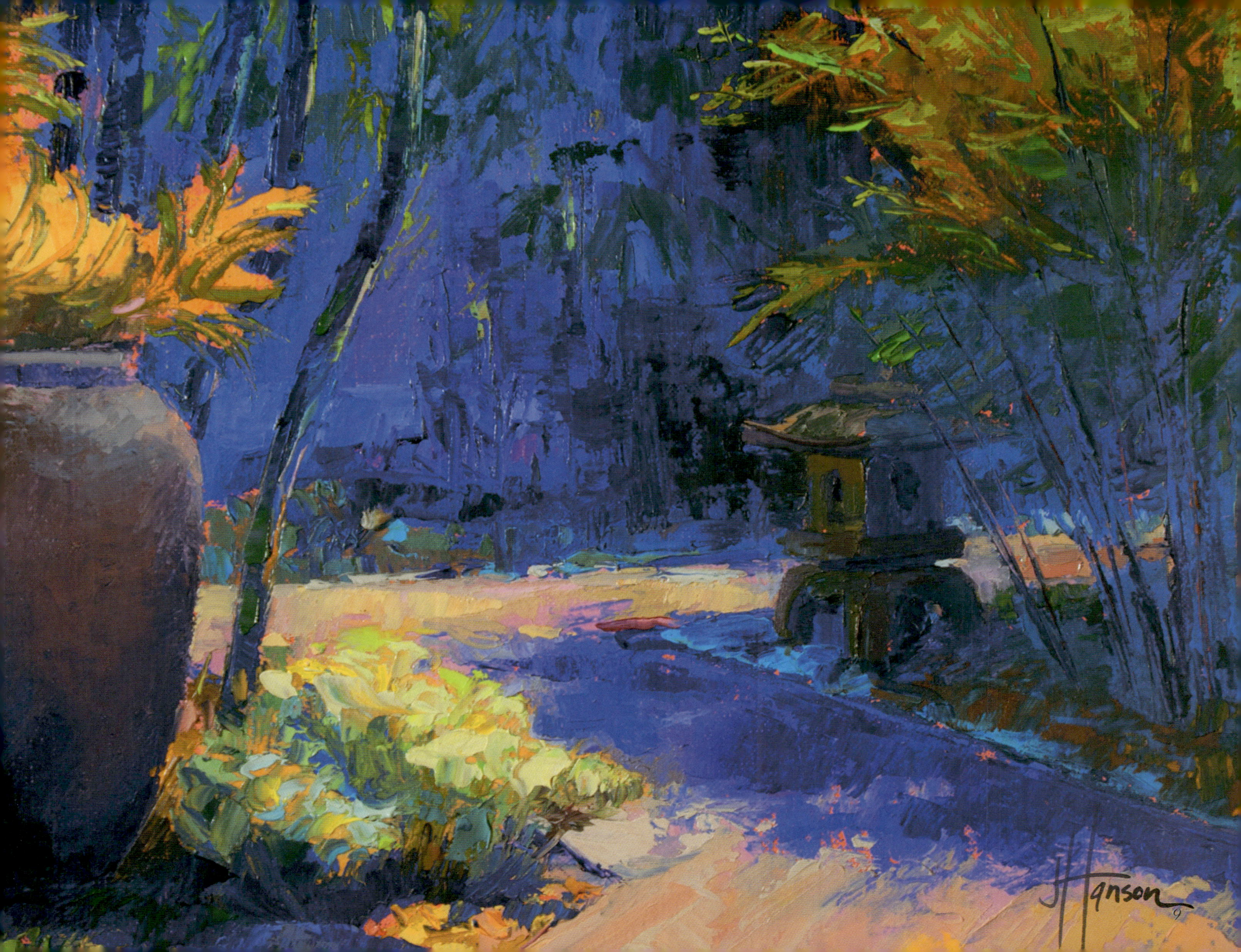
J Hanson

Chapter One

Light and Color

Let's start at the very beginning and look at the study of color with fresh eyes.

We could start by looking at the rainbow. You can clearly see each of the colors of the visible spectrum. Each color is clean and clear. It goes from red to orange to yellow to green to blue to indigo and then to violet. The infrared spectrum lies on the red side, while the ultraviolet spectrum is on the violet side. The wavelengths of these spectra are either too short or too long to be visible as color, leaving the seven colors of the rainbow as our color language.

Wouldn't it be nice if our paints were just like light, which produces the rainbow? Unfortunately, this is not how painters' pigments work. There are similarities, of course, because the color spectrum for the artist is the same as the rainbow.

Beginning color students are often surprised that the working properties of the paints in the tubes are not always what they expect. This is because each pigment used in the paints has its own working properties and is made from some element, natural or otherwise, that has a particular strength of color. For example, the sources could be as basic as sand for "earth" colors such as red oxide, yellow oxide, browns, and the like, whereas other colors, such as thalo and quinacridone, are manufactured especially to create vivid colors. While this is another fascinating subject, we will not go into detail here.

I think of these varied pigments as a family. Picture your family members at a reunion. There are the introverts (for example: lemon yellow), the extroverts (cadmiums), the ones who don't stop talking (thalo blue), and the quiet, shy ones who must be "brought out" (manganese blue hue). None of these pigments behave exactly the way light does. There are weak and strong pigments as well as opaque and transparent pigments. Beginning color students must practice with their "tools" (the pigments) to learn the behavior and strength of each tube of paint and each color ingredient. Until you have practiced, you will not achieve your expectations because you will not know how to control all of the personalities—in other words, how to bring out the best of each pigment.

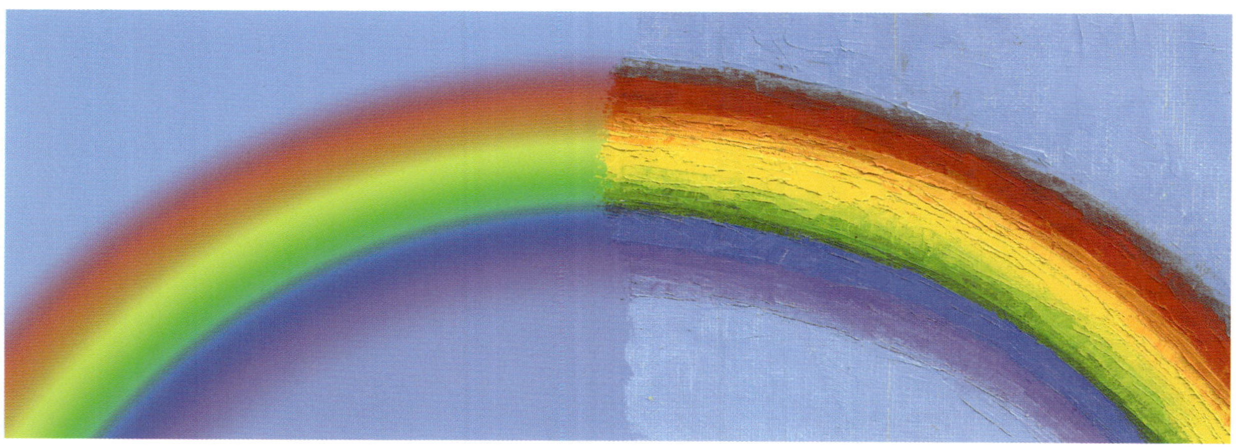

Rainbow of light and pigment.

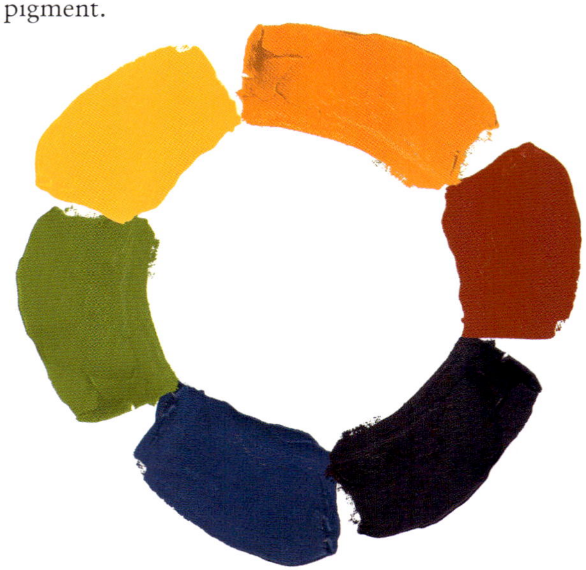

Colors of the rainbow.

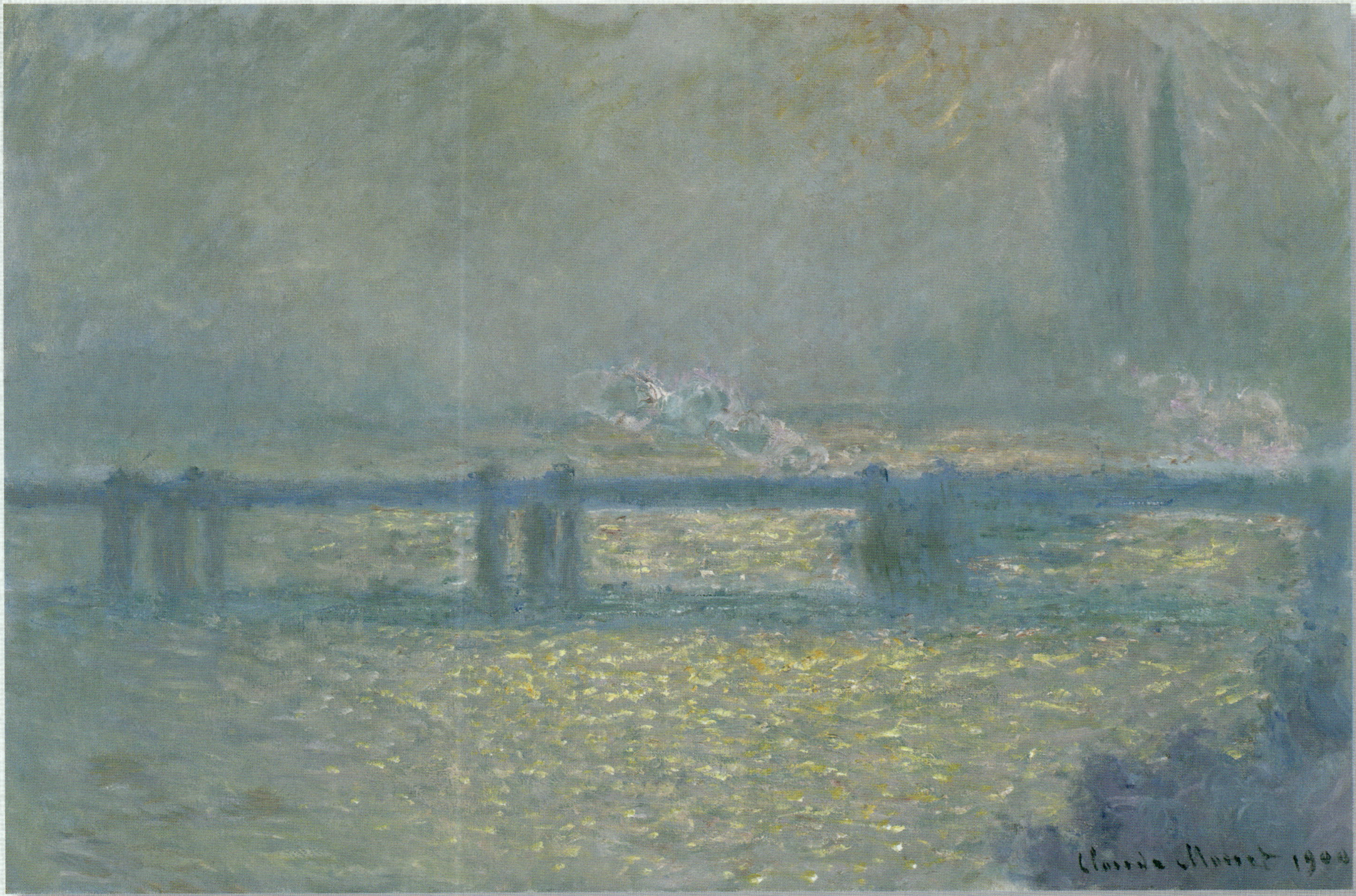

Charing Cross Bridge (overcast day)
by Claude Monet, 1900. Oil on canvas, 23.75" × 36".
Courtesy of Museum of Fine Arts, Boston

Notice how Monet uses color to capture the feeling of light.

Chapter Two

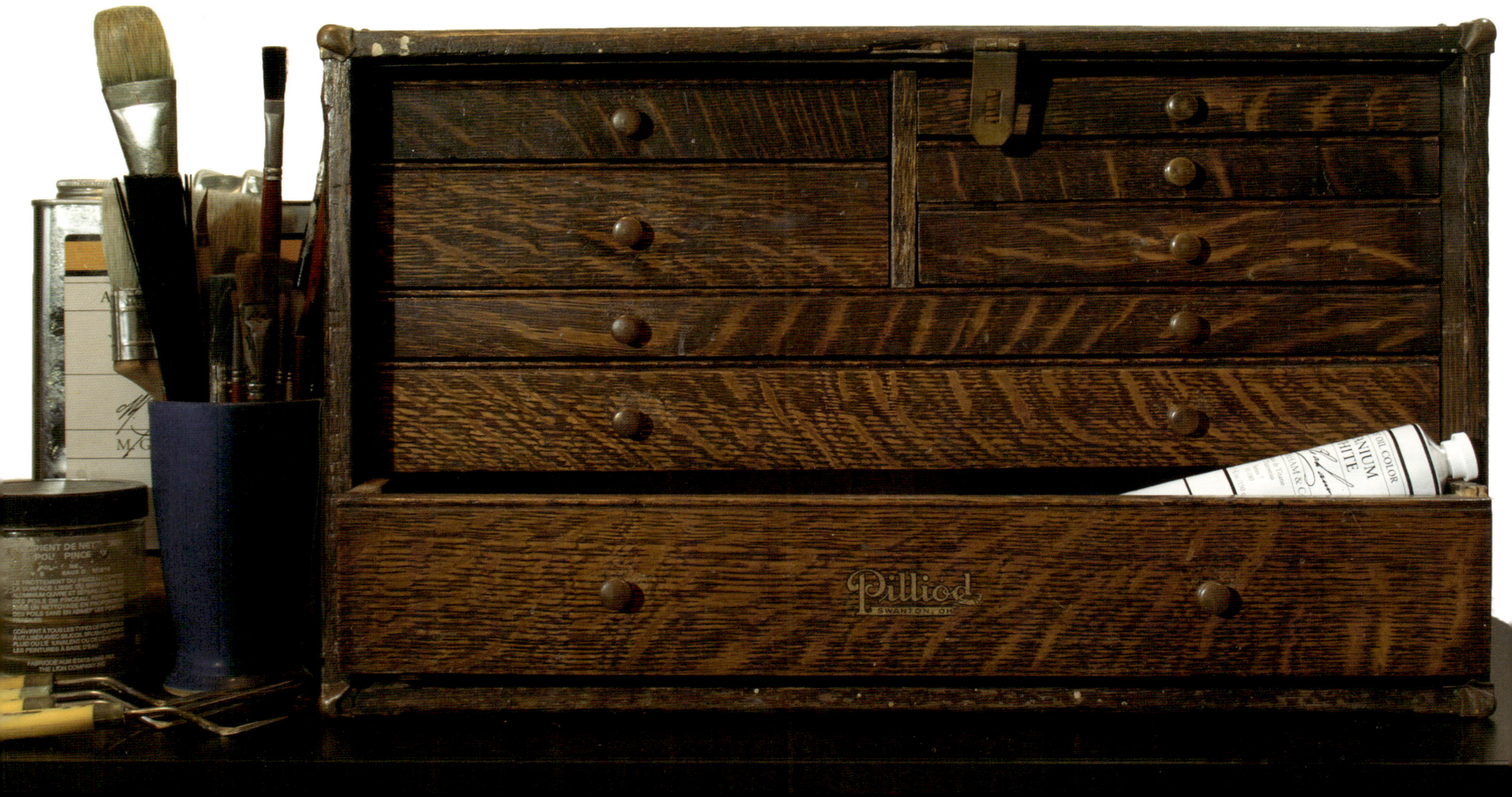

Preparation, Color Information & Exercises

My students always ask me for a supply list. What is the problem with this?

There is no standard paint color among manufacturers. For example, Grumbacher may call a color cadmium yellow medium. Winsor Newton can put cadmium in a yellow and also call it cadmium yellow medium. These colors can be different from Holbein's cadmium yellow medium. This creates no end of confusion for beginners. In addition, some pigments are used in only one medium, say, pastel or acrylic but not oil. There can be big differences across mediums in other ways as well.

In this chapter we will look at some of the different painting mediums and compare them briefly. Although this book is for any painter working in any medium, and the color principles are the same, there are subtle and not-so-subtle differences between mediums.

A painting medium is the substance you use to paint with. These mediums can be oil based, water based, or wax based. The most common color mediums include: colored pencil, conte, crayons, pastels, watercolor, acrylic, water-soluble oil, and oil. The most popular mediums and the suitability of their use with this method (temperature painting) will be discussed here briefly.

The term medium is also used to describe different types of additives you can mix with your paint colors to add gloss or take away shine. They can add texture or thickness and affect drying time. Each paint medium has its own "mediums" that you can add. They are not typically interchangeable.

Note: Many artists work with several mediums on one painting. This is called mixed media. You can put oil-based mediums on top of water-based ones, but you cannot put water-soluble mediums on top of oil-based ones. Oil dries with a harder finish, and the water-based mediums will probably not last as a top coat, because they will not "stick."

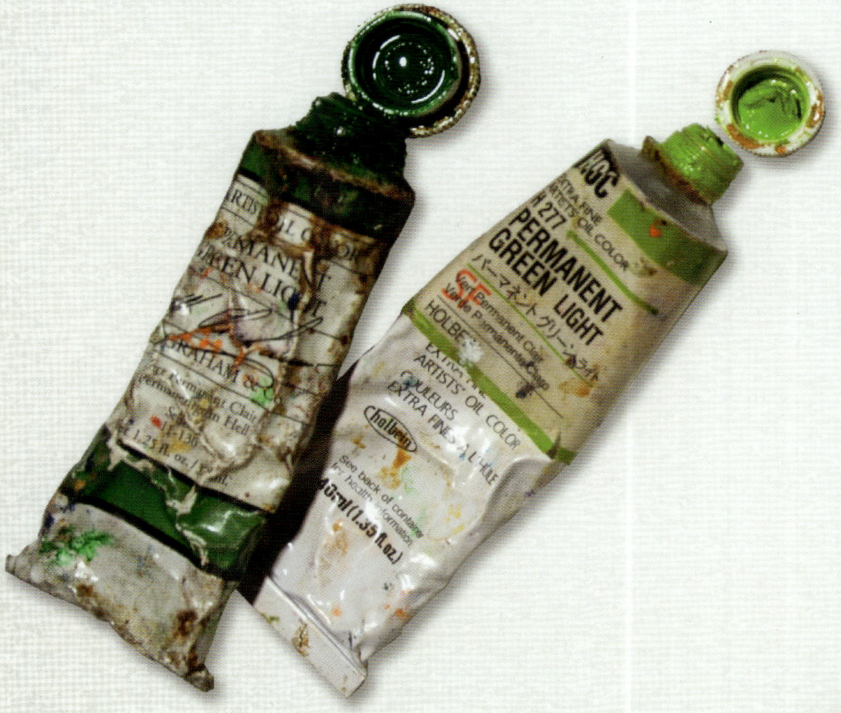

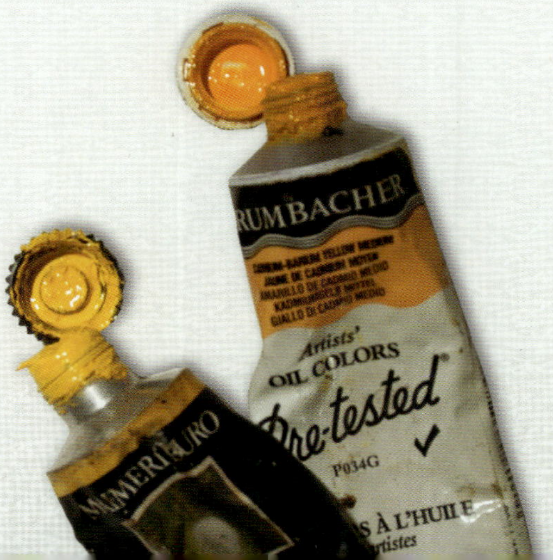

Permanent green light and cadmium yellow medium by different manufacturers.

PASTEL

Pastel is basically color pigment bound up in stick form. There are oil-based pastels and water-based pastels, and many different varieties and manufacturers. Water-soluble pastel can be thinned with water. Oil pastels need turpentine or something comparable to be thinned. Typically thinners aren't used at all. That is because the pastel is such a wonderful substance and is used directly on paper or textured paper made just for it. These papers are available with various coatings that "grab" the pastel and let you build up layers of color. If you choose to work with pastel, you will need to experiment with different types and colors of paper.

Pluses: The wonderful thing about working with pastel is that it is quick and easy, much like crayons and pencils, and relatively permanent when protected. It is lightweight (on paper) and the colors are vibrant, especially some of the newer pigments. There is a huge selection of color pigments available. They are all pre-mixed colors, ready-made!

Minuses: Finished work must be protected behind glass or Plexiglas. Working with pastel produces dust, which is harmful when inhaled. While there is an advantage to having premixed colors, the disadvantage is that you have to mix colors by layering on the surface. You are somewhat limited to mixtures if you have a limited supply of sticks. In the past there were fewer darks available and many of those darks were made with black. (Most impressionists do not use black.) Some wonderful darks have become available and now there are many more choices.

Pastel is an ideal choice for temperature painting if you have an adequate supply of similar value, different color sticks. Pastels are generally layered, and this method teaches you how to layer with beautiful, exciting color. For your choice of colors, refer to the supply lists for the other mediums and try to find a comparable color system, or refer to the pastel illustration in figure 1. For example, you will need a cool yellow (lemon) to pit against a warm yellow (cadmium). You will need a warm red (cadmium red light) to pit against a cool red (permanent rose, rose madder). You will need a cool blue (ultramarine) to pit against a warm blue (manganese, cerulean, or turquoise).

Combine new colors with the color collection you already have. Figure 1 shows some of the combinations I use. Note that each stick of color (hue) has its own distinct value. You must get several different sticks of varying values in the same color since you cannot mix them wet into wet (and therefore cannot change their value that way). This is very important so that you get a range of values in a range of colors, both warm and cool. So, put this on your Christmas list if you want to work in pastel!

There are a number of different color choices possible when working with the double primary palette. The goal is to have a warm and cool of each of the primaries. Look at your own paint supply and use what you have. The more contrast you pick between the two of the same primary, the more power you can get in your painting. However, the further they are from the pure color choice, the harder it will be to create the primary color by mixing the two choices. If this happens, you can always purchase the pure version of the color as well. For more explanation on how this palette works, see chapter 3.

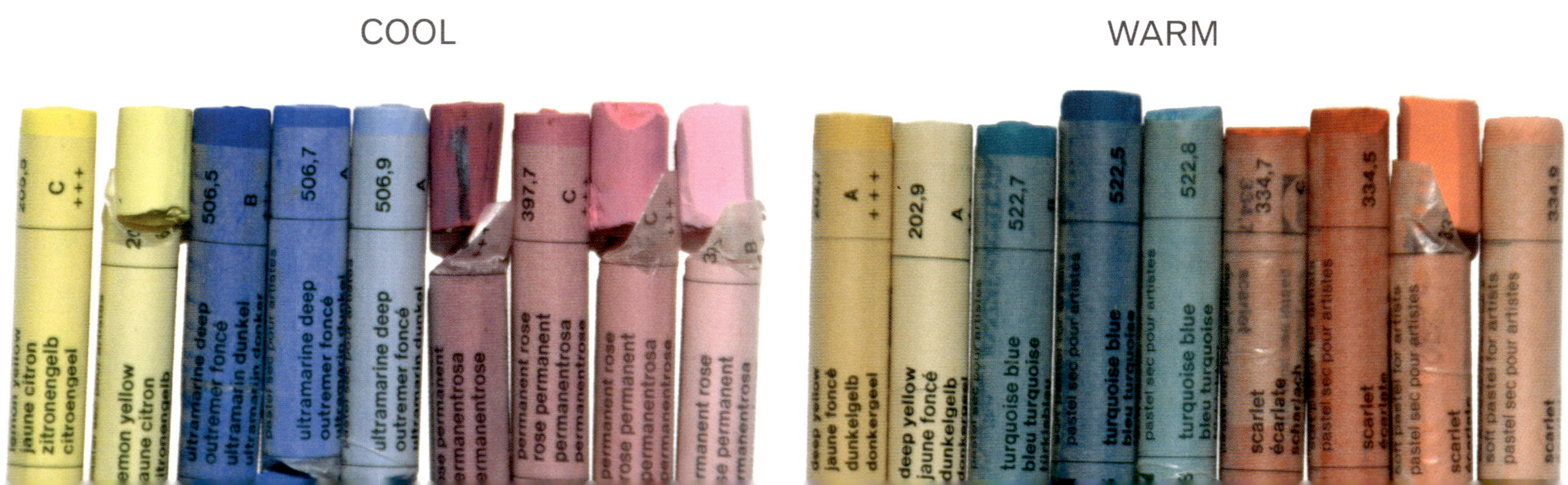

FIGURE 1.
Double primary palette for pastel.

WATERCOLOR

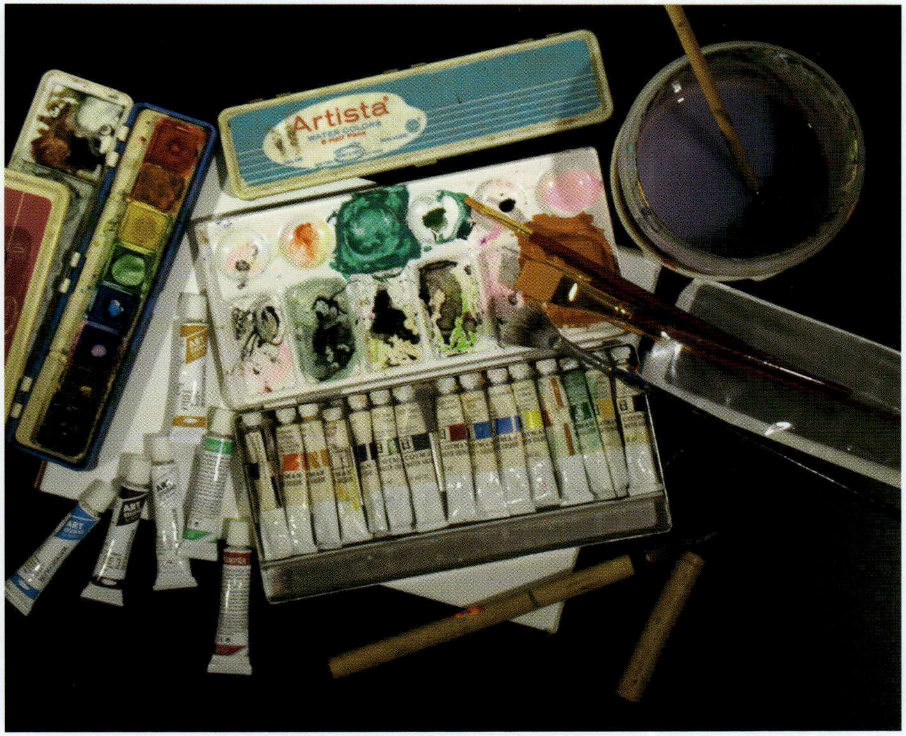

Watercolor is a wonderful medium, but not for temperature painting.

Watercolor is probably the most popular medium of all because water is all you need to thin your paint and for cleanup. It is easy to work with and less toxic than other mediums. The range of color is huge, and it is packaged in multiple ways. There are tubes you squeeze out and sets with hard powder, like those you used as a kid. There are dozens of manufacturers as well.

Pluses: Easy cleanup, not much odor, low toxicity, easy to transport, quick to dry, lots of working techniques, and huge color selection.

Minuses: Watercolor is fragile and must be framed to protect it.

Although watercolor is not a good choice for this method, the color knowledge that you will gain is significant. If you are comfortable with working in another medium to learn, you will find that your watercolor painting will be improved immensely.

OIL

Oil is considered the premium medium because of its longevity and the respect we have for artists from the past. Pigment is blended with linseed or another oil to produce a creamy, flowing medium that blends well, stays wet longer to aid blending, and is capable of great detail. It is considered the most permanent medium of all.

Pluses: Extreme mixability; infinite number of color mixtures available by mixing pigments wet; stays wet for days, allowing for easier blending when working on a painting over an extended period, but drying can be speeded with additives. A finished oil painting does not have to be framed because of the hardness of the finish, and a huge range of colors and mediums are available. It also has a smooth, creamy color consistency.

Minuses: Oil requires turpentine or another thinner for painting with a brush and for cleanup. Thinners are toxic to breathe and hard to dispose of. Oil is relatively heavy to lug around and the work is often wet during transport. Though listed as a positive, the slow drying time can be a negative as well.

Oil is my favorite medium to use with the temperature painting technique. I like the blending possibilities of working wet into wet. One of the main reasons I use a palette knife is that no thinner is needed.

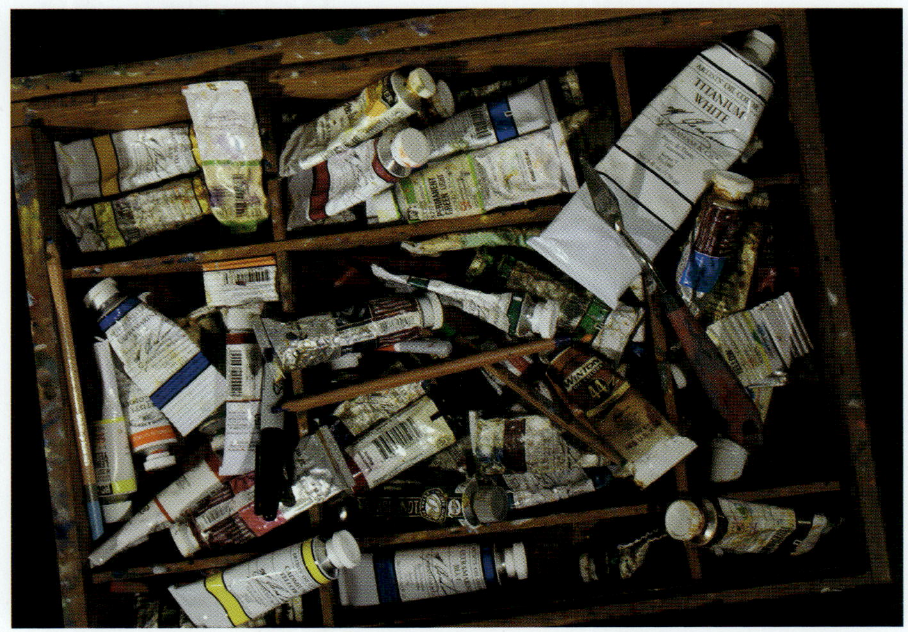

Oil color choices for the double primary palette:

Cool yellow: lemon yellow, hansa yellow, azo yellow
Warm yellow: cadmium yellow, cadmium yellow medium, cadmium yellow deep or dark
Warm red: cadmium red light, cadmium scarlet, scarlet lake
Cool red: permanent rose, quinacridone rose, alizarin crimson, rose madder, or other reds with blue content. There are lots of choices in this category.
Cool blue: ultramarine blue, ultramarine blue deep, French ultramarine, ultramarine blue red shade
Warm blue: manganese blue, cerulean blue, turquoise is a possibility or blue with yellow content
White: titanium is an opaque white, (zinc is a more transparent white you might want to try also)
Optional: burnt sienna

Suggested basic palette:

Lemon yellow (Holbein)
Cadmium yellow (M. Graham)
Cadmium scarlet (Winsor & Newton)
Permanent rose (Winsor & Newton)
Ultramarine blue (M. Graham)
Manganese blue (hue) (M. Graham)
Titanium white (M. Graham)
Optional: Burnt sienna (M. Graham)

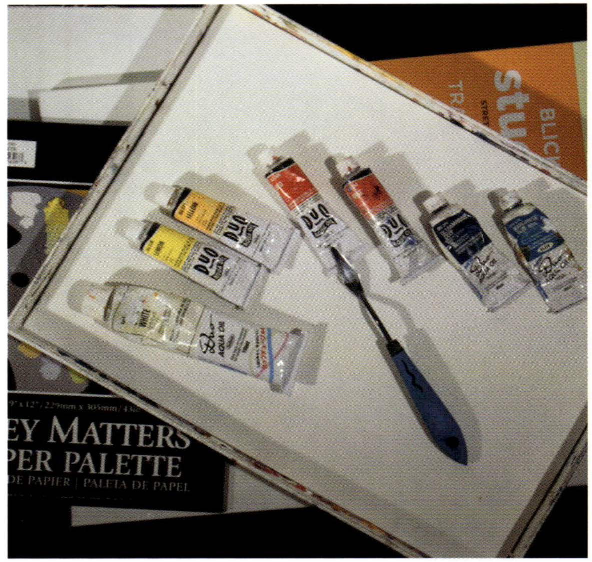

WATER-SOLUBLE OIL

This is a relatively new medium invented to reduce the toxicity of oil and preserve its blendability and creaminess. In short, it is designed to keep the good and eliminate the bad qualities of oil. It dries quicker than oil but slower than acrylic, which gives you more working time than acrylic. There are fewer colors to choose from than other mediums, but that is changing as more people use it. And, of course, cleanup with water is wonderful! I have to say I like this medium now, though I didn't like it much when it first came out.

Pluses: No turpentine, less odor, and more creaminess than acrylic.

Minuses: Not quite as creamy as oil and can get tacky too soon.

This is a wonderful medium for temperature painting because it is much like oil. It allows wet into wet mixing on the canvas and its consistency is great with the palette knife!

Water-soluble oil color choices for the double primary palette:

Cool yellow: lemon yellow
Warm yellow: cadmium yellow, cadmium yellow medium, cadmium yellow deep or dark
Warm red: cadmium red light
Cool red: permanent rose, rose madder, thalo red rose
Cool blue: ultramarine blue deep, French ultramarine
Warm blue: cerulean blue, manganese blue hue, turquoise
White: titanium is opaque, zinc is more transparent
Optional: burnt sienna

Suggested basic palette:

Lemon yellow (Holbein)
Cadmium yellow (Holbein)
Cadmium red light (Winsor & Newton)
Permanent rose (Winsor & Newton)
Ultramarine blue deep (Holbein)
Manganese blue nova (Holbein)
Titanium white (Holbein)
Optional: Burnt sienna (M. Graham)

ACRYLIC

Acrylic is a popular medium because it is water-soluble but more opaque than watercolor. It is very quick to dry and can be painted over easily. It is vibrant and fluid and comes in a huge range of colors, even neon and metallics. There is a large variety of mediums available to alter the paint quality, including gloss, matte, retardant, thickening paste, etc.

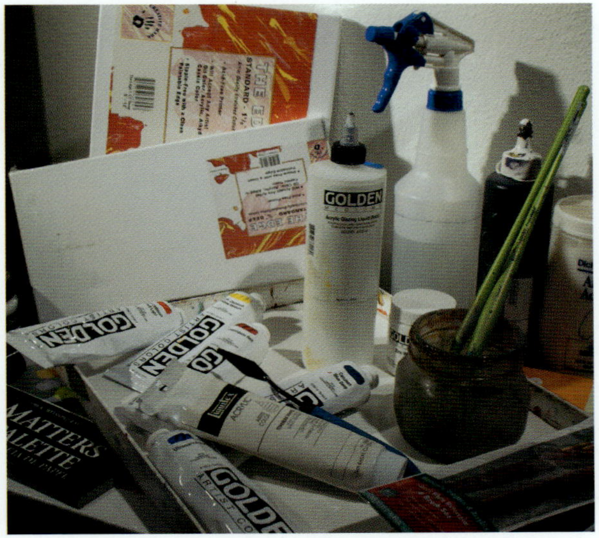

Pluses: Quick, bold, fast drying, easy to make changes, water-soluble (brushes clean with water), low odor, and less toxicity than oil. You do not have to put acrylic under glass, so framing is also easier.

Minuses: Acrylic has a plasticity that gives it a particular "feel" that some artists do not like. It also dries quickly, making blending more difficult. This aspect can make acrylic a difficult medium for learning, as by the time you get the colors figured out and mixed on your palette, they are too dry to use. Also, lightening colors on your canvas with acrylic is tricky because some of the whites are strong and other pigments are weak or transparent and can be overpowered by white, causing a chalky look.

Acrylic can be used beautifully for temperature painting. Because of its speedy drying time, however, I change my approach somewhat. When acrylic dries, it keeps its texture. If you paint the primary tones in acrylic, and they dry quickly with a lot of texture, it can be difficult to cover that texture with the final layers of paint. I recommend that students apply the primary tones with a brush (not as a wash as in watercolor, but strongly and opaquely, like you mean it!), rather than a palette knife. This keeps the texture to a minimum and lets the final layers with the palette knife produce the texture. I like acrylic and often use it to begin my paintings, especially for large canvases. Because I like the blendability of oil, I frequently switch to oil, applying it over the acrylic.

There are a couple of differences in names of pigments between mediums. For example, cadmium yellow medium is a rich, golden yellow in both oil and water-soluble oil. It is a much milder, middle-of-the-road yellow in acrylic. For this reason, I usually purchase cadmium yellow deep in acrylic to get the color similar to cadmium yellow medium in oil. This is not always the case, but remember, there is no standard between manufacturers.

Acrylic is a much more transparent medium than either of the other two wet mediums; therefore, some of the colors are not as dark. Ultramarine blue, especially, is not as deep a value in acrylic. For this reason, when working in acrylic, I often support that color and position on the color wheel with as dark a value pigment as I can find. I sometimes use anthraquinone blue, dioxazine violet, or thalo blue, but make sure it is not thalo blue green shade or you will not get a good contrast with your warm blue because the warm blue has yellow content. Because I don't normally use black, I often use ultramarine blue, since it's the deepest, darkest color in the palette for making my darks. When ultramarine blue doesn't come dark enough, I find I am unable to make darks dark enough unless I supplement that color. I would like to emphasize again that it is less important to have the exact pigment on my supply list than it is to have the correct relationship between your warm and cool primary colors and their placement on the color wheel. There is more information in the following chapters to help you with this.

Acrylic color choices for the double primary palette:

Cool yellow: hansa yellow light, primary yellow, azo yellow
Warm yellow: cadmium yellow deep or dark, if you have cadmium yellow medium, be sure it is dark enough to provide contrast to your cool yellow
Warm red: pyrrole red light, cadmium red light
Cool red: quinacridone rose, permanent rose, napthol crimson, or any red with blue content
Cool blue: ultramarine blue. If your blue is not dark enough in value to create strong darks, you will need to supplement this color. You can use anthraquinone blue.
Warm blue: primary cyan, cerulean blue, cerulean blue chromium, manganese blue hue, cobalt turquoise, or any blue with yellow in it
White: titanium and zinc. Titanium is stronger and more opaque but I recommend using both whites when working in this medium. Zinc is weaker and is useful when working with final details.

Suggested basic palette:

Cadmium yellow (Holbein)
Cadmium yellow medium or deep (Golden)
Pyrrole red light (Golden)
Anthraquinone blue (Golden)
Manganese blue (Golden)
Burnt sienna (Golden)
Titanium white (Golden)

Pigments for All Mediums

Let's talk about our family of pigments in general. The following section outlines the qualities of the pigments we discussed, as well as additional colors I use with temperature painting in Part Two. If you are a beginner, refer to the suggested basic palettes on the previous pages.

Titanium white. My palette starts with titanium white, which I use for almost everything. While I occasionally use zinc white in oil, I find it used more often in acrylic. Zinc white is a little weaker and a little more yellow, so it can be helpful to slightly lighten something in acrylic so that the color is not as apt to get chalky. Acrylic titanium white can be really strong and overpower the pigments.

Lemon yellow. The color in this position needs to be a yellow that is beginning to move toward blue or has a green content. My lemon yellow is fairly weak and transparent. I like those qualities as well as the blue content because this yellow distances well.

Pure yellow. I try to find a yellow across all the mediums that has neither red nor blue in it. Buy the purest one you can find; it will likely be made from cadmium.

Cadmium yellow medium or deep. My cadmium yellow medium is a full step darker and warmer than my pure yellow. I like each color to be clearly different from the one before in both temperature and value, to help me as I choose the colors for my painting.

Cadmium orange. This color is pretty consistent across mediums. Cadmium orange is actually our middle value color. Cadmiums tend to be very strong and opaque and will overpower lots of weaker pigments. If you work with a gray paper pad to mix your paint on, cadmium orange is the same value as the gray paper pad which is number five value.

Cadmium red light or cadmium scarlet. This color is the workhorse of the entire palette of colors. It is so strong that often only a "toothpick" amount is needed when using this in mixtures. When I'm working in acrylic, I often use pyrrole red light.

Bright red. Try to find a red that has neither yellow nor blue in it. This is not easy, as most reds, in my opinion, contain blue. In acrylic I usually use pyrrole red. In oil, I use Holbein's bright red, which I believe is also pyrrole.

Permanent rose or quinacridone rose. There are a lot of colors that fit here. You can use alizarin crimson, which is more transparent and a little brownish; several of the napthol reds or crimsons; rose madder; or a red that's beginning to move toward the blue primary. I prefer permanent rose because it is strong and clean and "fights" to set off cadmium red light (its warm counterpart). It also makes some beautiful pinks and purples.

Permanent magenta. This pigment is reddish purple, strong and transparent.

Dioxazine violet. This color favors the blue side of purple. It is very dark and strong and one of the best choices for darks.

Ultramarine blue. This should be the darkest blue on the palette. It is usually very transparent and makes the most wonderful clean, distancing colors imaginable.

Cobalt blue. This color is usually opaque and is considered the purest blue as it contains no yellow or red.

Manganese blue. I sometimes use cerulean or even turquoise for the blue in this position on the color wheel. Remember, this is a blue with yellow in it. I am actually using manganese blue hue in my oil palette. It is weak and transparent, but I prefer its color more than the more opaque, grayer cerulean.

Note: When you see "hue" on the pigment name, it means it is a weaker version of the regular color. One of the reasons the manufacturer does this is to keep the cost down. The hue usually looks identical to the color when you open the tube, but it will usually be less potent and will most likely be overpowered by the regular pigments when mixed.

There are many other optional colors. Turquoise is usually strong and is often made with thalo green or blue. Viridian is a gorgeous dark green that can be tweaked into amazing greens by adding yellow and is incredibly cool when mixed with white. It tends to be weak. I often put burnt sienna, terra rosa, English red, or one or two earth colors on my palette when I work because of the convenience they provide when cooling down a color, softening something, or establishing a mood quickly. I also sometimes use permanent green light, which is an incredibly strong yellow-green. Often I mix my own greens using the three blues and the three yellows on my palette.

Note: I usually avoid working with the thalo colors, especially in oil, as they overpower the other colors. I rarely use black, as I prefer to make my own darks and make them either warm or cool.

There is a lot of information here about color. Let's keep it simple. Imagine that you are climbing a ladder. The first step is learning the use of the primary colors: red, yellow, and blue. This first rung is absolutely essential. With every additional step, complexity is added. Much of my color theory will be discussed in-depth in the following chapters. There will be additional colors added at the beginning of the temperature painting method in Part Two. For this stage I would like to keep it simple. As far as pigments go, your supply list includes lemon yellow as your cool yellow, cadmium yellow medium as your warm yellow, cadmium red light as your warm red, permanent rose as your cool red, ultramarine blue as your cool blue, and manganese blue as your warm blue. This is a basic double primary palette (two sets of yellow, red, and blue) and the beauty of it is that it gives you a warm and cool choice for each of the primary colors (more on this in chapter 5). It enables you to pit a warm against a cool and gives you more color options. Add to this white, and possibly burnt sienna (which helps you mix a super-dark color), and it's really all you need for temperature painting.

SUPPLIES

In addition to paint, you will need something to mix your paints on, something to paint on, and something to paint with.

Pastel

Pastel is in its own category because it is not wet, and therefore not blendable except by stroking other colors into and on it. Experiment with different pastel papers. Use your fingers to apply it and your fingers or blending tools to move it around. A small area of your working paper or a scrap of the same paper can be used to try out colors.

You will also need a container to keep your sticks handy and in order. I break my sticks in half and put the labeled portion in a safe place for reference when replacing the stick. I use a compartmentalized container and divide my sticks by color and temperature so that I can think about the pigments the way I see them in other mediums on my palette. Keep a jar of salt or rice handy, and when the stick is dirty from other colors and you can no longer see what color it is, put it in the jar, shake, and it comes out clean! Other supplies you might want to have on hand are kneaded eraser and tortillon (stump) for minimal erasing and blending. A chamois is also helpful for softening.

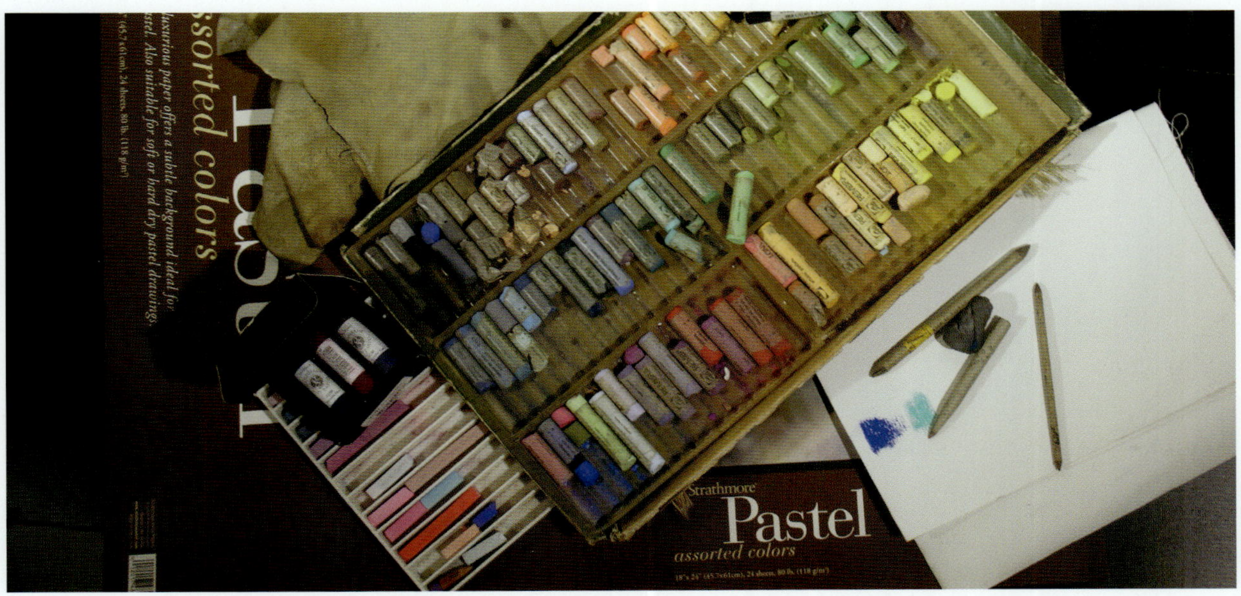

Wet Mediums

For the wet mediums, you can paint on paper, canvas sheets in a pad, inexpensive panels, stretched canvas, or any surface, really. The secret is to make sure the surface is gessoed. You can buy all of those materials pre-gessoed or gesso them yourself. Gesso is most often acrylic based, though oil-based gesso is also available. It is normally white, but you can get it in black and sometimes a few other colors. You can also mix pigment into it and color it yourself. Gesso comes in various size jars or gallon containers. It provides a protective coating for the support itself, "holds" the paint, and prevents the surface from degrading from the paints and their mediums and thinners.

For class work I suggest that my students buy pads of gessoed canvas. They come usually ten sheets to a pad, and many sizes are available. When working with a palette knife, I usually recommend the twelve-by-sixteen-inch size. If your canvas is bigger than that, it takes too much time to cover in a three-hour class; too much smaller and the work is too tight. Be sure you purchase genuine artist canvas. These pads are the least expensive for class work and is easily thrown away. If you do want to save something, you can always glue a backing to the canvas and then frame it.

Canvas boards are a little more expensive than the pads, and they are firm to work on. Unfortunately they can warp in humid situations. I prefer stretched canvases, which can be purchased in a larger quantity for a good price. You can also paint on store-bought hardwood panels or make your own inexpensively. Purchase one-eighth-inch-thick hardwood panels, cut them to a variety of sizes, and apply several coats of gesso. You can sand these to make them smooth or leave the brush texture on them or create your own texture.

When working with the wet mediums, you will need a palette to mix your paint on/in. I use the Masterson palette, which has a snap-on lid. It measures twelve by sixteen inches, and I have several for each medium, as I work in all three wet mediums. When working in oil, I use a pad of disposable twelve-by-sixteen-inch sheets and set that in the palette box. I set up my paints and use it for mixing, and as the sheet fills up I transfer my wet paint to the sheet below and continue. The same can be done for water-soluble oil.

When working in acrylic, use a palette box equipped with a thin sponge that lies at the bottom of the box. Lay a single sheet of acrylic palette paper over the moistened sponge. This keeps the paint and palette box moist, and the acrylic paint remains wet for days. When you're done working for the day, snap the lid on tight. If you have access to an extra refrigerator or freezer, you could store these palette boxes there and the paint would remain moist indefinitely. You will have to thaw it prior to working, but it's a wonderful way to keep your paint from drying out. I don't recommend putting it in the refrigerator or freezer that you use for food unless it is completely airtight. You do not want any outgassing—these pigments are not meant to be eaten!

There are many different palettes on the market. A visit to your local art supply store will show you some options.

I love the palette knife for working and also use brushes. There are numerous kinds of palette knives, and while the larger ones are made for larger painting sizes, the palette knife most comfortable to me is the diamond shape, about two and a quarter inches long. Get several different sizes and experiment with them.

I don't recommend a particular brush manufacturer. This is because I don't use brushes a lot, and brush quality is not consistent. In general, oil brushes are long-handled and have stiff bristles. You can use the same type of brush for water-soluble oil that you do for oil, because it takes a stiff brush to move that medium as well. However, I do not recommend switching back and forth between mediums with the same brush. Some artists use acrylic brushes for water-soluble oil. That type of brush can be used for different mediums. Acrylic brushes also tend to be long-handled, but because acrylic has a softer consistency, you can also use a softer brush. There are some wonderful soft synthetic brushes that work very well for acrylic. Short-handled brushes are typically for watercolor, but there is lots of crossover between brushes now.

Try experimenting with different styles and sizes of brushes. My favorite brushes are the flats and the brights. These are brushes with a flat ferrule so that when turned on their side they can make a narrow brush stroke, and when laid flat they can color in large areas at a time. Brights and flats make a crisper edge. This helps to avoid too much blending so that plane changes remain crisp and visible. You should also have one or more filbert brushes. These brushes also have a flat ferrule but instead of a square shape at the end of the bristle, the sides have been curved. This makes a softer stroke and aids blending. Small detail brushes are called rounds because the ferrule has not been crimped. The bristles come out in a round form with a tapered tip. It is also called a detail

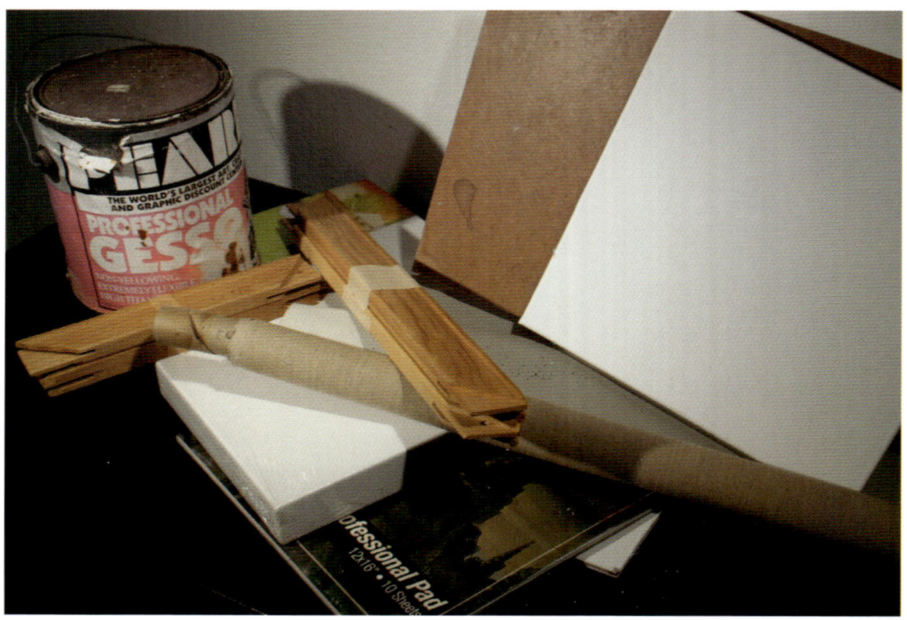

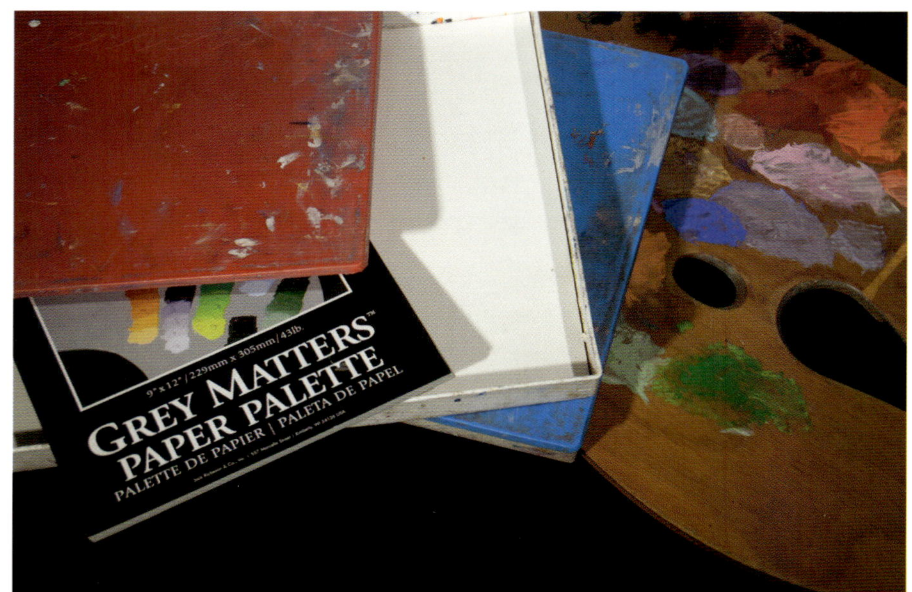

brush and you need this for smaller strokes as well as for signing your name. Although I only use the rounds for detail, they are available in many larger sizes for other applications as well. Other brushes that are helpful are one- to three-inch-wide brushes for "massing in" large areas. They are less costly at hardware stores, though the quality is lower.

Note: Students often ask how to use a brush. While I can show them how to hold it for painting (instead of like a pencil, as is their first instinct), brush style is a personal statement. I let them find their own unique painting style or language. I do not like to teach students to paint the way I do. Art needs to be a vehicle for each of us to find our own individuality, not an exercise in copying someone else, even though sometimes that's a great way to learn!

Oil

For wet painting, you will also need a vessel to hold your thinners and mediums. I use two jars (with covers that don't leak). One holds my thinner and one holds my fat (medium)! In my opinion, the most toxic elements of painting come from continued exposure to the odors of the thinners and mediums, especially in oil. Some are much worse than others. Although I do love them, I try to use them as little as possible. I do not use thinners at all when I paint with the palette knife, but when I paint with brushes, especially in the studio, I recommend using only Gamsol. It is truly odorless. (I remember years ago, thinking I was getting a good deal at my local big box hardware store on "odorless thinner" by the gallon. When I got it home and opened it, I discovered it had the most ghastly strong odor imaginable! Was I naïve?!?) My "fat" is walnut oil. I sometimes use liquin and sometimes other mediums for different effects. There are many mediums that affect oil paint's consistency, drying time, sheen, etc. Experiment to see what works best.

As for cleaning my oil brushes, I wipe them as clean as possible with a paper towel first, then I use walnut oil or Gamsol to get most of the paint color out, and finally I use soap and water. Murphy's oil soap works great, as do some of the commercial brush cleaners from an art store. I often do not clean my brushes daily or even weekly, as I should. But I find that the walnut oil keeps my brushes fairly well lubricated until I can do a thorough cleaning.

Students ask if there is anything that can be done with a hardened oil brush. If the Murphy's oil soap doesn't soften it, try soaking it in tri-sodium phosphate. It requires many days of soaking and working the brushes, but with persistence, they will soften. However, the bristles get pretty beaten up and, honestly, I don't think it is worth it.

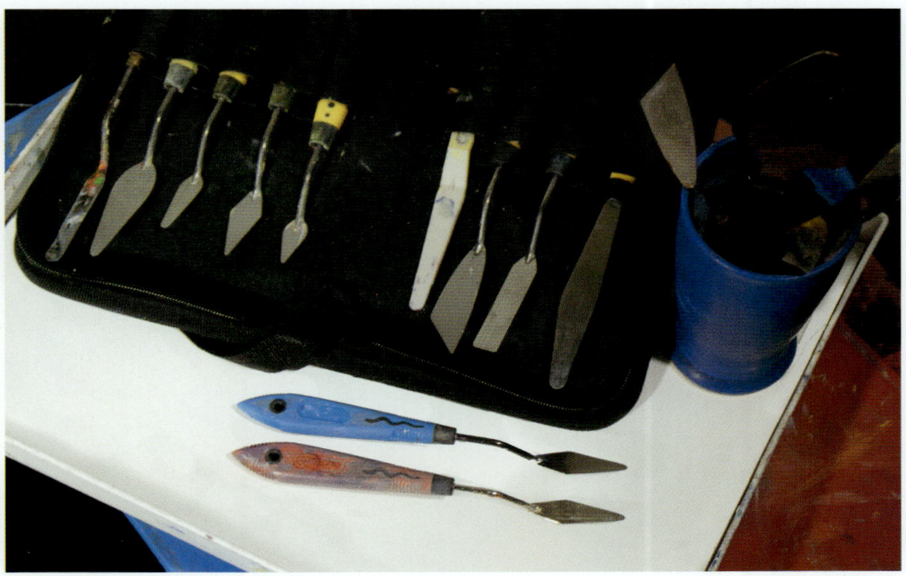

My favorite painting knife.

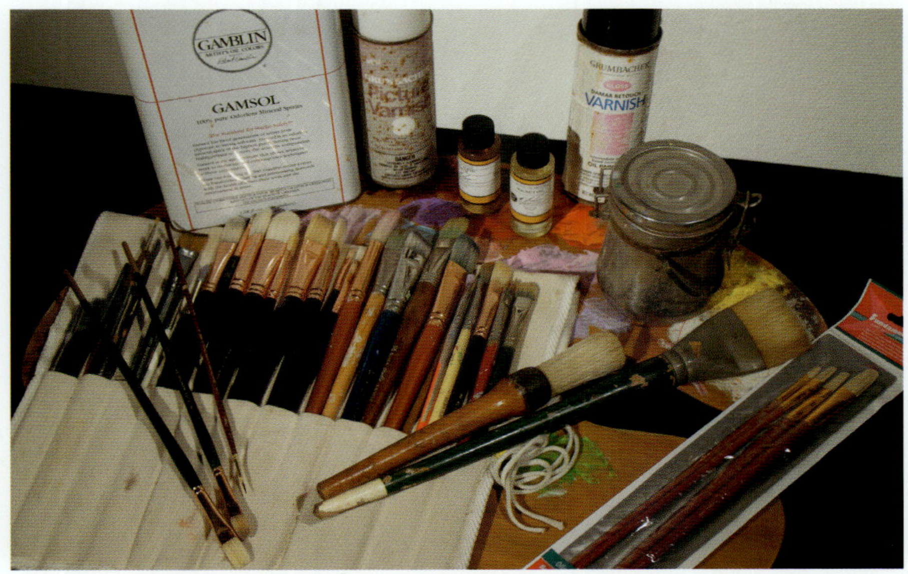

Water-Soluble Oil

Use a large plastic container for water, since water is the thinner and a large container keeps your brushes cleaner. I use a medium called linseed oil for water-soluble oil, which makes the paint creamier and easier to spread. I usually pour a small amount out on my palette surface when working with a brush. For some reason this method works better for me than if it was put in a cup. There aren't a lot of choices in mediums for water-soluble oil, but that will likely change as this medium gets more popular.

Can you blend water-soluble oil with oil? Yes, but when you mix oil into water-soluble oil, you lose the ability to clean your brushes with water. At that point, you may as well be working entirely with oil paint.

Acrylic. Fill a large container with water, which is the thinner for this medium. My favorite medium when I work with acrylic is a clear gloss glazing liquid. There are many manufacturers of this product. As with water-soluble oil, I usually squeeze this out on my palette rather than putting it in a cup, but it can be done either way.

Note: More than oil, pastel, or watercolor, acrylic offers the largest variety of mediums with all kinds of working properties including special effects.

If your brush hardens (it can happen so quickly), soaking it in rubbing alcohol will bring it back. Incidentally, that is how you can tell if your house paint is oil or latex. If the color rubs off on a cloth soaked in alcohol, it is latex. If, after being rubbed briskly, the color comes off on a cloth soaked in mineral spirits, it is oil paint. And remember, you cannot paint latex over oil. But you can paint oil over latex without it peeling later.

Note for all wet mediums: Traditionally we are taught to work "lean to fat" with oil. This means the paint is thinned or "cut" at the beginning of a painting, whether with turpentine, mineral spirits in oil, or water in the water-soluble mediums. After these initial layers are applied and the composition and drawing is sorted out, the painter begins applying the finishing coats, and these paint layers would use the fat or the medium, not the thinner. The thinner's job is to break down the paint and the fat's job is to build up the paint. This strengthens the paint and the painting by putting a coat on top that is permanent and retains a finish.

Varnish

Should you varnish your finished work? Artists have different opinions on this. Some pastel artists refuse to put a finish on their pastel because they fear the finish will decrease the luminosity of the color (and it can). Some pastel artists swear by finishing their work so that it will not continue to powder (pastel dust dropping away into the finished frame over time). I recommend practicing with products from an art supply store and making your own educated decision.

For oil painters, varnish is recommended as the final coat so that dirt and ultraviolet damage will occur in that layer and not in the oil paint itself. For these reasons, and to get a consistent sheen in the final finish (since not all of the pigments dry the same way), I use spray varnish. Varnish can be brushed on as well. It is available as a final varnish and as a retouch coating. The finished oil painting should be protected with the final varnish. But this varnish should never be put on the final painting until that painting is thoroughly dry. Because I work with the palette knife and use lots and lots of paint, my paintings could appear dry on the surface but the oil paint might still be wet underneath. It takes months, if not years, for oil paint to dry. So, I often use the retouch varnish, which breathes just enough that the drying paint underneath will not crack and blister the final coat. For a commissioned piece of work that needs to be delivered when it is complete, I use a coat of retouch varnish with the stipulation that one to two years down the road, it will receive its final coat of varnish. Several manufacturers make quality varnishes.

Water-soluble oil paintings should also be varnished. They dry faster than oil, so the final varnish can be applied sooner. Because temperature painting involves thicker paint and a palette knife, be careful to let the underlayers dry thoroughly.

While acrylic paint has longevity, particularly if a good fat medium is used with it, the medium has not been around as long as oil, so we don't really know how long it will hold up. I use varnish on acrylic paintings. Remember that the purpose of the varnish is to protect the paint underneath.

PRECAUTIONS

Take steps to minimize exposure to the toxic qualities of paint mediums. While this is a serious concern, particularly for people with compromised immune systems, I believe the risks can be overcome.

Skin is the largest organ in our body that exposes us to toxins. So keep paint off your skin by investing in a pair of gloves. There are many kinds of gloves, from lightweight gloves you can wear while you paint to "gloves in a bottle" or "liquid gloves" that you rub on your hands like hand lotion. It creates a film so your skin doesn't absorb chemicals from the materials you're working with. I don't like the feel of gloves on my hands when I work, so I use the liquid product. I also use an air purifier to remove fumes from my workspace. Good ventilation is important, too, especially when working with pastels. There should be enough air current to take the dust away so you don't breathe it in.

EXERCISES

The following are exercises I give my students, and they have told me how valuable they've found them to be. The exercise in figure 2 is excellent for teaching you to control the value of your color and recognize value differences. It will also show you a lot about the personality of each pigment in the double primary palette. When you complete it, keep it in your paint box and refer to it as needed. The goal here is to find middle mixtures between two parent colors. One set of parents is on the left vertical column and the other set of parents is on the top horizontal row. One way of looking at it is that the intersection where those two meet is the offspring. You will notice that the bottom left segment is a mirror image of the upper right segment. There is no point in mixing two identical halves of the chart with the same mixtures. So, in the quadrant on the bottom left, why not add white to each mixture and find the pastel version of the middle mix?

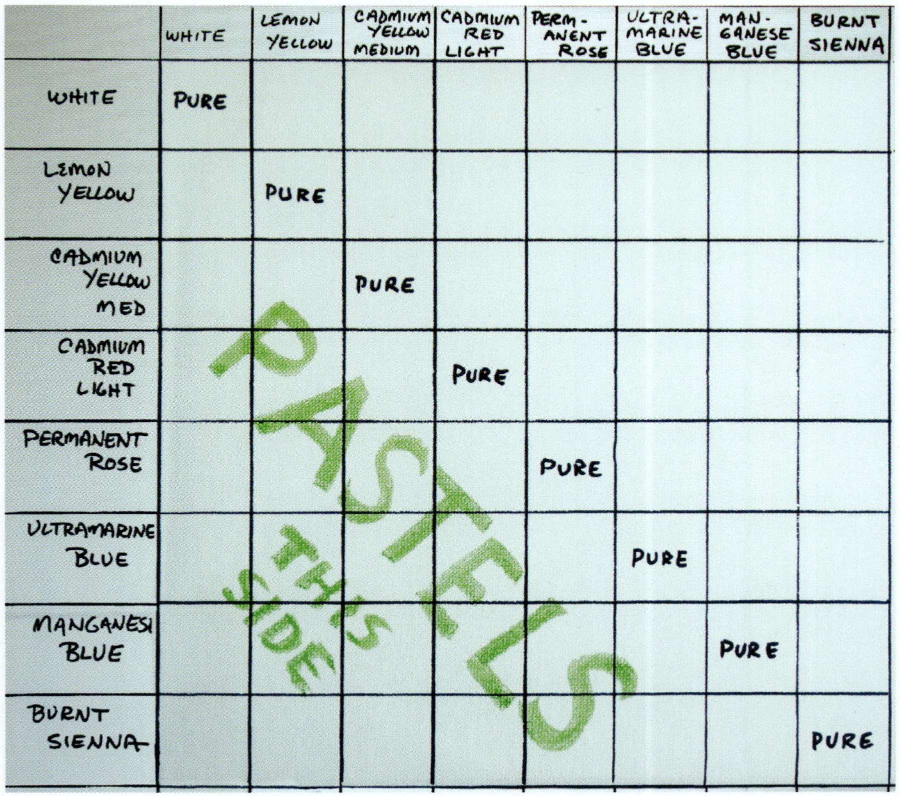

FIGURE 2.
Exercise for making "middle" mixes.

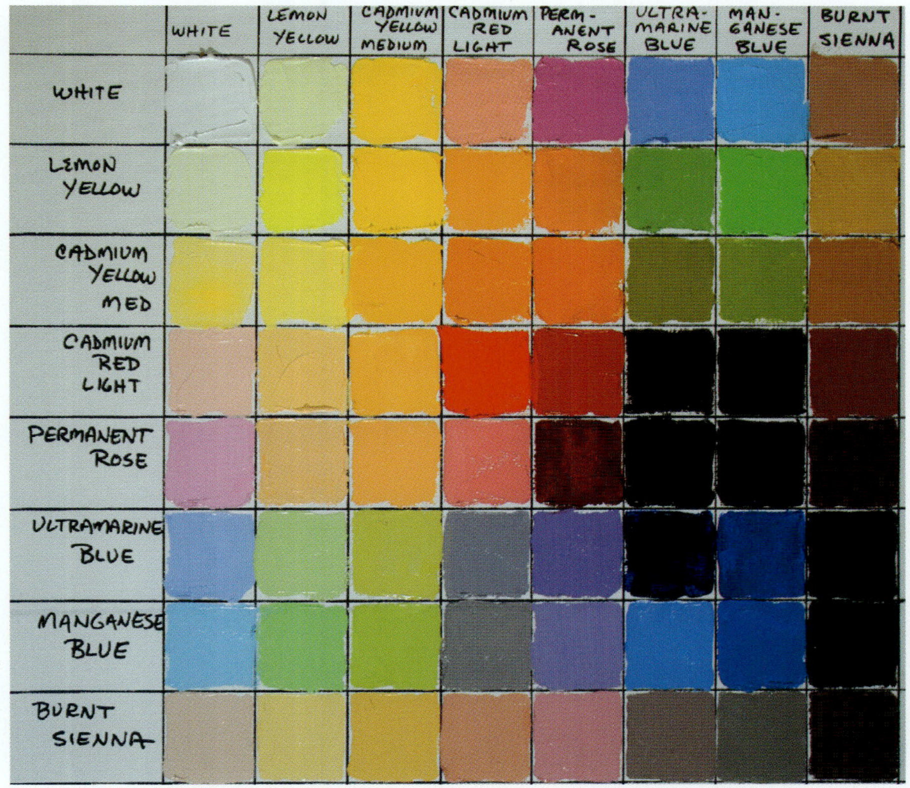

FIGURE 3.
Use this completed chart to see if your middle mixes are accurate. Note that the printer inks shown here may not match the actual paint colors.

Note: A middle mix (figs. 3 and 4) is not created with a teaspoon of this and a teaspoon of that, as in cooking. Rather, it is a visual halfway, and since each parent color has a different strength, you must make a judgment call. This will quickly show you something about your powers of discernment! But relax, it gets easier with practice. Here's a tip: Notice that I put one of the parents on each side, leaving a space between to paint the mixture itself. By doing it this way, I can compare the value difference more easily between each parent side.

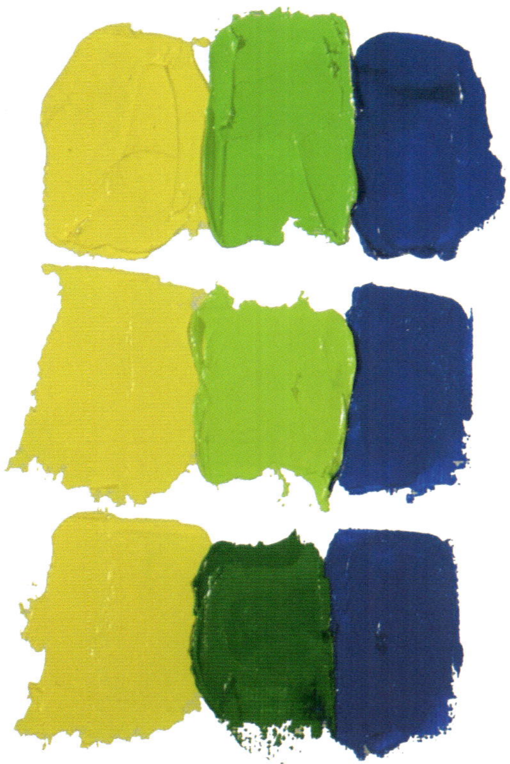

FIGURE 4.
You can see the setup here with the parent colors on either side, leaving a space for the middle mixture. The mixture on top is the best. The mixture on the bottom is too dark, while the mixture in the middle is too light.

The next exercise asks you to mix your own earth colors (since they are not included in the double primary palette) and how to mix a warm and a cool version, plus a "pure" and a pastel version (figs. 5 and 6). You can leave an extra column on the right for possible other mixtures. A couple of colors that come to mind are Paynes gray (from black) and Naples yellow (from yellow ochre). There are dozens. Almost all of the earth colors from art supply stores are mixable if you know how. Some earth colors have other valuable properties, such as transparency, that cannot be duplicated very well. If you've grown accustomed to using them for those reasons, don't give them up. Actual formulas are given in chapter 6.

OUT OF THE TUBE		PURE	WARM	COOL	PASTEL	OTHER
	BLACK					
	GRAY					
	R. UMBER (brown)					
	B. UMBER (brown)					
	BURNT SIENNA					
	YELLOW OCHRE					
	YELLOW					
	ORANGE					
	RED					
	PURPLE					
	BLUE					
	GREEN					

FIGURE 5.

This is the proper way to lay out your selection of colors on your palette if you are new to working with the double primary palette (fig. 7). This arrangement will teach you how to "see" color temperature and figure out which colors to mix together to create what you want in your painting. Let the color of the pigments guide you along the way. Notice that I did not puddle the colors as I squeezed them out, but "pulled" them out instead. This can be helpful for keeping the stable of colors clean on the palette. When you dig into a puddle of color with the palette knife, sometimes you deposit a different color into the pigment, polluting the entire pile of paint. This is less likely to happen with a stretched out line of paint. Notice, too, that I put the yellows next to the white, then the red, and finally the blue. This helps to keep the lighter mixtures toward the white end of the palette and also helps to prevent polluting your pigments. This is particularly helpful given the wet nature of acrylics.

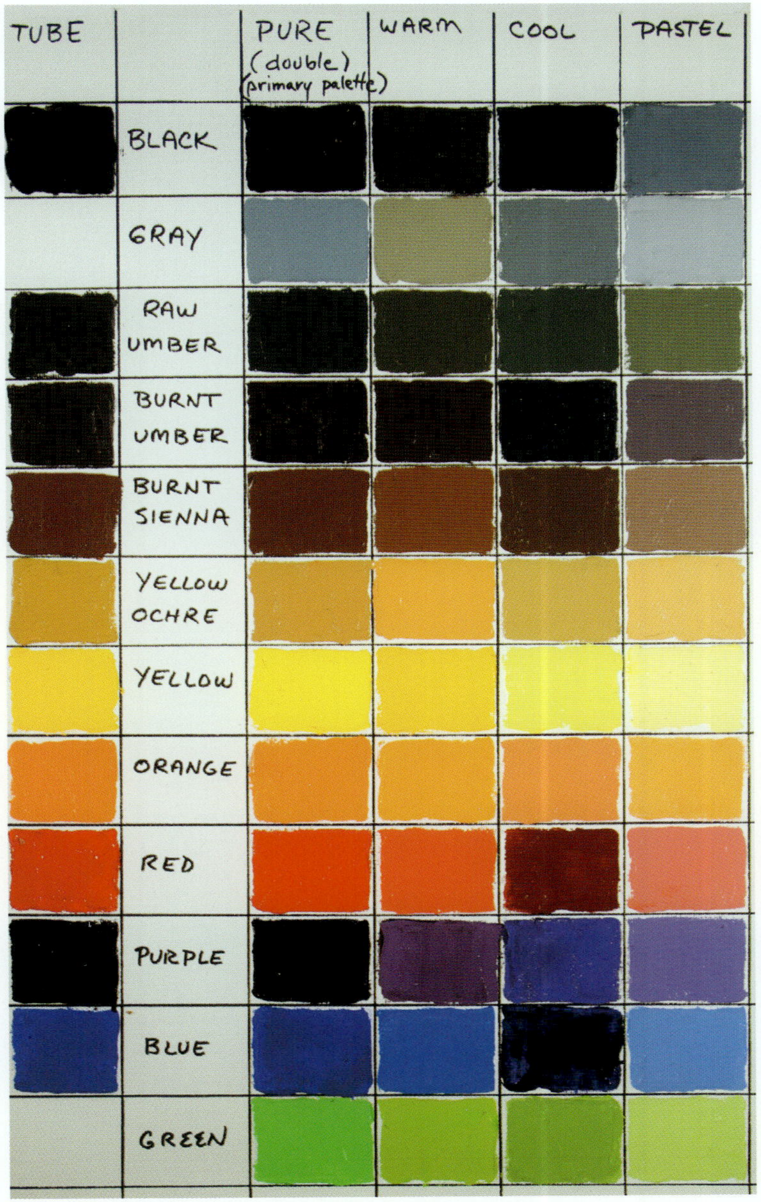

FIGURE 6.
Use this completed chart as a guide.
There is a wide variety of possibilities here.

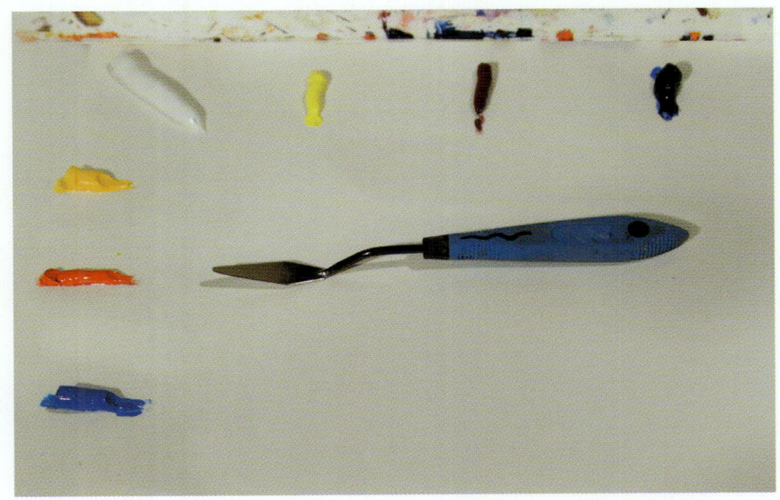

FIGURE 7.
Proper palette layout for the double primary palette suggested for the beginning student.

Chapter Three

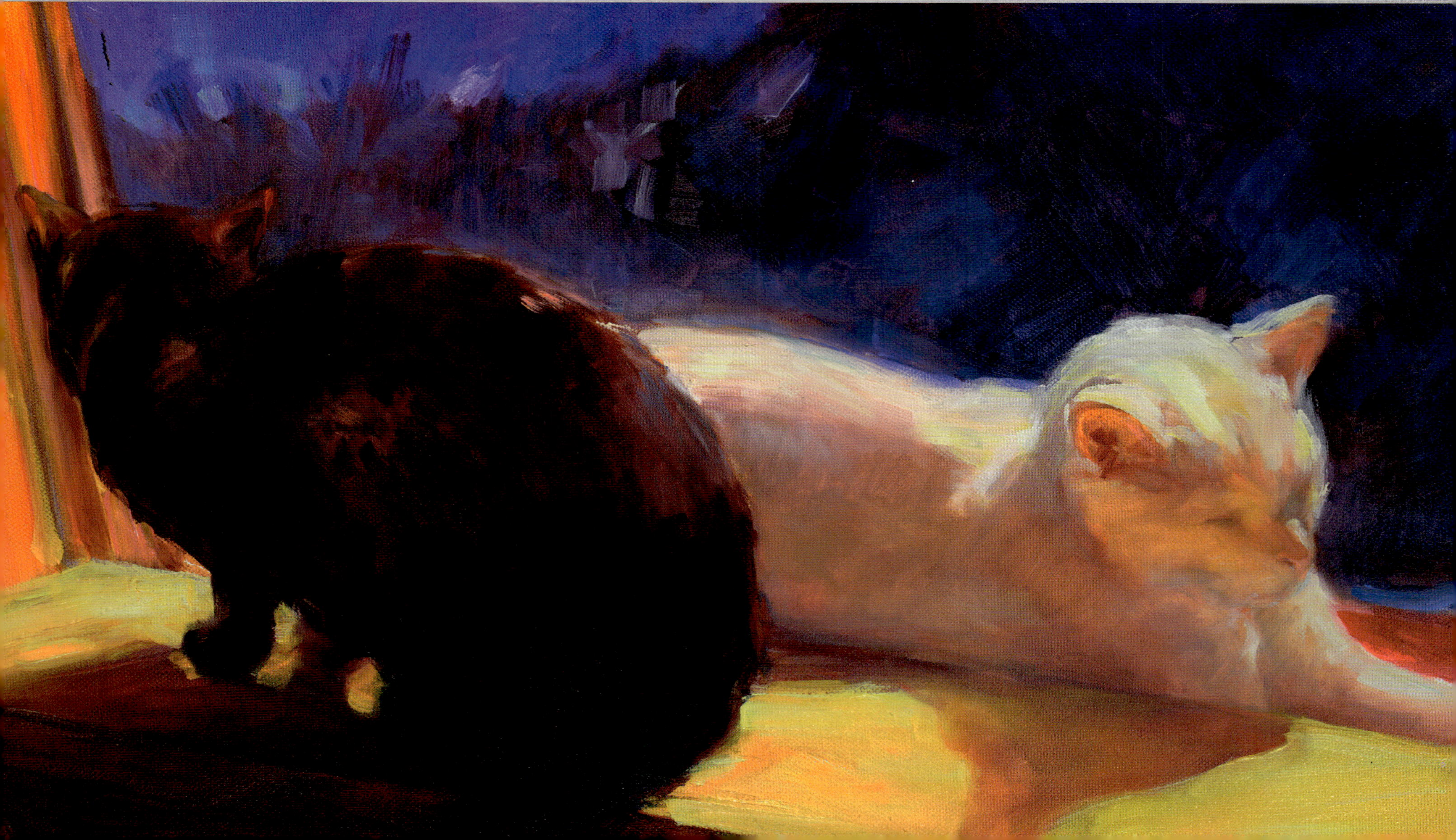

Primary Colors

Now with all this information, what is the beginning color student to do? Well, let's keep it as simple as possible.

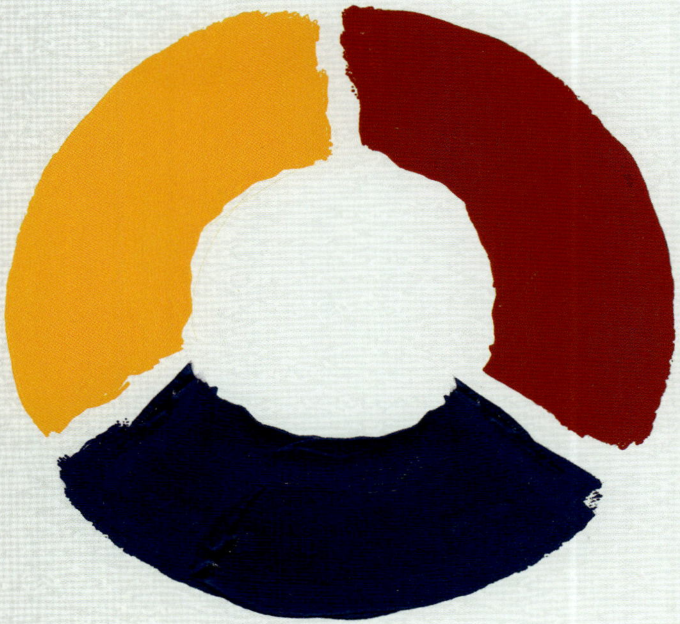

FIGURE 8.
Primary colors.

OPPOSITE:
Two Cats on the Windowsill by Julie Hanson, 2005.
Acrylic, 12" × 24".

Look at the color wheel again and find its most basic elements (fig. 8). The first thing you notice is that there are three colors that are very different from each other. These colors are red, yellow, and blue. They are called the primary colors because no other colors can create them, and they are the colors from which all other colors are made.

Let's worry about the names of the pigments later. You can refer to the lists of pigment names in chapter 2 any time. For now, just think about red, yellow, and blue. Remember, the entire color world can be simplified down to these three colors, each with distinctive working properties.

Since color is important to you as a painter, it is very important that you begin to see the world *right now* in various subtle and not-so-subtle variations of just these three colors. Everything you see, ask yourself, is it red, yellow, or blue? Which color is it mostly? This is always your starting point. But remember, each color has physical working properties that "confuse" the colors and the clarity of the mixtures (like the clarity of light). You will still need to practice with the individual pigments in your collection to learn what secrets each brings to the table. Refer back to chapter 2 and do the exercises. Practice mixing color!

I am always surprised to find students who know that the primary colors are red, yellow, and blue, and yet don't have a clue about how to use these colors in painting. So let's look at this again carefully. Each of the primary colors has a role to play in your painting. In fact, they are your painting's subject; you just may not realize it. *No matter what the color of the object you are painting, you will be using red, yellow, and blue to bring it forth.* So, let's repeat that, because it is important! For the colorist, no object, scene, or subject can be fully expressed in a three-dimensional way, no matter what color it is, without red, yellow, and blue working in balance and doing their jobs. That is almost more important than the subject. (An artist can draw well and use value to bring forth the subject, but the emphasis here is on the use of color to do it).

Yellow is easy, as it is the light! Most of the time, yellow represents the parts of the subject that are receiving light or being illuminated (fig. 9).

Blue is easy too. Most of the time, blue represents the part of your subject that is shadowed or not illuminated (fig. 10).

Red is the challenging one. What does it do? It warms something. In the words of an artist who was one of my favorite students, it creates "roundidity." In painting, that is what makes something come forward, have volume, or look three-dimensional (fig. 11).

You now know how to paint any object. You just need to make sure red, yellow, and blue are doing their jobs no matter what the actual local color is. This is an oversimplification but this point needs to be made strongly because without this, your color will probably be off balance . . . period. Most likely, the weakest link will be your use of red.

Because we "see" the visible spectrum, it is our only visible language; therefore, in your painting you must represent this balance fully. A good painting has this balance!

You know that in art, every rule ever discovered can be broken. But if we teach you the broken rules, you will not see the simplicity and the immensity of the rules. So, learn the rules first . . . then break them in style. Your own!

Remember: this is as simple as painting in color can be. As we go further into the book, if you get confused, come back to chapter 3. This is the first rung of the ladder. Now, let's climb.

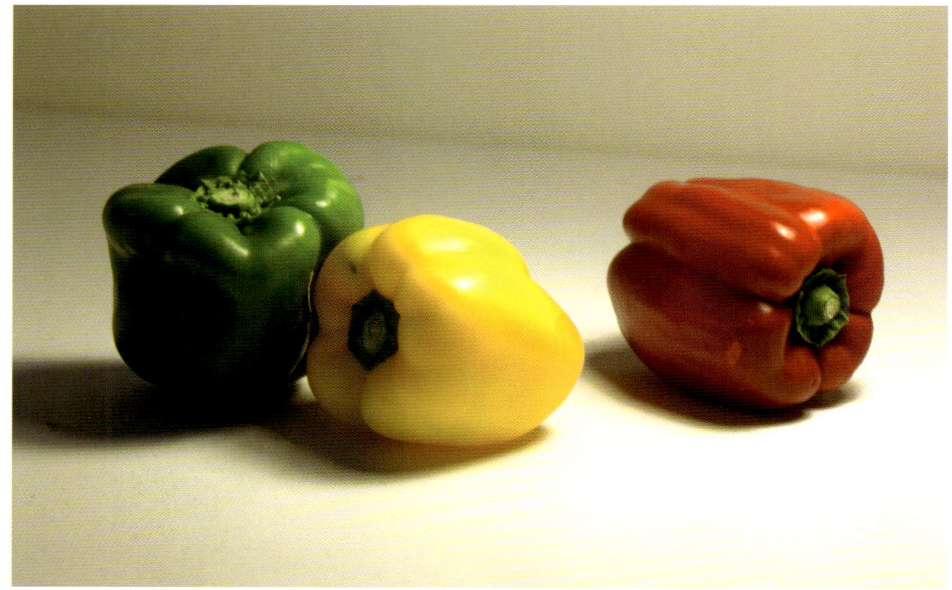

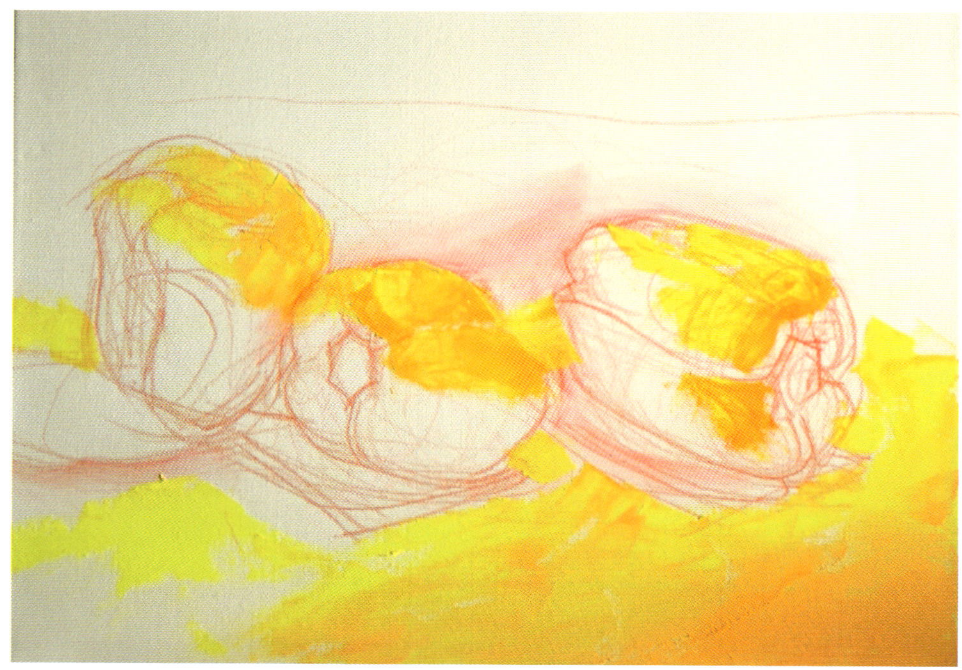

FIGURE 9.

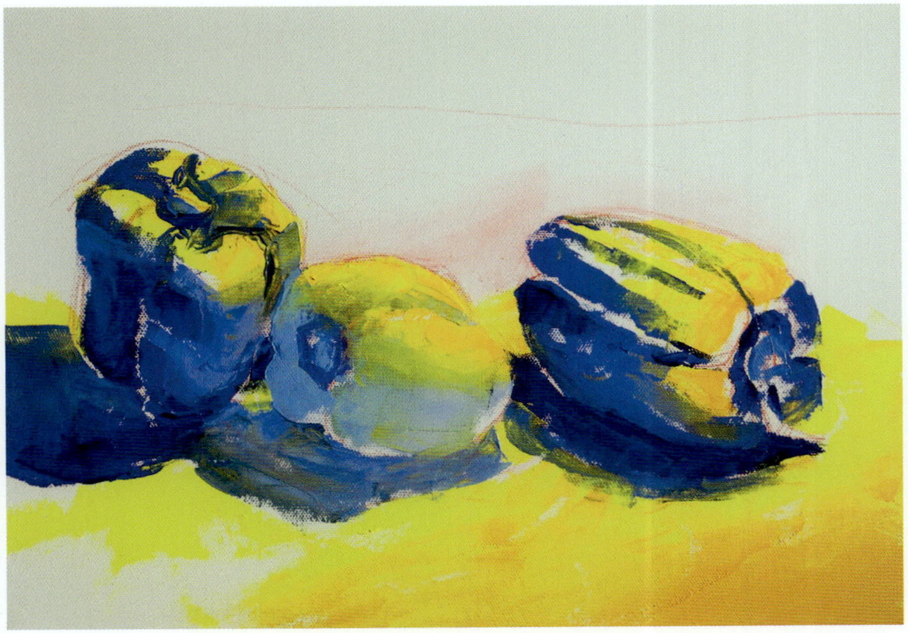

FIGURE 10.

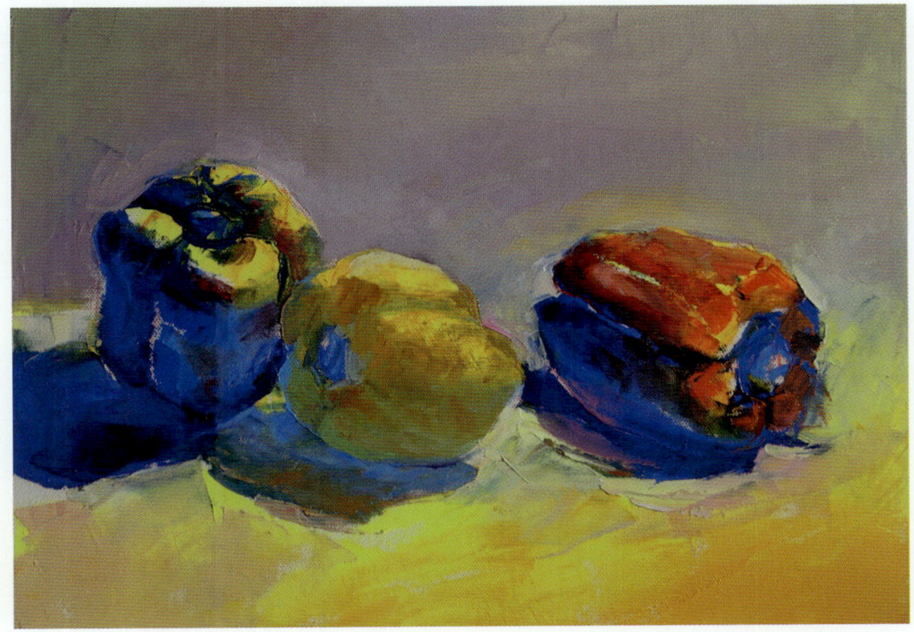

FIGURE 11.

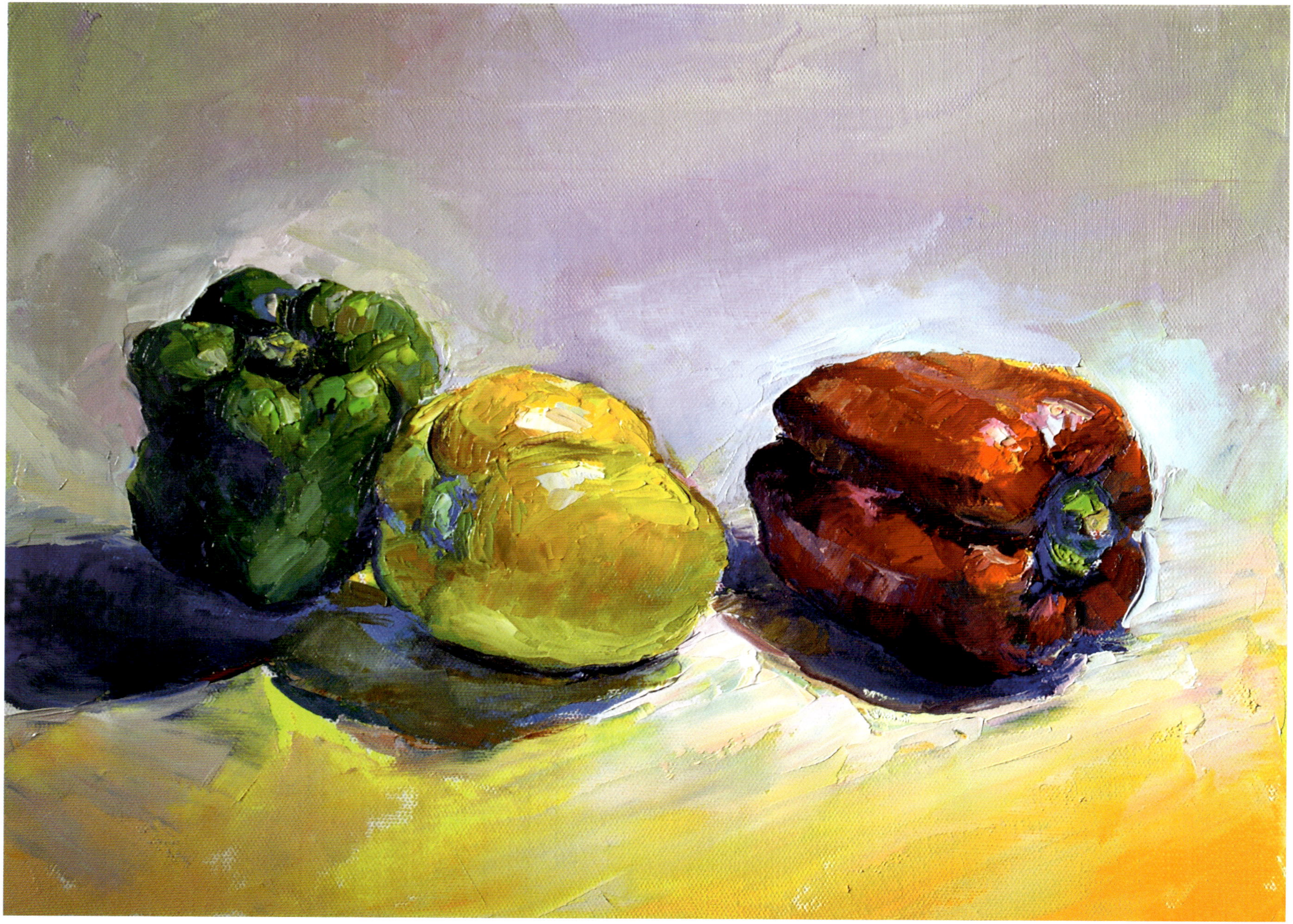

In the finished painting of the peppers, you can see how all three primaries are handling their jobs with the different local (actual) colors of the peppers.

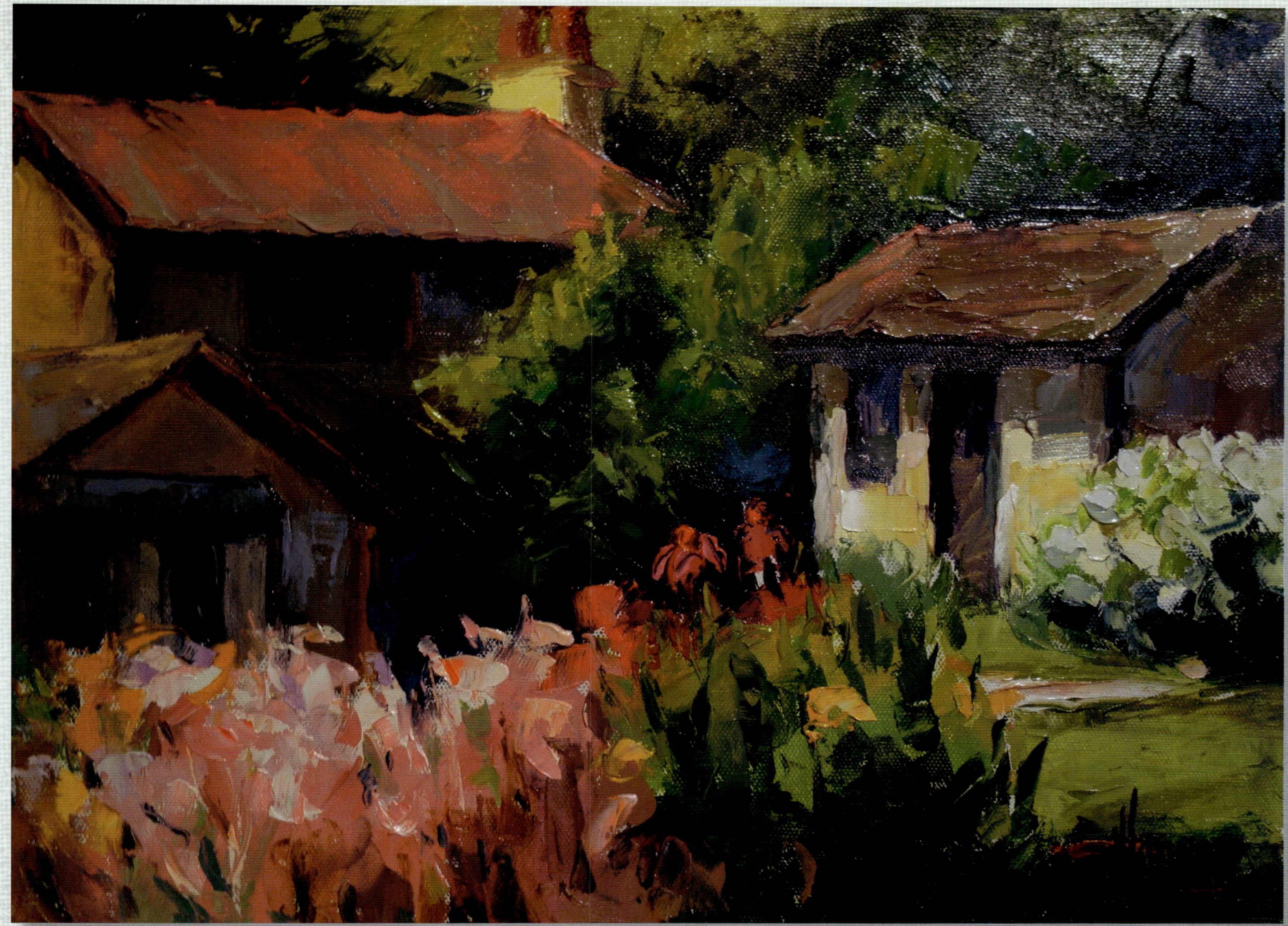

Edgewood by Julie Hanson, 2014. Oil on canvas, 12" × 16".

Chapter Four

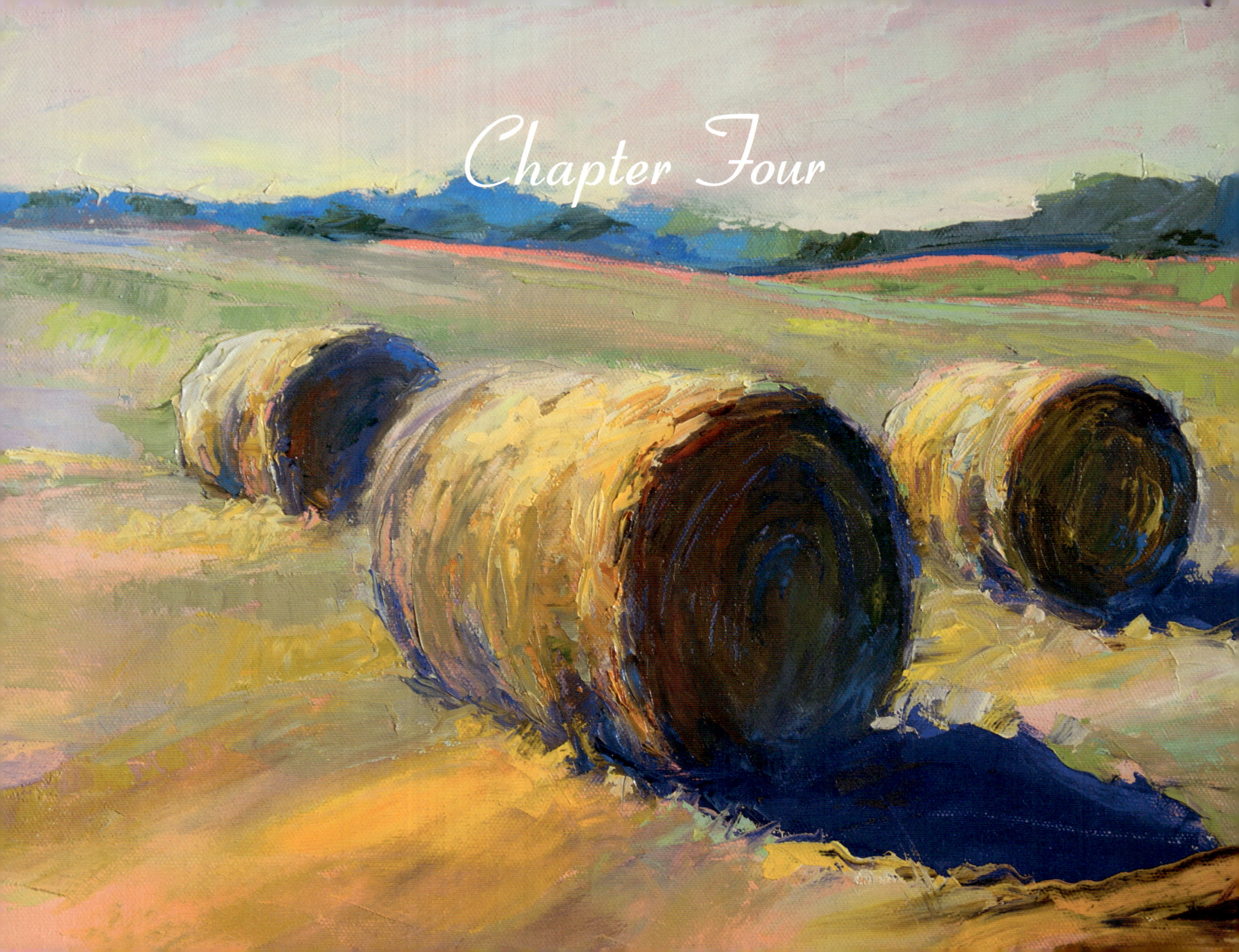

Three-Dimensional Form —Keep It Simple!

When you begin to study form, you realize that one of the tasks is to show the three-dimensionality of forms in a painting.

Because the painting surface is flat and therefore merely two-dimensional, you can see that when the third dimension is added and the flat plane becomes three dimensional, the simplest possible form is the cube (figs 12 and 13). Thankfully, there are very few basic three-dimensional forms for the painter to learn.

Before we go deeper into the study of color, let's look at these three-dimensional forms in the simplest possible way, just as we looked at color in the simplest possible way in the previous chapter. The reason is that you will be painting three-dimensional subjects on a two-dimensional surface. That means you will need some magic tricks to pull it off. So, what are the most basic forms in nature? See if you can figure this out before you look ahead.

FIGURE 12.
Two–dimensional form.

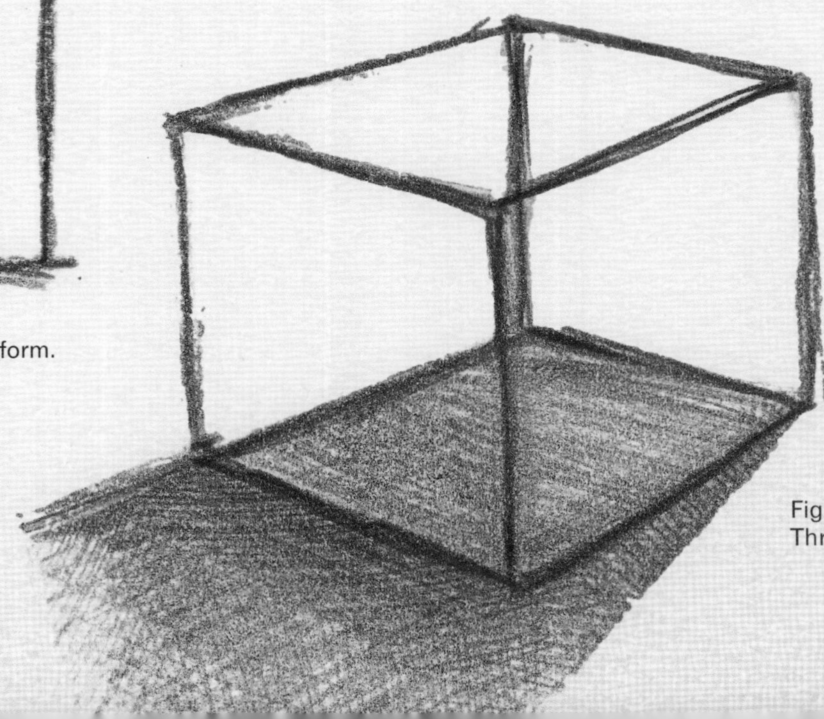

Figure 13.
Three–dimensional form.

OPPOSITE:
Hay Bales by Julie Hanson, 2011.
Oil on canvas, 12" × 16".

DO YOU NEED DRAWING SKILLS?

Most of my students lament the fact that they aren't as good at drawing as they would like to be. Is it true that to be a good painter, you have to know how to draw? Well, yes. But, if you truly "feel" color and can "weave" the threads of red, yellow, and blue, even with poor drawing skills, you can be a decent painter. There are many artists from earlier times who are considered great but did not have superior drawing skills. We love them for other reasons. Look at Renoir's ladies. Sometimes it is hard to find the skeleton under the beautifully painted flesh. How about Van Gogh's drawings of the potato eaters? They are spectacular probably because of the distortions.

Of great interest to me is observing how students use their left or right side of the brain. The right side is typically thought to be the intuitive, touchy-feely side, the side of emotions, spatial concepts, and color. The left side is associated with logic, order, drawing, scientific research, knowledge, and learned skills. Many people are drawn to art to find a voice for the right side because our culture can be out of balance and tends to be very left-brain oriented. These folks need to loosen up, get into the flow of things (right side), not think so much. I always tell them that both sides are needed, because balance is good! Some folks are so right-brained (natural artists) that they cannot draw a straight line even with a ruler. These folks need to find left-brained skills. We need to strengthen our weaknesses in painting, whatever they may be. But don't let your weaknesses stop you from finding your strengths! So, take a drawing class, too. Learn how to render the underlying forms of nature. If you can render them well in value (dark and light) by doing pencil studies and charcoal studies, it will probably be much easier for you to translate that into color.

CUBE, SPHERE, CYLINDER, AND CONE

To create three-dimensional form, I used six values for the black-and-white renderings (fig. 14). One is the highlight or lightest, two and three are the mid tones or local color, four is the shadow, five is the reflected light, and six is the cast shadow or darkest.

These are the basic forms of which all of nature is made. There are, of course, variations on these forms such as the pyramid, which is a combination of a cone and a cube; the doughnut; and probably others; but these can be simplified back to the original four. For example, trees are cylinders with a sphere on top, buildings are cubes with difficult angles (pyramids) for roofs. We will choose the cube for much of our discussion because it is the easiest of the four three-dimensional forms to "build" in a painting. Because the cube has three flat planes needed to create three-dimensionality, using the three primaries does the job. When you paint the other forms, you must blend the colors evenly and carefully because of the rounded sides. This can take lots of practice to get it to look even and truly believable. Practice!

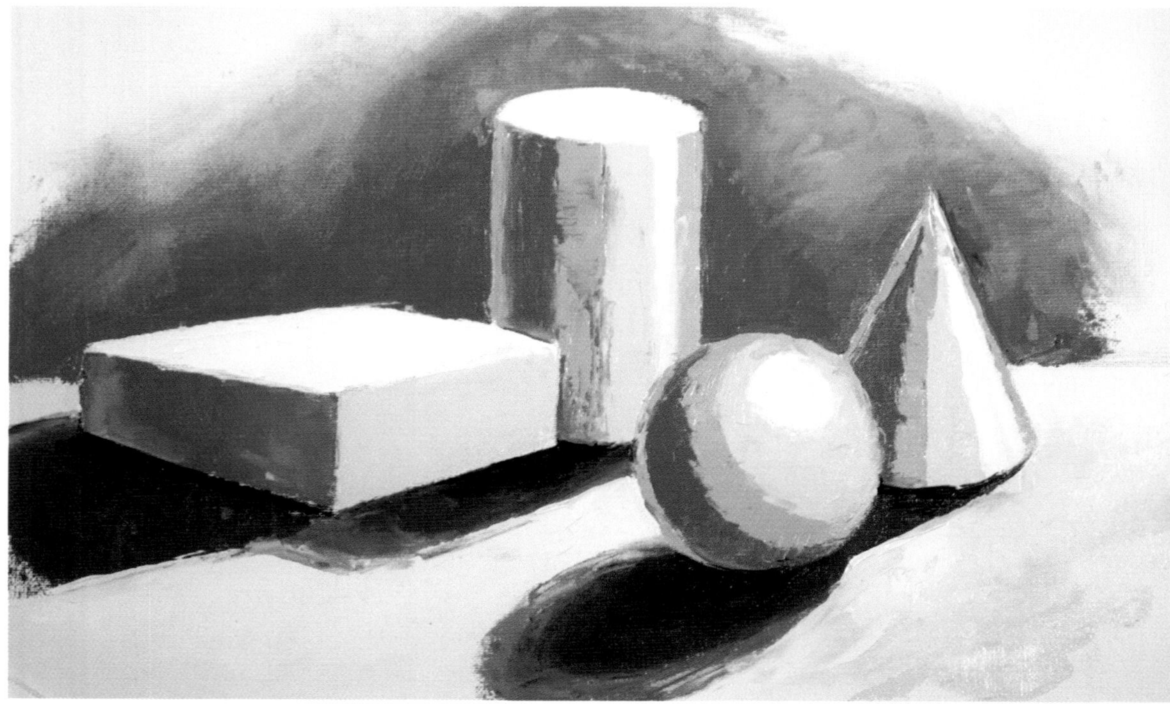

FIGURE 14.
Study of basic forms in value only.

What is value? Remove the color. Remember that value is to drawing as color is to painting. But this value study gets the point across, doesn't it?

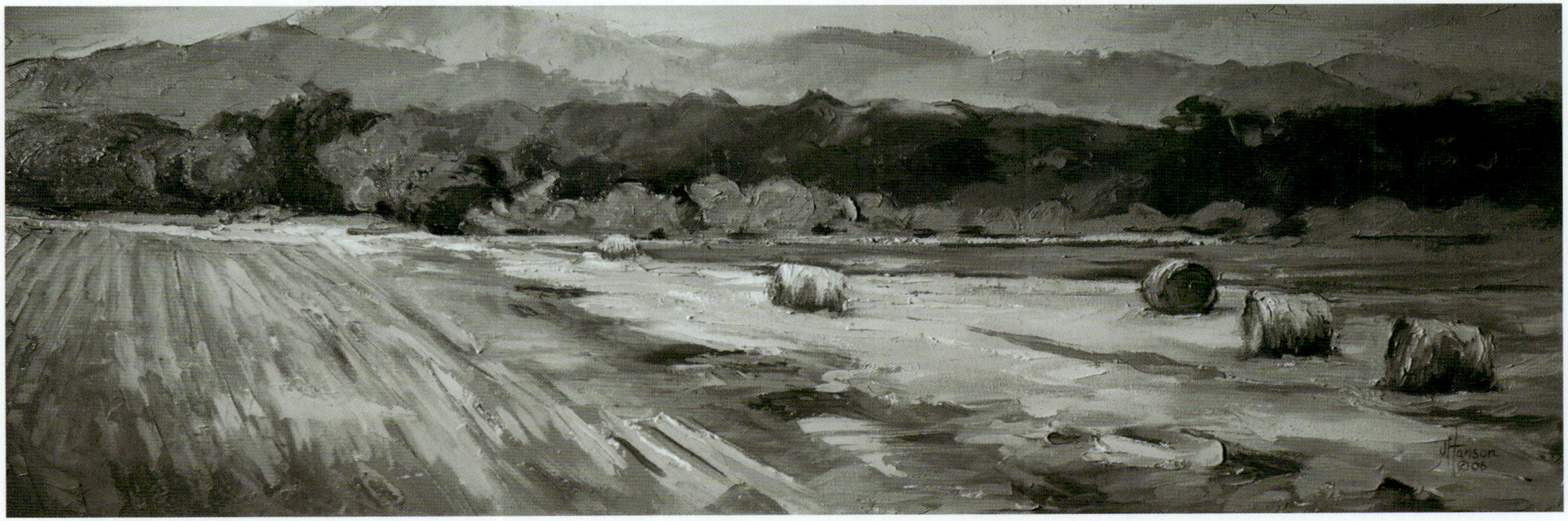

FIGURE 15.
Country Farm by Julie Hanson, 2010. Oil on canvas, 12" × 24". Value only, color removed.

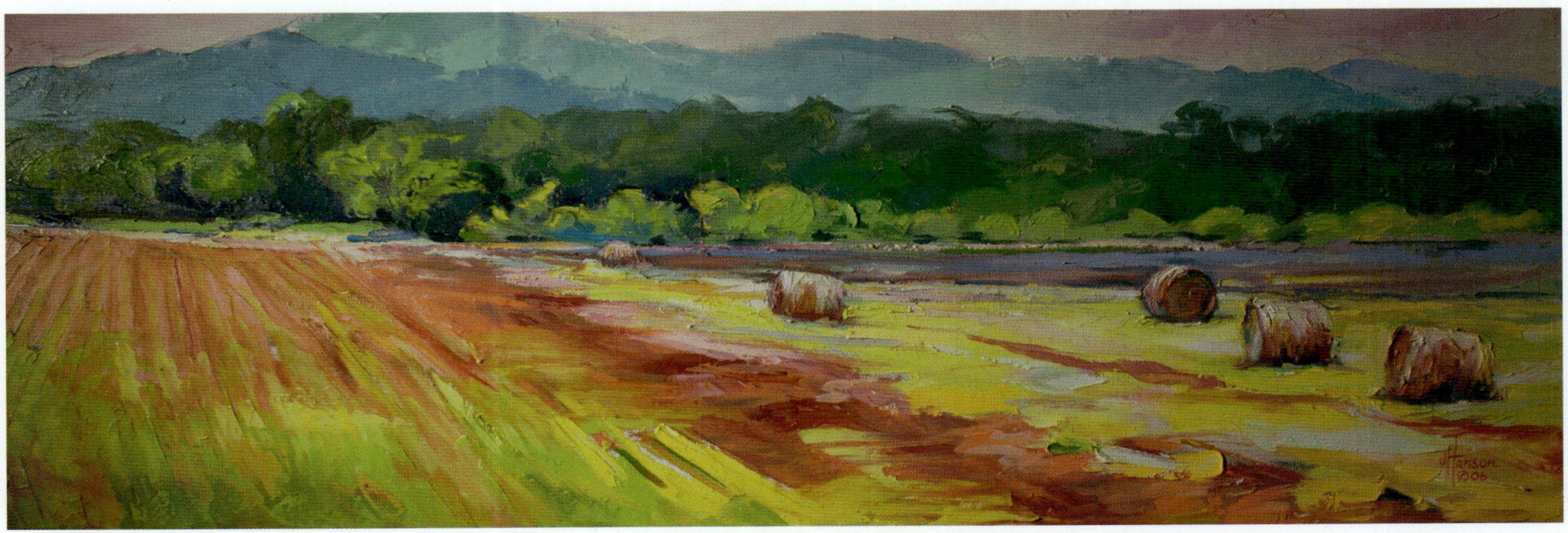

FIGURE 16.
Country Farm by Julie Hanson, 2010. Oil on canvas, 12" × 24".

When considering the cube, you are looking at one of the simplest forms in nature just as you have looked at the simplest use of the primary colors. It is time to put them together.

If the most basic form has three sides for us to paint, then to make something visible in a painting as a form with width, height, and depth, you need all three sides of the form. I repeat: *you need height, width, and depth to show three-dimensionality. Remember that you need red, yellow, and blue to convince us that something on a two-dimensional surface is real or three-dimensional.* That is what color does! So? There are three basic colors you need to make something three-dimensional and there are three sides to your basic form . . . any light bulbs going off yet?

This is extremely basic stuff, yet this is where it all begins. Directions for mixing colors in the four forms in figure 17:

1. yellow and white highlight
2. and 3. red, yellow, and blue and white midtone or local color
4. blue and white shadow
5. blue and more white than shadow color for reflected light
6. blue and a touch of red plus less white than in shadow color cast shadow.

I like painting white forms, as they are a neutral playing ground for red, yellow, and blue. But go easy on the red! In a stronger-colored object, for example, it can sometimes be a little easier to manipulate red, yellow, and blue to do their jobs. I added a touch of red to the blue to darken and alter the color of the shadow to set off the objects. The background is painted a fairly dark green since that color would also set off the objects. Because painted white objects don't typically have strong reds, yellows, and blues in them, adding a green background gives more power to what little red is in the color.

Simply put:
Yellow is the lit side.
Blue is the shadowed side.
Redis the side you need to pull forward or give body with its warmth, or to give "roundidity."

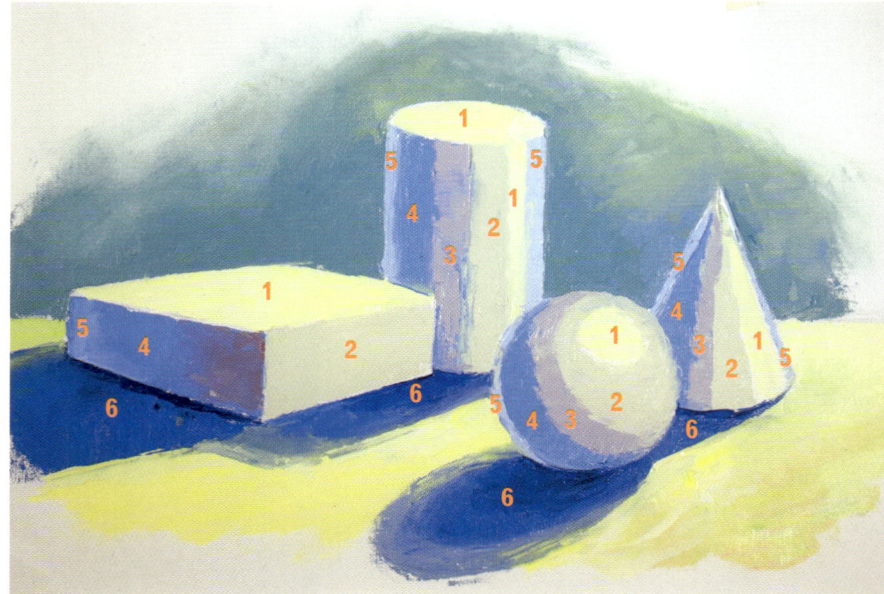

FIGURE 17.
Study with yellow, blue, and red to show three-dimensional form. 1) yellow and white highlight; 2 and 3) red, yellow, and blue and white mid tone or local color; 4) blue and white shadow; 5) blue and more white than the shadow color for reflected light; 6) blue and a touch of red plus less white than in the shadow color.

This is not an exact science, but it is a science that works when you get the hang of it. Sometimes you have the shadow side coming toward you, so that means blue, doesn't it? Yes, but the blue will have to be combined with red in some way so that the red can do its job to bring the object forward. You must weave the threads! If you remember the colors and their jobs, you will usually find your answer to mixing a successful color. Some forms are more difficult than others, of course, just as some actual colors are more difficult to paint. All of the forms need to have the colors used effectively to make them three dimensional. More blending is required on the rounded forms, so, in my opinion, they are more difficult to paint or, at the very least, more time consuming than the cube. And, too, some objects have more difficult local colors than others.

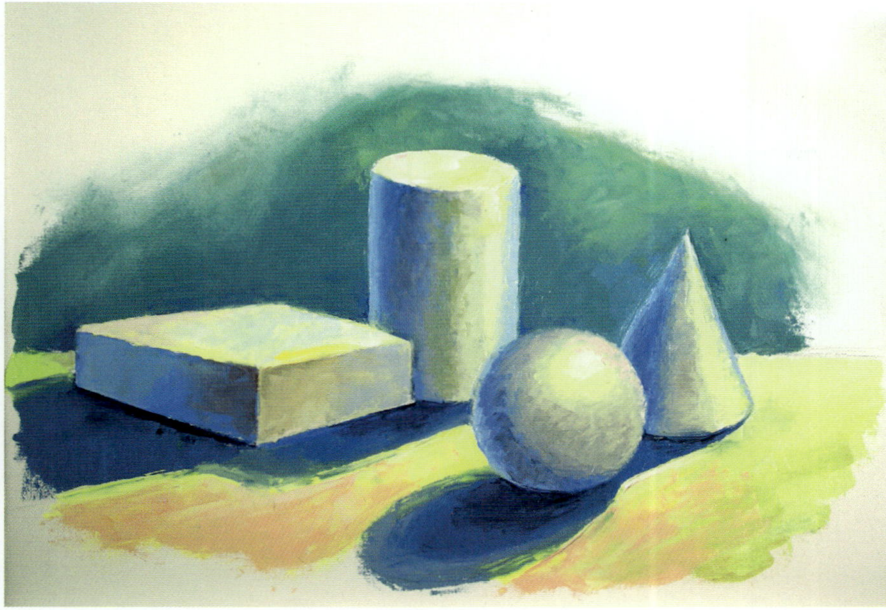

FIGURE 18.
More color added to create the local color white.

In figure 18, the colors are smoothed as evenly as possible. I found that red had to be added to the shadow color on the rounded forms to help them pull forward and turn. This creates the core shadow. I also added red on the cube to pull the front corner forward.

Because the local color on these forms is white, the three primaries have to be blended together to be kept neutral enough to represent white.

Red was added to the mix on the right side of the block to pull the corner forward. I added red to the front of the table to help pull that forward and to balance the yellow. I lightened the back edge of the block on the left side. A couple of crisp edges in the background help the objects pop, and a small bit of permanent rose and white on the back edges of the objects also helps to pop them out from the green behind them. Finally, the back edges of the lit sides were cooled down to help them recede.

One more time, let's look at the roles of red, yellow, and blue. *The simplest way to illustrate form in a painting is to use yellow for the light source, blue for the shadow or absence of light, and red for body.* Body could be defined as warmth, "roundidity," or bringing something forward. If you look at the color wheel again, the role of yellow is pretty easy to see and so is the role of blue. The role of red is a little harder to see, but after you light an object and a shadow is created, your next job is to make it round or three-dimensional, and that is red's job.

If the first rung of our ladder was to see red, yellow, and blue in every object, the next rung is to look at the actual (local) color of the object you are painting. Now red, yellow, and blue have to work to give three-dimensionality to every color imaginable. This is when the tough get going and the fun begins. This color system now goes to work. With each new actual or local color of your subject, you must find a way to make it look lit, shadowed, and coming forward out of the flat, two-dimensional surface of your canvas.

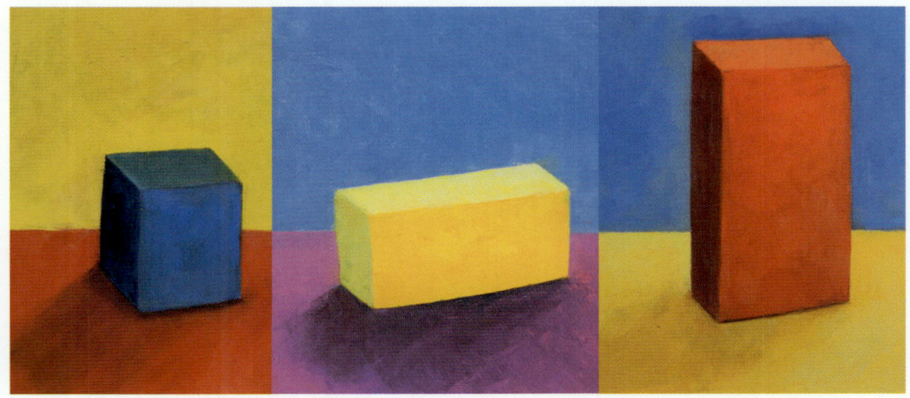

Block Studies by Candi Russell, 2014.
Oil with palette knife on canvas pad, (3) 12" × 16".

Why do we do this? The beginning color student thinks the goal of painting is to match the color of the object they are painting. You think if you get that right, the painting will work, and sometimes it does. But for the artist seeking good color balance, the truth is that if you get the three primary colors to do their jobs accurately, your painting will be successful. So, again, practice this and paint many simple forms to strengthen your skills with underlying form.

These paintings all express three-dimensional form made exciting by the use of color!

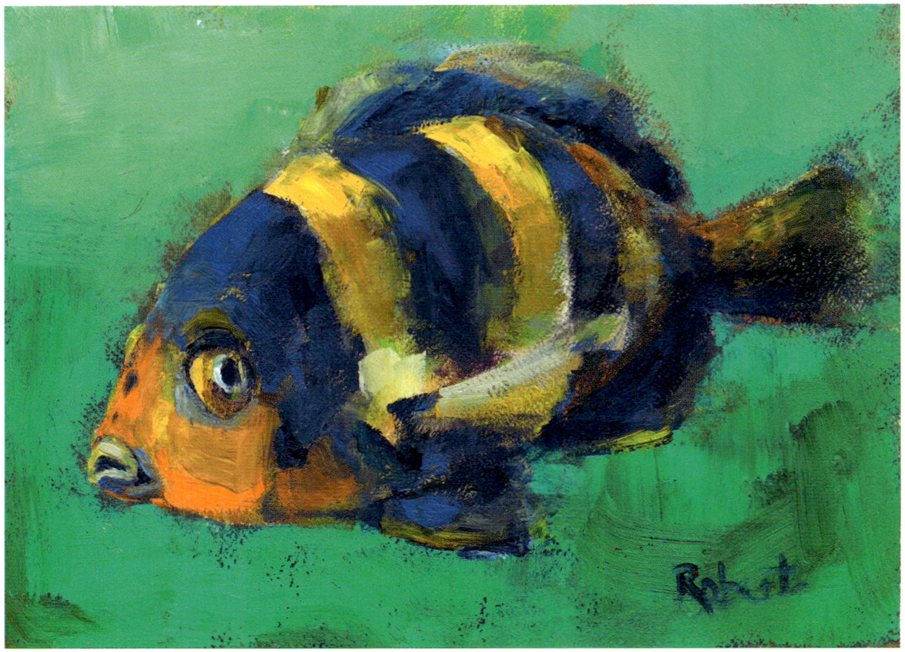

Sidney by Joan Roberts, 2010. Acrylic, 9" × 12".

Are you getting the picture? Notice that each primary color is doing exactly what it does best.

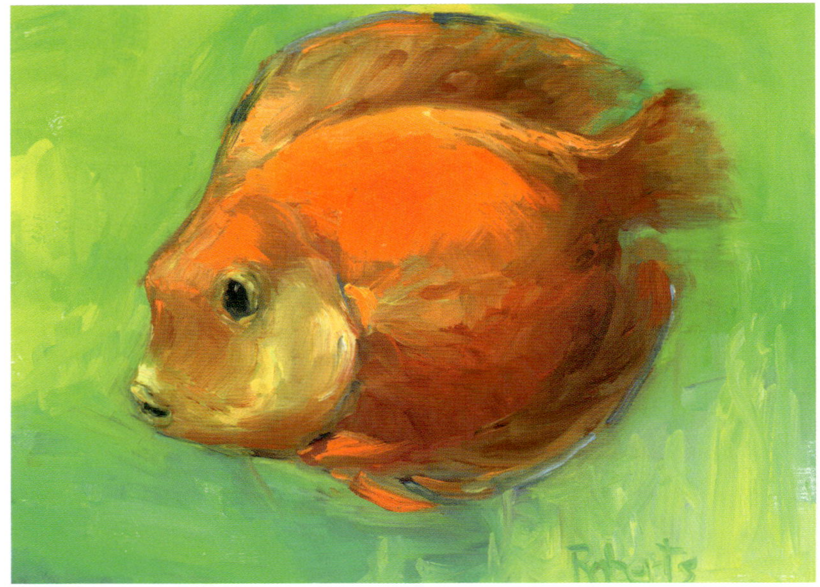

Wanda by Joan Roberts, 2013. Acrylic, 9" × 12".

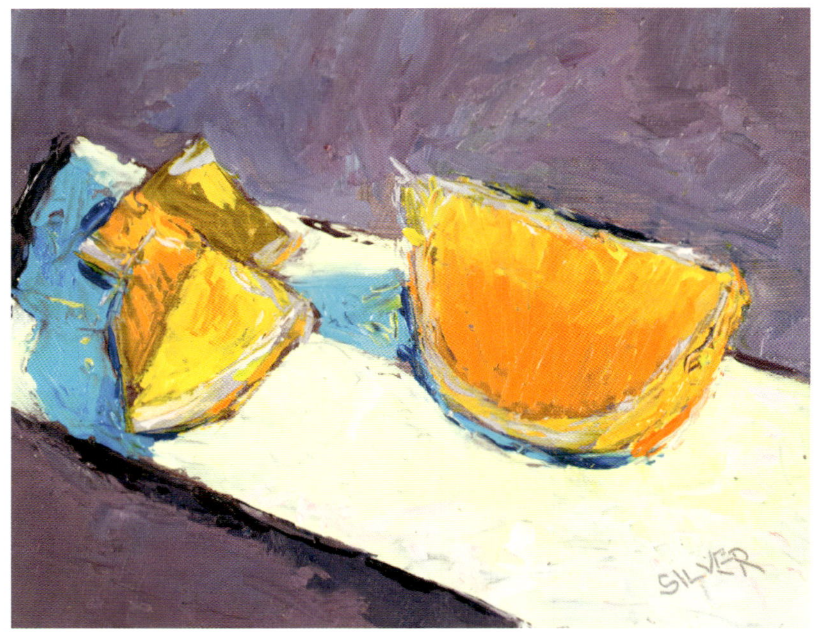

Slice of Life by Judy Silver, 2015. Water-soluble oil, 6" × 7".

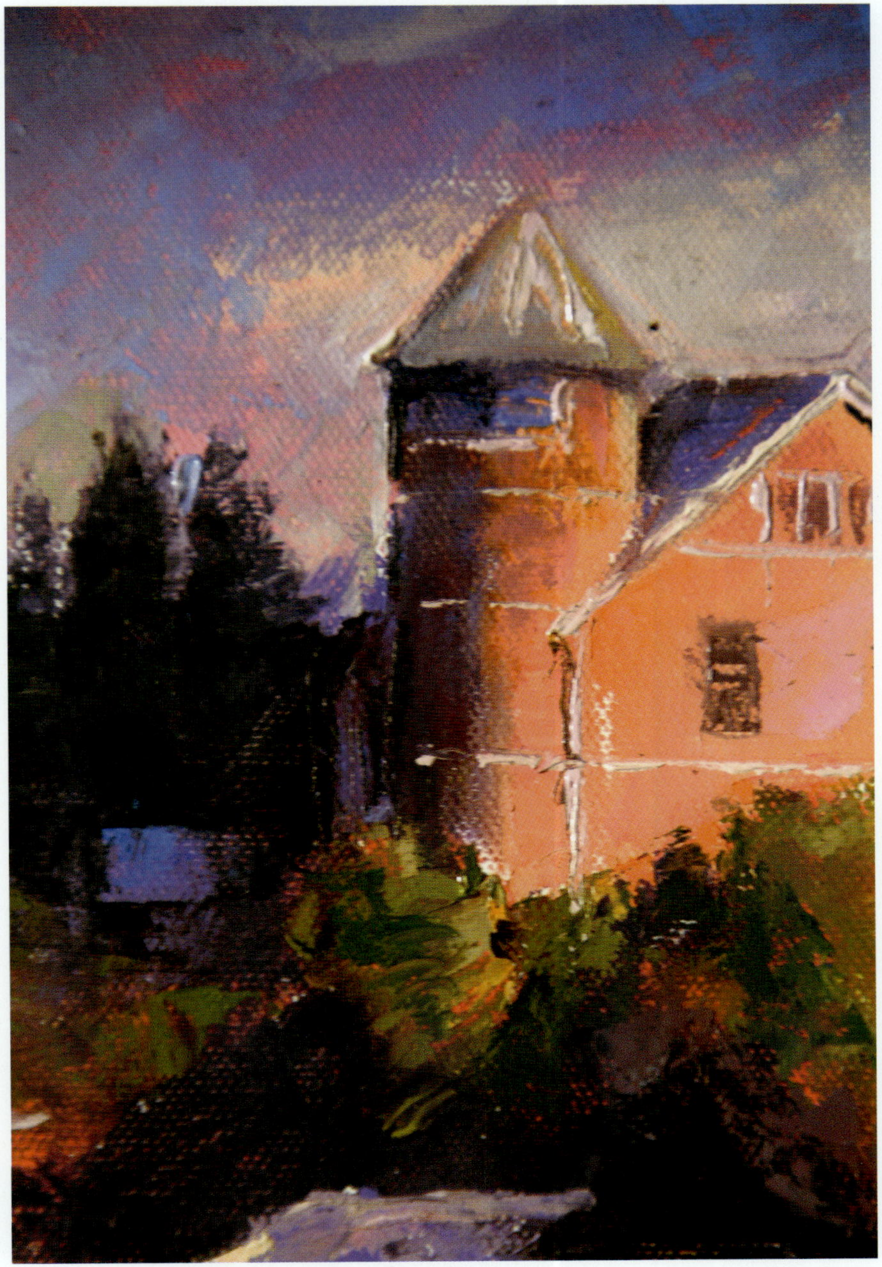

Close-up of *Maine Shore* by Julie Hanson, 2013.
Oil on canvas, 12" × 16".

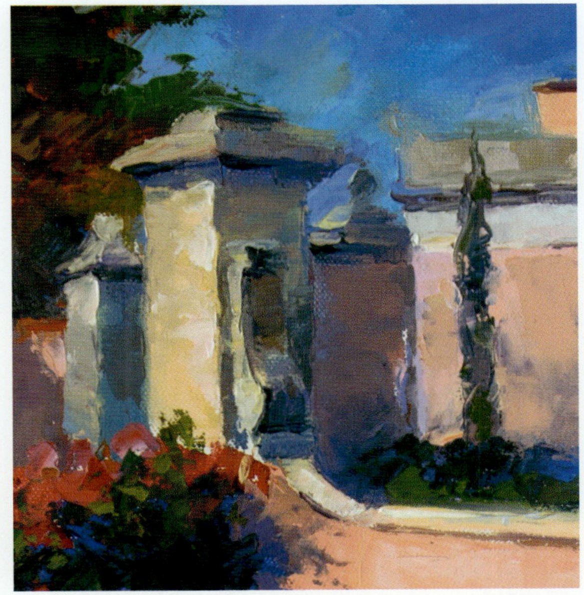

Close-up of *Ringling Museum* by Julie Hanson, 2008.
Oil on canvas, 12" × 16".

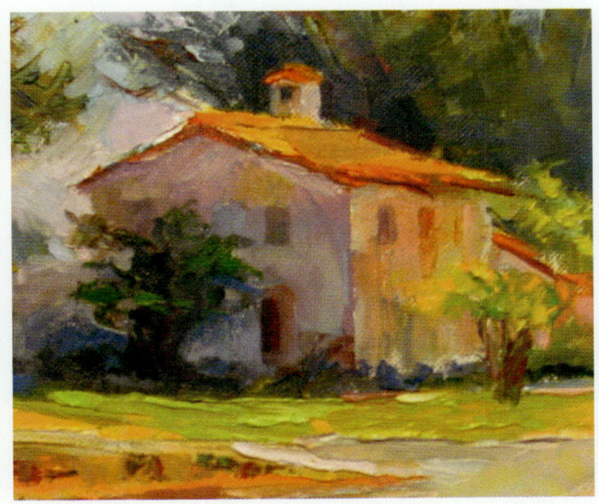

Close-up of *Corner House in Venice* by Julie Hanson, 2007. Oil on canvas, 12" × 16".

Chapter Five

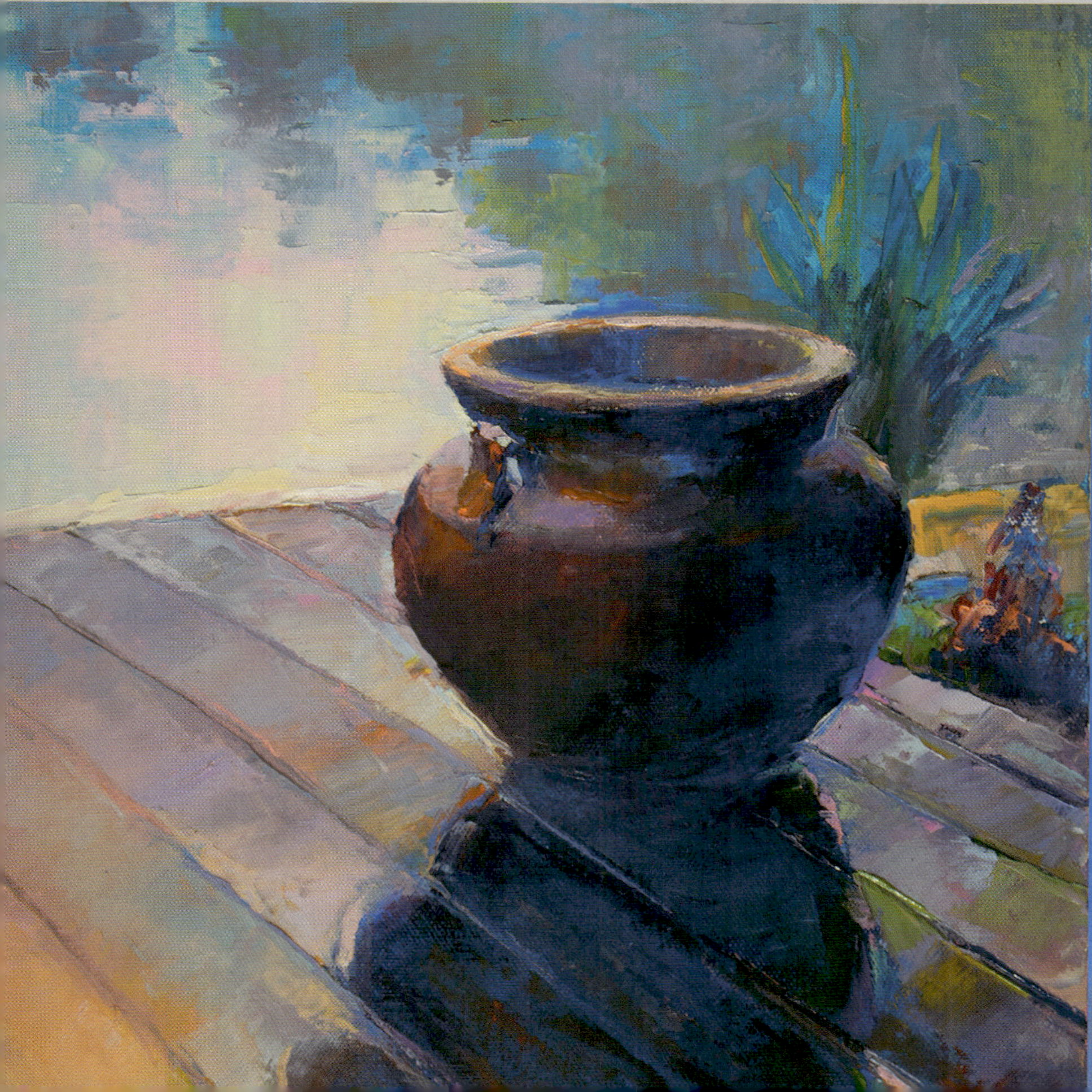

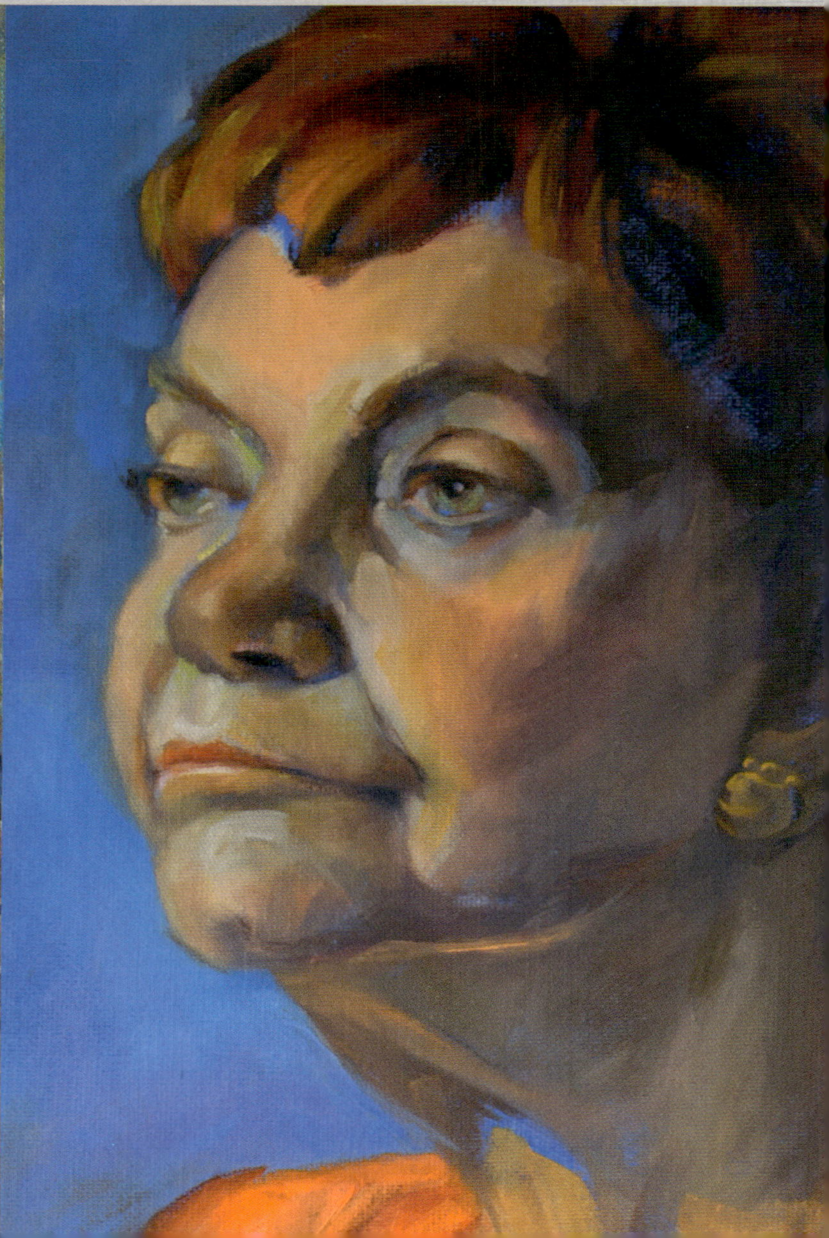

Warm & Cool Colors

Let's climb another rung of our ladder. As a painter, you need to know how to pit a warm color against a cool color to make something exciting happen. Not only that, but every time you want to create a plane change, you need to pit one color against another or one value against another. To the colorist, warm and cool is almost a complete painting language. If you look at the basic color wheel, you can probably tell very easily which colors are considered warm and which are considered cool (fig. 19). Let's look closer. When the color wheel is simplified like this, it is easy to see which colors are warm and which colors are cool.

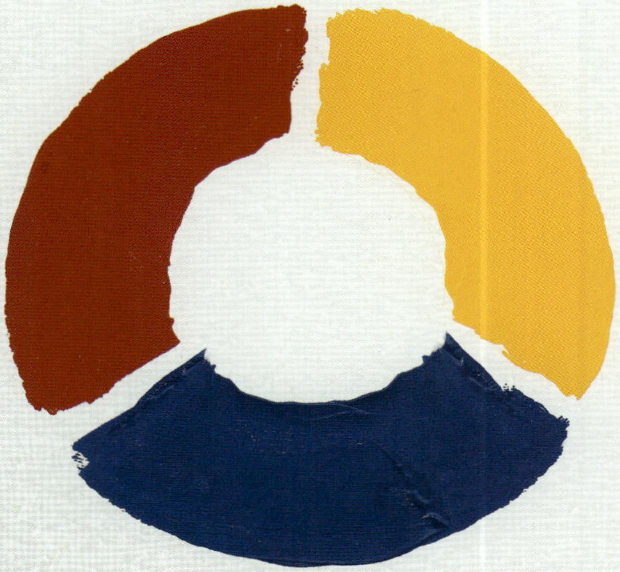

FIGURE 19.
Blue is the *only* cool color. Red and yellow are both warm.

OPPOSITE:
Portion of *Lady in Red* by Julie Hanson, 2014. Oil on canvas, 16" × 20".
Portion of *Rainy Day Color* by Julie Hanson, 2011. Oil on canvas, 12" × 16".

Blue represents cool elements (water, ice). Red represents warm elements (heat, fire). Yellow also represents warmth (light, sun). This is an important point, since we need to know this to paint form. And this brings up another important point for the painter.

Julie's Rule #1: Warm colors come forward and cool colors recede.

If you want a color to come forward, it must be pitted against another color to make that happen. If you want a color to recede, you must set up the appropriate relationship with another color that comes forward. It is your job to do this when you paint.

Painting in color is always about the relationships you have developed. As I said, it is the change in color from, say, warm to cool color (hue) or light to dark (value) that is the language of painting. The colors have their own working relationships that the colorist must learn. When we stop forcing them to do something for us and instead become sensitive to their qualities, magic happens.

So far, we have looked only at the three primary colors. To get the secondary colors—purple, green, and orange—we will need to mix one primary color with another primary color (fig. 20).

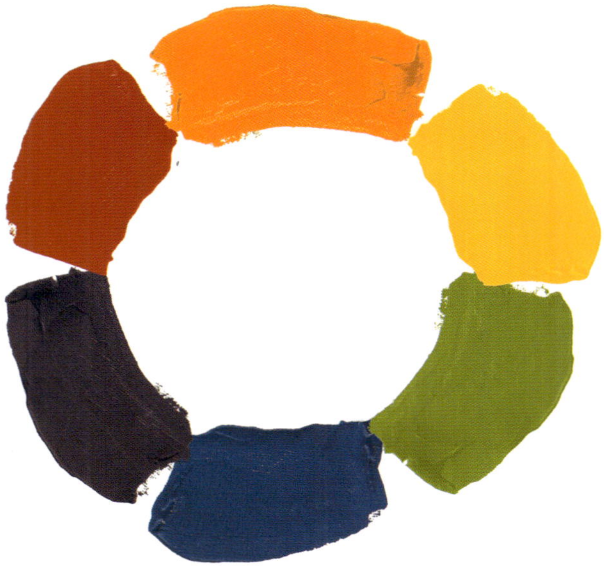

FIGURE 20.
Mixed secondary colors added.

These three secondary colors are also part of the main colors of the rainbow, but they can be mixed from the three primary colors. However, the primary colors cannot be mixed from these. The purity and other characteristics of these color mixes have many of the working properties of the parent colors and so are dependent on which red, yellow, and blue you choose. More on that later.

Here's another rung. Which of these secondary colors are cool and which are warm? If you guessed orange is warm, green is cool, and purple is cool, you are right. Why? If you start with yellow and move toward red, you are warming up yellow because red is the other warm primary. Orange is warm. If you move from yellow to blue and get green, you are adding blue, which is cool. If you start with red and move toward yellow, you are staying warm. If you move from red to blue and get purple, you are adding blue, so the color is considered cool. The biggest problem is with blue, the only cool primary. If you move toward red, you are warming it up. If you move toward yellow, you are also warming up blue, but blue is still in the mix, and that makes green and purple cool. So, when we look at the color wheel this way and split it in half, we now have three cool colors and three warm colors. It's a great balance (fig. 21).

Simply put: Colors containing blue are considered cool. Colors containing red or yellow are considered warm.

Now look across the color wheel at the color on the opposite side. These opposites are called complementary colors (fig. 22). They complement each other because they are completely different from each other (not containing any part of the other); each one is pitted against or opposite the combination of the other two. This is something you will want to memorize (and keep a color wheel handy). The three sets of complementary colors are:

Yellow – Purple
Orange – Blue
Red – Green

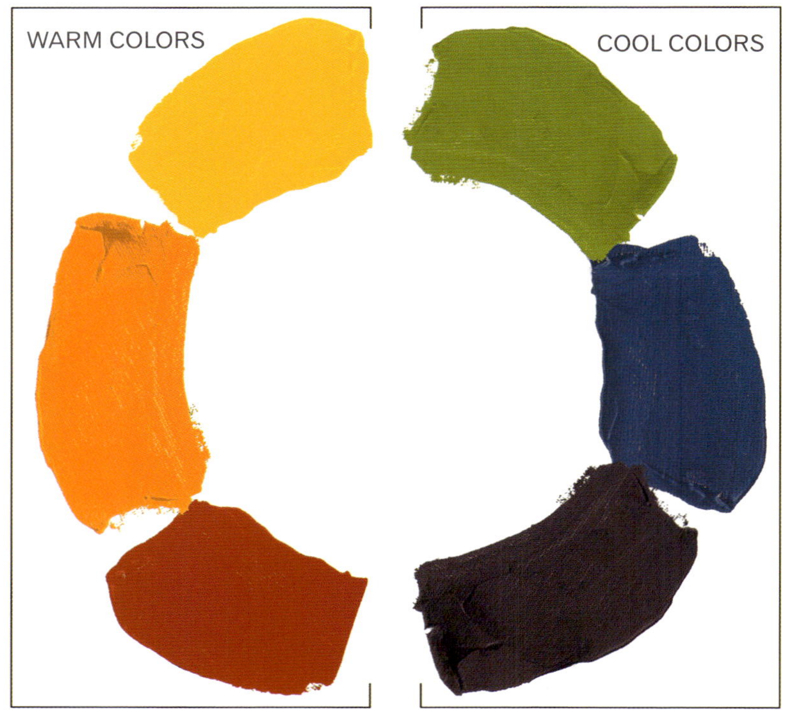

FIGURE 21.
Warm and cool colors of the color wheel.

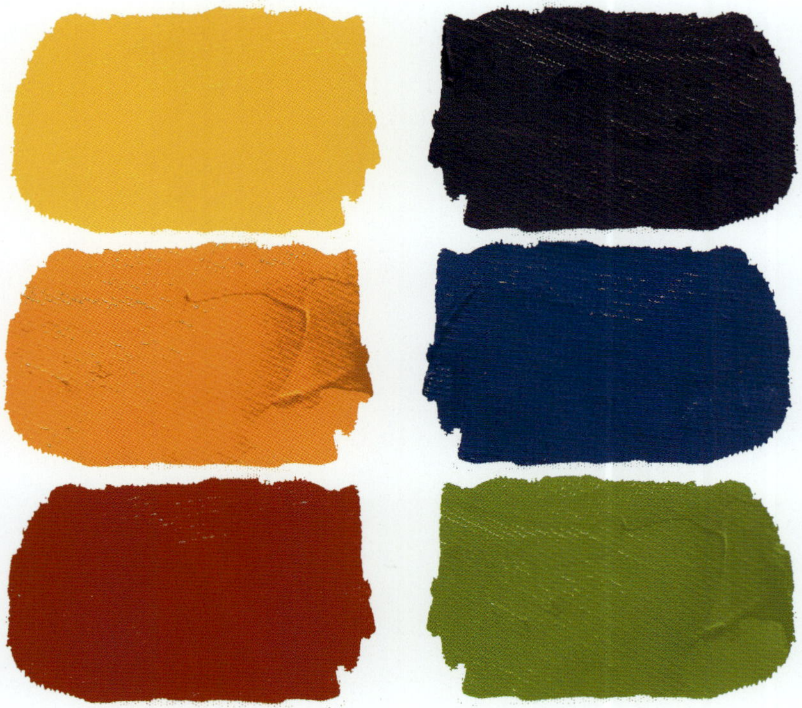

FIGURE 22.
The three sets of complementary colors.

To recap, you need to pit a warm color against a cool color to make something exciting happen in your painting. And you'll want to use color to create three-dimensionality as well. Let's go further into the study of warm and cool color relationships and how they can be fully developed by the pigments we choose when we paint. Let's look at the double primary palette.

As we saw earlier, it is very hard to get one perfect red, blue, or yellow to make those nice, clean mixtures that contain the qualities of light. The pigments don't behave the way light does, so we need to find a better way to mix a variety of beautiful, clean colors.

Again, Julie's Rule #1: Warm colors come forward and cool colors recede.

In figure 23, I have divided each slice of the pie for each primary into thirds. You can see the names of the pigments that belong in that part of the color wheel. All of the pigments, pure or otherwise, that you can buy at the art store fit somewhere inside the color wheel. You can probably figure out by comparison the colors not shown here (or listed in chapter 2). Now that you are familiar with the color wheel, you can use it to decide if a tube of color is warm or cool. Remember, it is the relationship to another color that determines whether a color is warm or cool, and that may change any time you add another color to your painting.

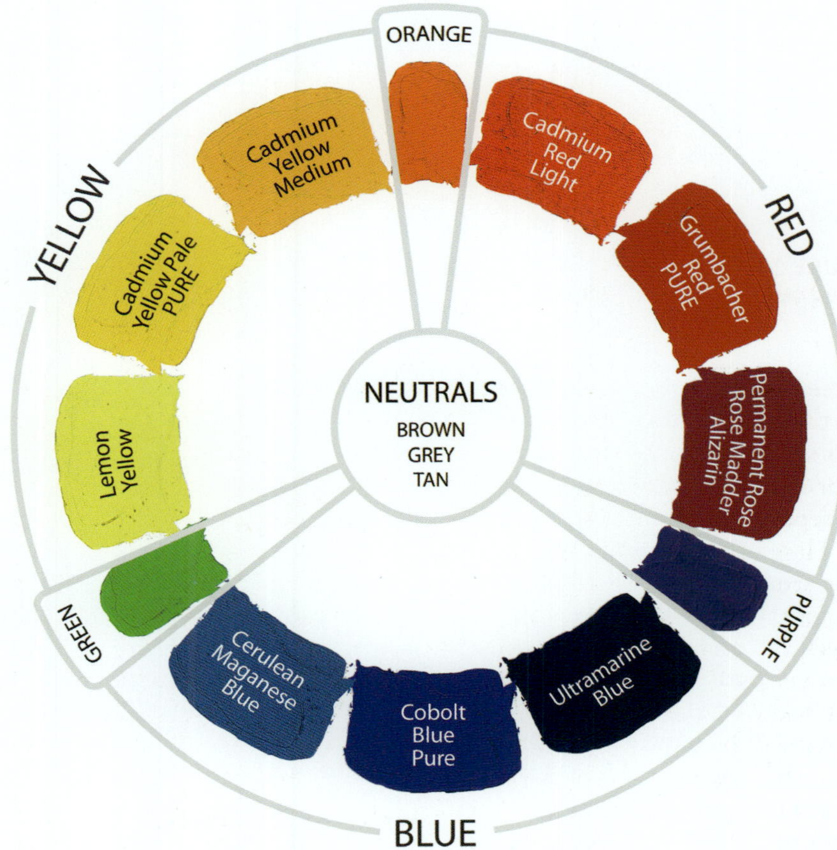

FIGURE 23.
This is the complete color wheel, including the double primary palette. It includes all of the colors discussed so far.

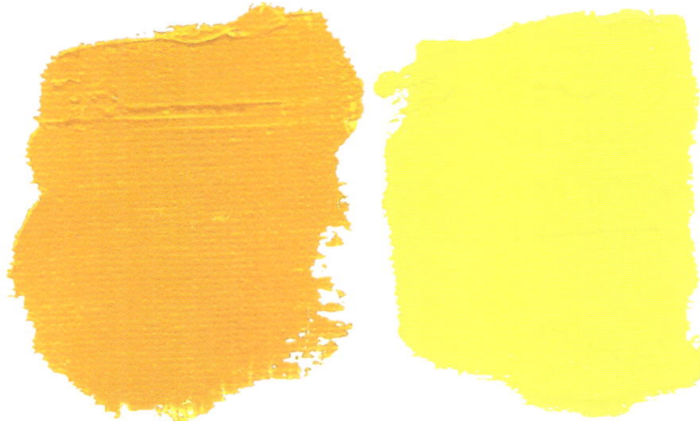

FIGURE 24.
When the yellow in the middle of the color wheel is removed, you can see by comparison that the cadmium yellow medium on the left is warm and the lemon yellow on the right is cool.

Notice also on figure 23, starting with yellow, the color in the middle is considered pure (no red or blue in it). The yellow on the right is beginning to move to the other warm primary, red, which makes that color warm, right? The color on the left of pure yellow is beginning to move to blue. That makes it cool, right? Figure 24 shows warm versus cool yellow.

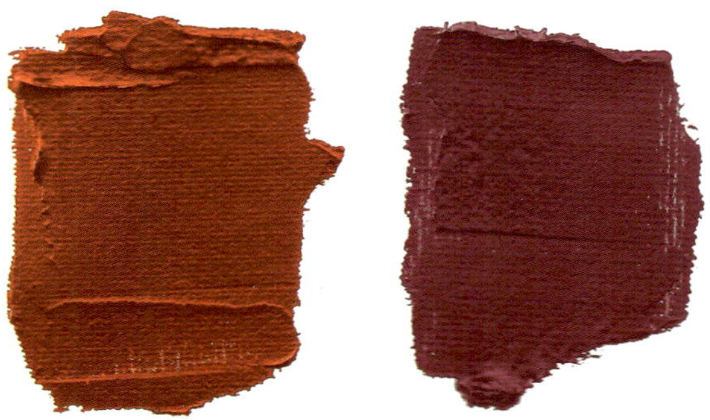

FIGURE 25.
When the red in the middle of the color wheel is removed, you can see by comparison that the cadmium red light on the left is warm and the permanent rose on the right is cool.

Now look at red (fig. 23). The color in the middle is considered pure (no yellow or blue in it). The color to the left is beginning to move toward yellow, which keeps it warm. The color on the right is moving towards the cool primary, blue, so it is cool. Figure 25 shows warm versus cool red.

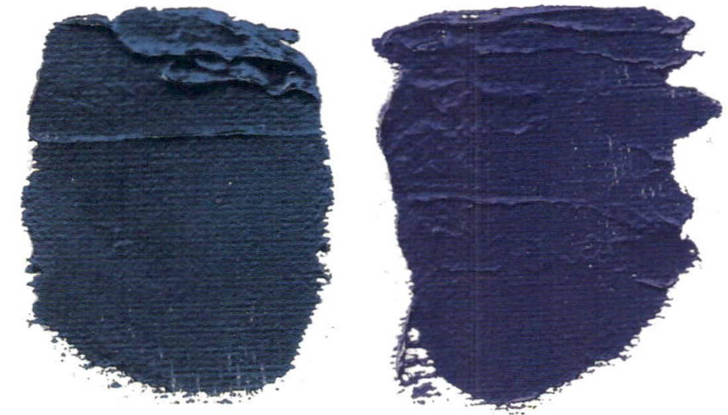

FIGURE 26.
When the blue in the middle of the color wheel is removed, you can see by comparison that the manganese (or cerulean) blue is warm and the ultramarine blue is cool . . . or is it?

In Figure 23, notice that cobalt blue is considered to be our pure blue (does not contain either red or yellow). It is confusing now to decide what blue is doing as it moves to the other primaries, isn't it? That is because when blue moves toward the red primary, it is being warmed by red, but when it is moving toward the yellow primary, it is also warming. So, which is the warmer of the two? That is a continued source of disagreement between artists. There are other factors at play as well, which we will discuss later. For now, I will be referring to manganese blue as the warmer of the two and ultramarine as the cooler. One reason for this is that manganese blue has more yellow in it than ultramarine blue has red. Another way of explaining it is that ultramarine blue is closer to cobalt (pure blue) in appearance and working properties than manganese. Also, because ultramarine blue is a darker value than manganese blue, you must add white to ultramarine (thus cooling it further) when comparing its equal value to manganese (fig 27).

This then, is the double primary palette (fig. 28). It does not contain the pure red, yellow, and blue, but includes only the warm and cool version of each primary color. Here is the magic you need to develop rich and glorious color in your paintings!

FIGURE 27.
The first two colors are our double primary palette blues. White has been added to ultramarine blue on the bottom right swatch to equalize the values of the two blues. Because we can't darken manganese to equal the value of ultramarine, we must lighten ultramarine blue to equal the value of manganese. Now which is warmer and which is cooler? The answer becomes more clear.

Simply put: You now have a way to have a warm yellow and a cool yellow to pit against each other. You have the same with red and blue. Another way of saying this is that you now have a warm blue, a cool yellow, and a cool red, whereas before you only had one temperature for each color.

When you look at the color wheel again, I bet you can now see which of the primary colors (divided in thirds), when mixed together will give you the most vivid secondary colors—vivid orange, brilliant green, and vibrant purple. It is the slice of the two primaries, closest to the secondary color!

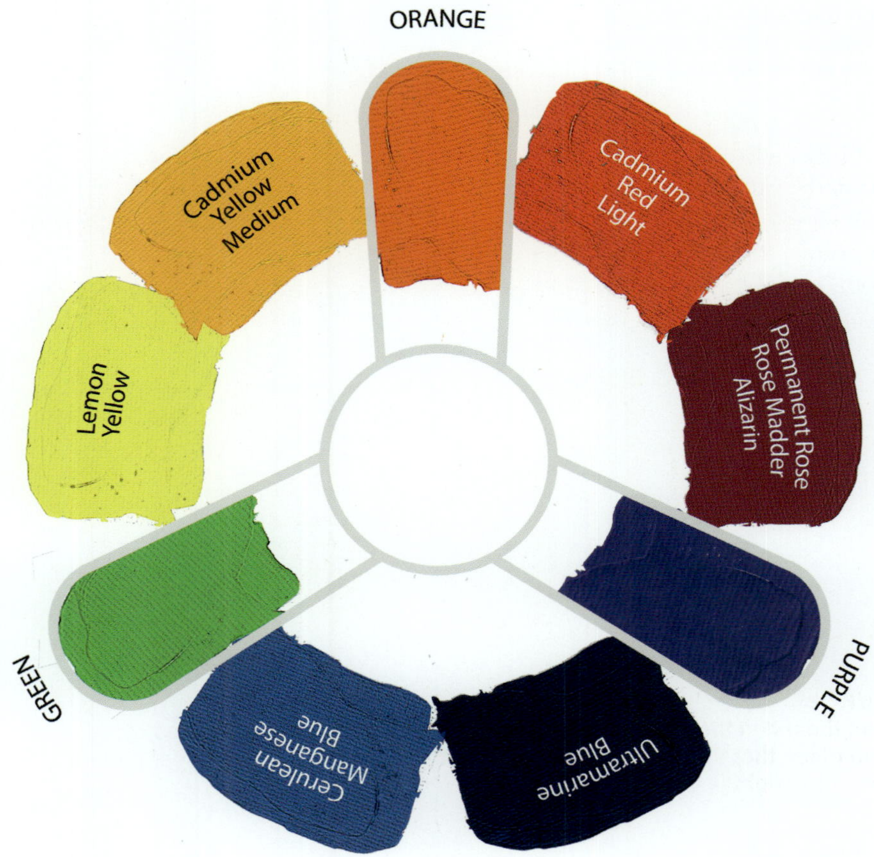

FIGURE 28.
Simplified double primary palette showing secondary colors.

SECONDARY COLORS

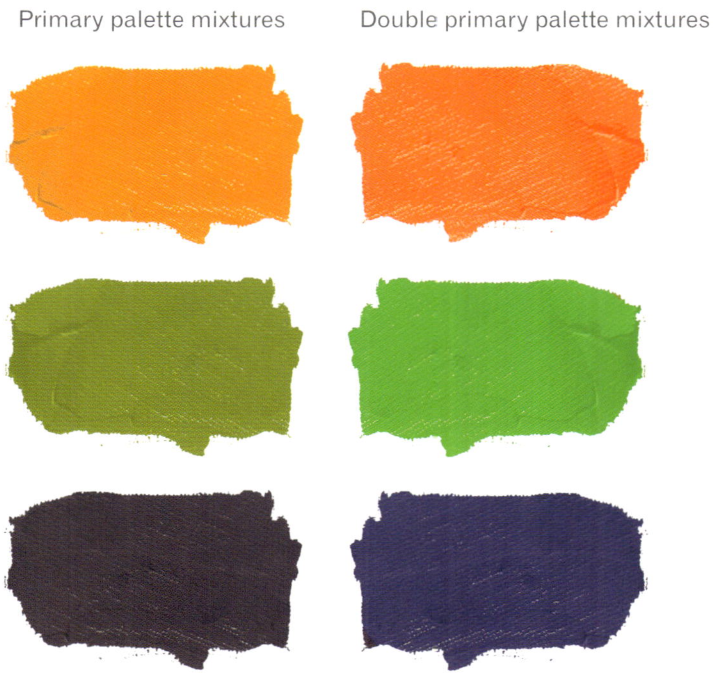

FIGURE 29.
The double primary palette produces much more vivid secondary colors than the three primaries alone.

The double primary palette will help you mix those beautiful, clear colors of the rainbow (fig. 29). This illustration shows the secondary mixtures of orange, purple, and green made from the pure primary colors, and the new mixtures made from the double primary palette. A picture is worth a thousand words!

Julie's Rule #2: Pure color comes forward and mixed color recedes. Pigments right out of the tube, or exceptionally clean, pure colors, or any of the more vibrant mixtures, want to come forward in your painting. The more heavily mixed pigments, earth colors, less vibrant tube colors, and colors with white added recede.

This illustration shows the comparison between pure cadmium orange out of the tube (on the left) to the orange that was mixed by adding yellow to red (on the right). It also shows the difference in purity **(Julie's Rule #2)** between the two blues of our double primary palette—ultramarine and manganese right from the tube.

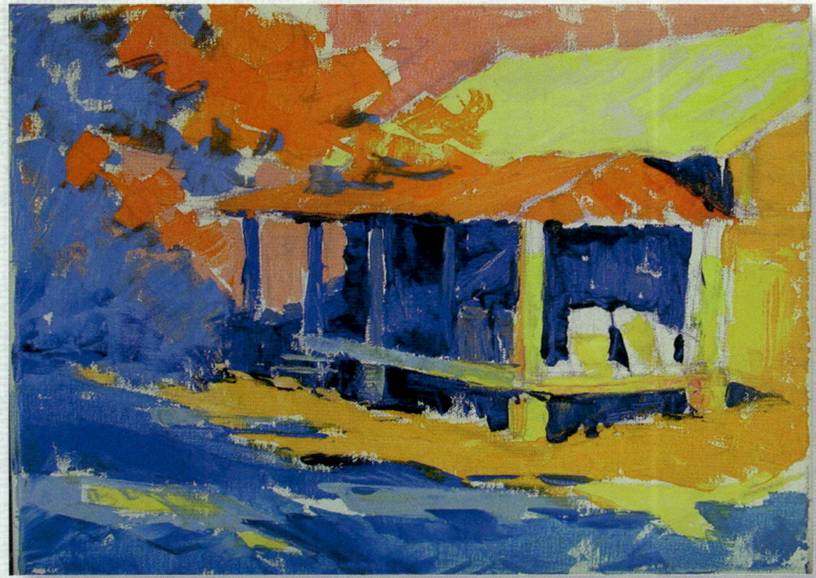

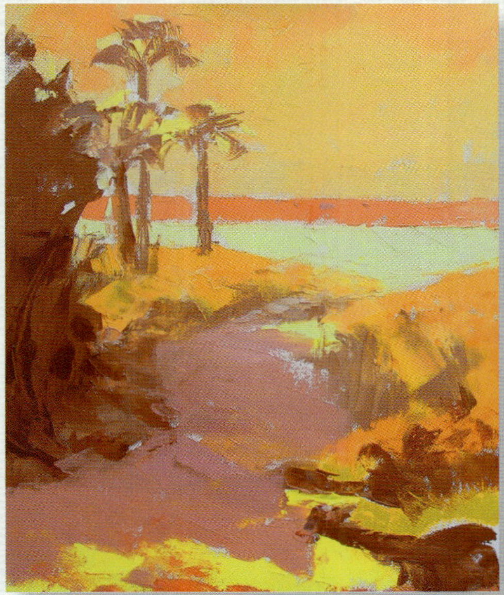

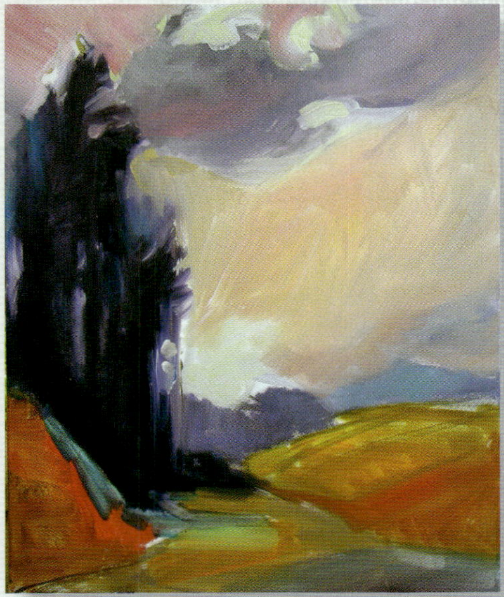

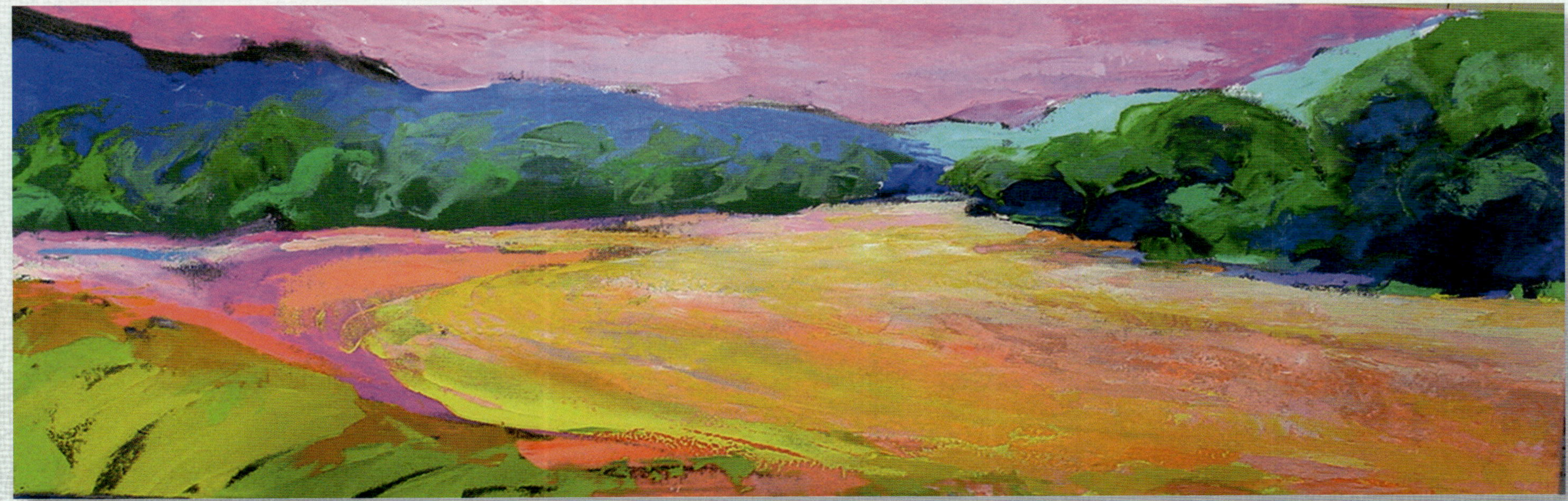

Julie's color studies.

Chapter Six

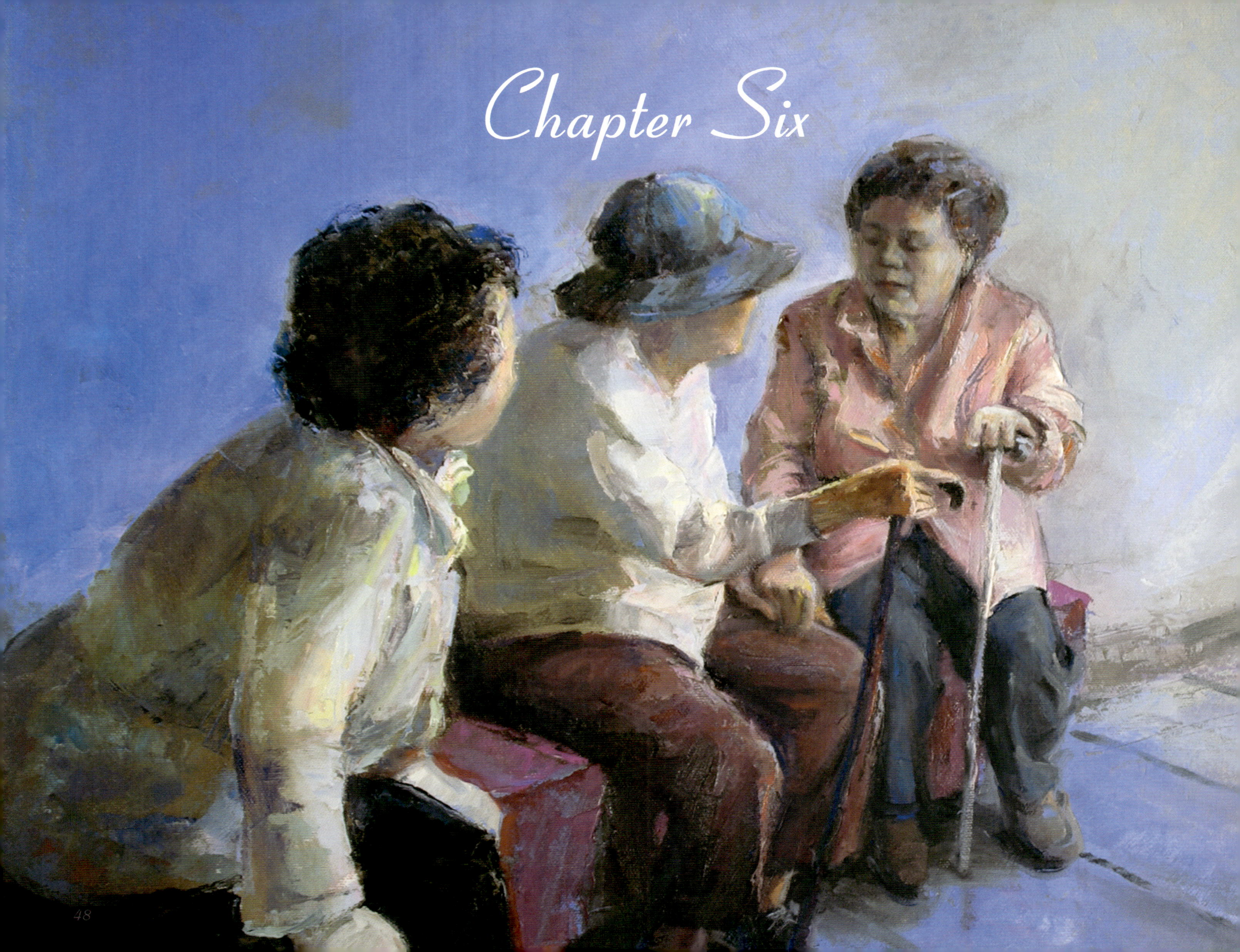

Earth Colors & Neutrals

The double primary palette will help you mix those beautiful, clear colors of the rainbow, and it will also help you mix your dull or neutral colors including the earth colors—browns, grays, and tans.

MUDDY COMPLEMENTS

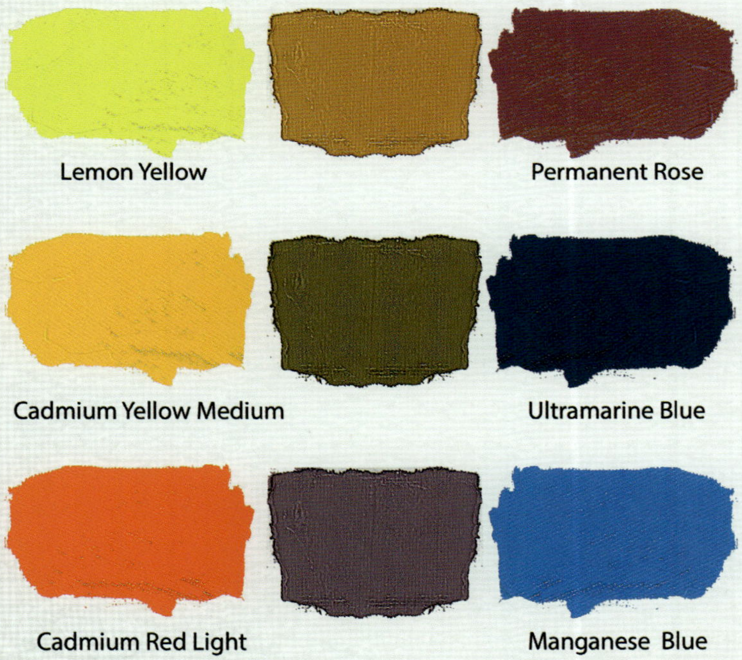

Neutrals can be very important, as they give the eye a rest. They harmonize the other colors and set off the brighter colors and more extreme values. You could say they set the stage for the play. The better the stage set, the better the entire performance.

Now let's put the double primary palette to work. We learned that to make a brilliant orange, we would mix the yellow closest to orange on the color wheel with the red closest to orange. What happens if we mix the yellow furthest from orange with the red furthest from orange? We get a muddy orange (fig. 30). This is because both the yellow and the red we used contain blue. Blue is the complement of orange, hence the orange is muddy, dull, or neutralized. Another way of saying it is that blue kills orange and orange kills blue.

Try now to get a muddy or dull green. Red kills green (it is the complement), so a good way of getting a dull green is to introduce red. How about if we mix ultramarine blue (blue containing red) with cadmium yellow medium (yellow containing red)? Try it.

And to get a muddy purple, you will be amazed at what cadmium red light and manganese blue give you. Try it and see. Manganese is a blue containing yellow; cadmium red light is a red containing yellow. Yellow kills its complement, which is purple.

As you make these non-pure mixtures, note that these are the colors that illustrate **Julie's Rule #2: Pure color comes forward and mixed color recedes.** This is how you fully use this rule. When you mix these paints, you will learn so much about your family of colors and why mixing good color is not the same as a "rainbow of light."

There are many more gifts from the color wheel.

FIGURE 30.
Heavily mixed secondary colors orange, green, and purple mixed from two primaries, both containing the third primary.

OPPOSITE:
Saying Goodbye by Julie Hanson, 2014.
Oil on canvas, 18" × 18".

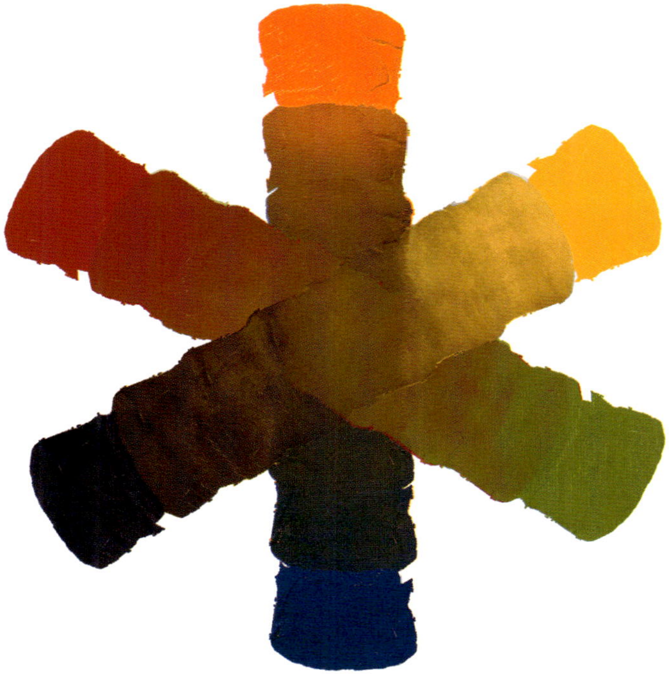

FIGURE 31.
This illustration shows where the neutrals are found on the color wheel.

You now know how to neutralize color. Neutrals are essentially all three primary colors mixed together. Add white and the color is even more neutralized.

How do you make neutrals such as tans, beiges, browns, and grays?

Tan, beige, or gold neutrals are made with yellow to start. Mix them using warm or cool yellow depending on whether you need them to be warm or cool. Next, this yellow needs to be softened, neutralized, or "killed." Your choices are to add a warm or cool blue and a warm or cool red. This is because the complement of yellow is purple, and purple is made by mixing red and blue. You would choose cool blue and red to cool yellow if you are looking for a cool tan. You would choose warm red and blue if you are looking for a warm gold. Then you "season to taste." Neutralized yellows have more yellow, but also both of the other primaries. There are exceptions to this depending on your source colors, but this is the general concept. Add white and it is even more neutral.

Browns are made by starting the mixture with either of the reds, depending on whether you want a warm or cool brown. The complement of red is green, which is a mixture of blue and yellow. You then add to your red choice the warm blue and yellow for warmth. For a cool brown, add the cool red and blue. Browns and red-flavored neutrals have more red, but also both of the other primaries. Beyond that, you must season to taste. There are exceptions to this depending on your source colors, but this is the general concept. Add white, and it is even more neutral.

Grays, blue-grays, green grays, and warm grays start with one of the blues, depending on whether you want a warm or cool gray. The complement of blue is orange, which is the red and yellow primary combined. If you wanted a warm gray, you could choose the warm red and yellow added to the warm blue. For a cool gray, start with ultramarine blue and add the cool red and yellow. Sometimes you have to mix the warms with the cools to get the color you are looking for. *Most grays also need white added to the mix.* This sets gray apart from the other neutrals. White is the final ingredient.

These colors share the quality that they are not pure. Pure pigments (the colors of the double primary palette we discussed) cannot be made from earth colors. Most earth colors can be made from pure color.

Earth colors are called that because they are made from duller pigments. Many of these pigments come from the soil or earth elements. These pigments are usually less pure than pigments manufactured in other ways and tend to be less expensive because they can be found in soil, rock, etc. They include siennas, umbers, ochres, some blacks, grays, and even earth reds, greens, and yellows, not to mention the oxides or transparent pigments. There are an abundance of earth colors.

These colors are traditionally taught for use in developing an underpainting or tonal study of the subject to begin a painting. They are a good choice for this use because of their less pure, more neutral, sometimes weak or transparent nature. But most can be mixed readily from the primary colors. Not only can the majority of earth colors be re-created this way, but often they can be improved so much more when you know what primary colors went into making them. This gives you power—the power to warm them up or cool them down. This information tells you quickly how one compares to another. So why fill up your palette with tube colors when you can make them much more simply yourself from the primary colors?

Sometimes a color has properties other than just its appearance or temperature. It has strength/weakness or transparency/opacity or other attributes that make it an important selection on your palette. Sometimes it is just easier to use earth colors. But for now, and for simplicity's sake, let's mix our own earth colors.

When we look at the illustration of the color wheel in figure 31, we can see how the neutrals or earth colors can be mixed. Browns favor red. Beige and tan favor yellow. Grays favor blue. Colors that aren't pure are simply made by mixing several colors together. Most of the earth colors contain all three primary colors. Now look at figure 32 to see what colors were mixed to approximate some common earth colors.

I found a tube of Holbein transparent black oil. I used that for my black and squeezed some right out of the tube. To match it, I started with ultramarine blue. I then mixed in a small amount of permanent rose and an even smaller amount of lemon yellow. The idea was to keep it dark but knock the blue back with its complement, orange, which is a combination of red and yellow. My black is even more luminous than the black from the tube.

I did not have a tube of gray. My raw umber is M. Graham oil from the tube. To match it, I started with permanent rose. I then added ultramarine blue and a very small amount of cadmium yellow medium. This gave the greenish look, but be careful not to add too much cadmium yellow!

My burnt umber is M. Graham oil. To match it, start with cadmium red light. Then add ultramarine blue. Perfection!

My burnt sienna is M. Graham oil. To match it, start with cadmium red light. Add manganese blue and it will be very close.

My yellow ochre is also M. Graham oil. To match this one, I started with cadmium yellow medium. It was too warm, so I added permanent rose. Then I found a tiny bit of cadmium red light was needed. To gray that down, I added manganese blue. My color still was not as dull as the tube color, so I added a bit of white. It matched!

Remember that no two tube colors from different manufacturers are going to match anyway. In other words there is much wiggle room here. My point is that it is easy to mix the earth colors. What is more important is that, rather than matching them, you learn how they work and how to mix your own warm and cool versions.

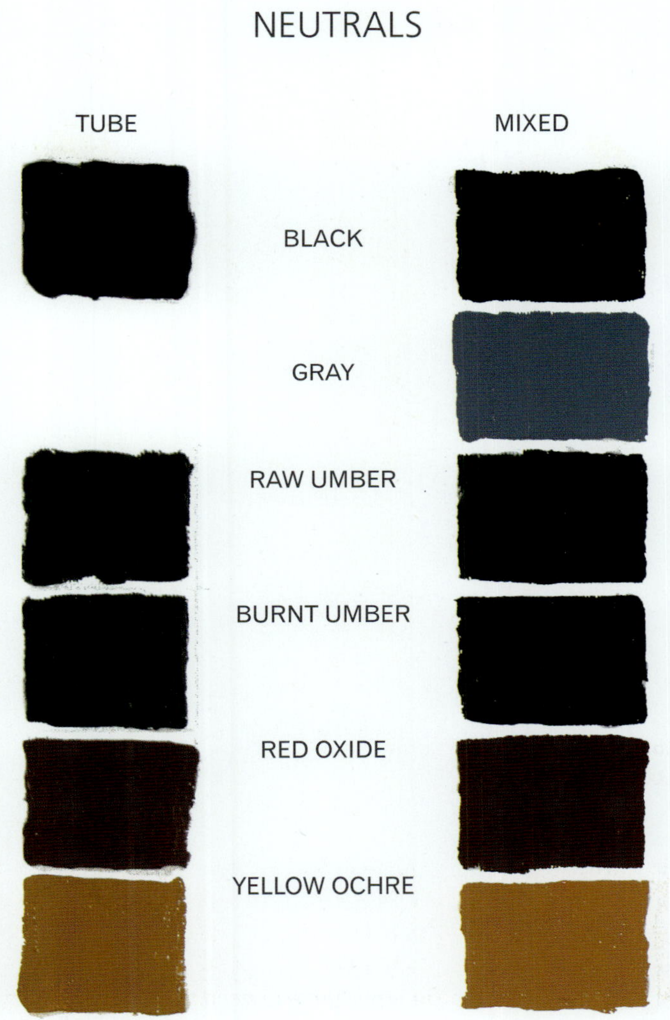

FIGURE 32.
Samples of tube colors vs. mixed (from the double primary palette). The colors shown are dependent on the reproduction process and may not be represented accurately.

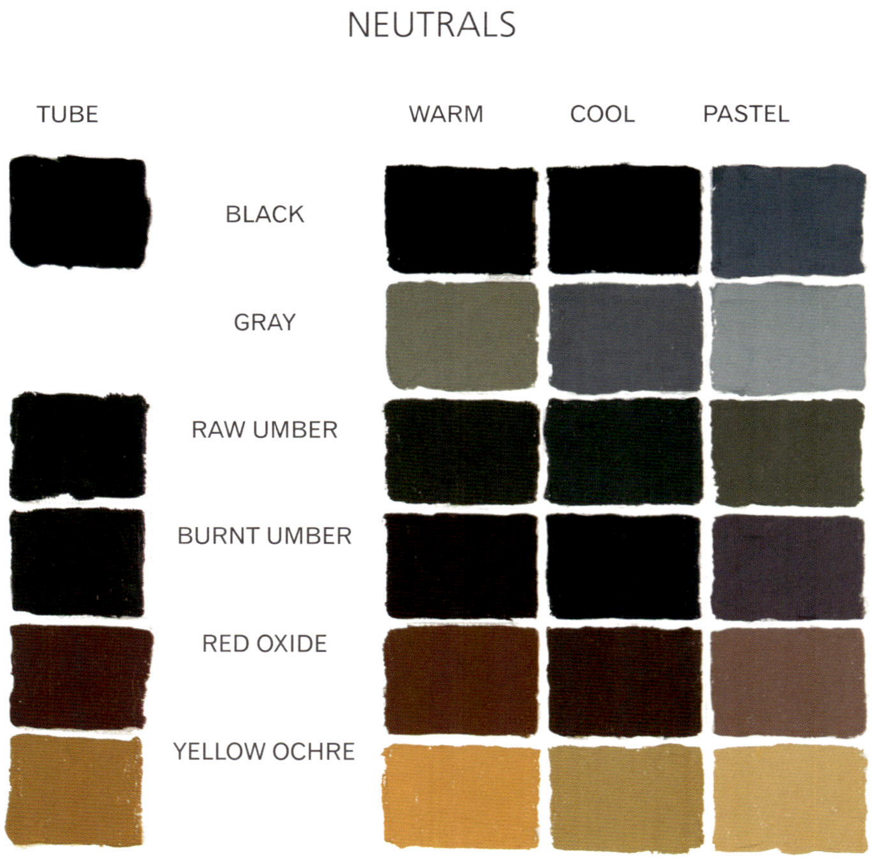

FIGURE 33.
Examples of warm and cool mixtures using the double primary palette. White was added to show a pastel version as well. The colors shown are dependent on the reproduction process and may not be represented accurately.

Warm black: ultramarine blue and cadmium red light.

Cool black: ultramarine blue, permanent rose, lemon yellow.

Warm gray: ultramarine blue or manganese blue and cadmium red light and white.

Cool gray: ultramarine blue, lemon yellow, permanent rose and white.

Warm raw umber: permanent rose, less ultramarine blue than with the cool formula, cadmium yellow medium.

Cool raw umber: permanent rose, ultramarine blue, cadmium yellow medium.

Warm burnt umber: cadmium red light, ultramarine blue.

Cool burnt umber: less cadmium red light than the warm formula, ultramarine blue, tiny touch of white.

Warm burnt sienna: more cadmium red light than the cool formula, manganese blue.

Cool burnt sienna: less cadmium red light than the warm formula and manganese blue.

Warm yellow ocher: cadmium yellow medium, permanent rose, manganese blue.

Cool yellow ocher: cadmium yellow medium, lemon yellow, permanent rose, ultramarine blue, plus a tiny bit of white.

For the pastels shown in figure 33, I just added white.

These formulas are not carved in stone, but they give you the general idea of how to make earth tones. We are always looking at what is warm, what is cool. The most important point is that your warms and cools are in relationship to each other. It is this contrast that helps to create the excitement in your painting. You can see how to make warm and cool browns, tans, and grays. Can you see how much more power you can achieve by controlling your mixtures with your use of warm and cool primaries? Again, your control here is almost more important than the actual color of your subject, but there is no reason why you can't have your cake and eat it too.

Note: It isn't the exact color of something that matters as much as it is the relationships set up using contrasting hues, temperatures, and values.

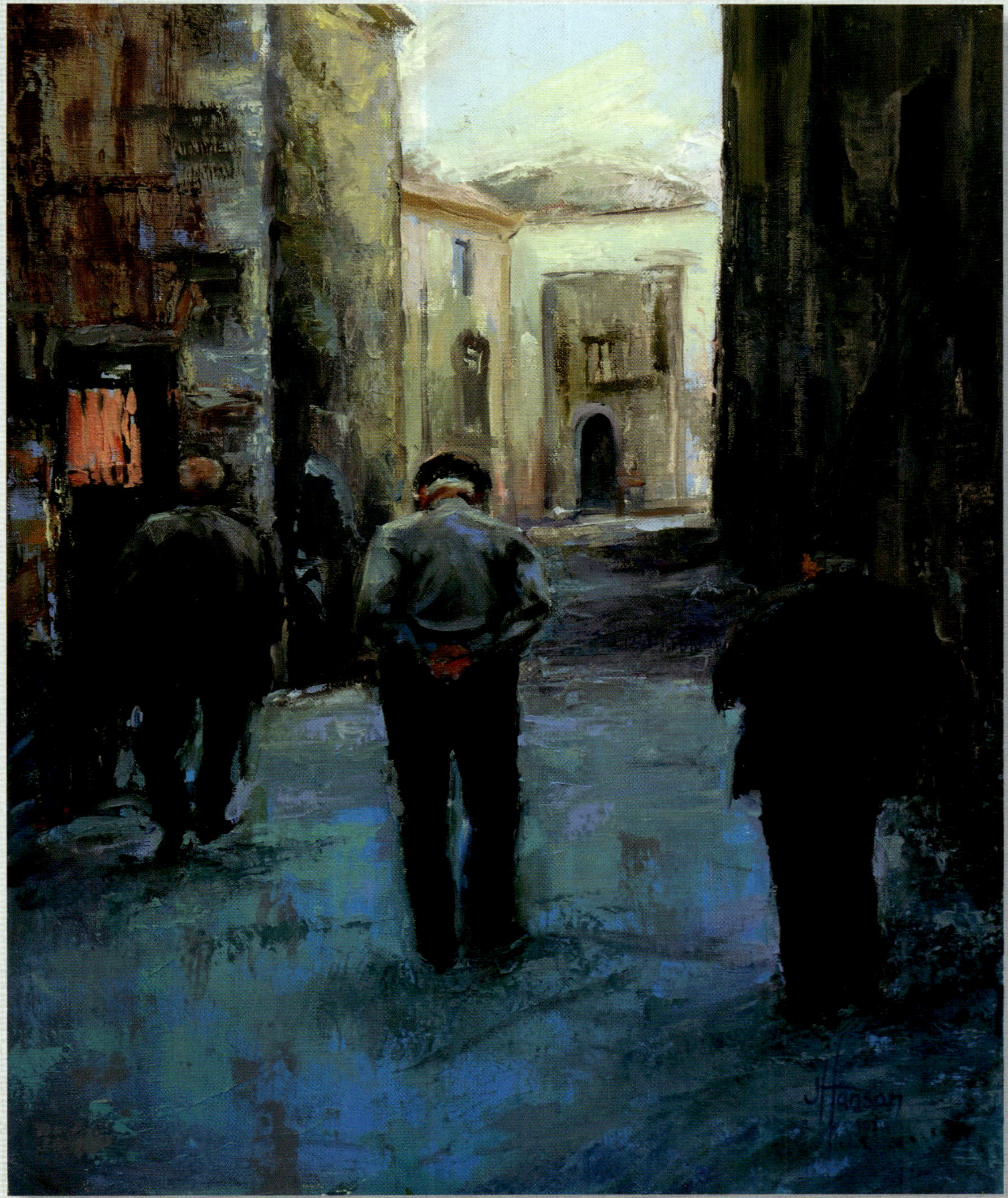

Old World, 2015. Oil on canvas, 18" × 18".
No earth colors were used in this painting.

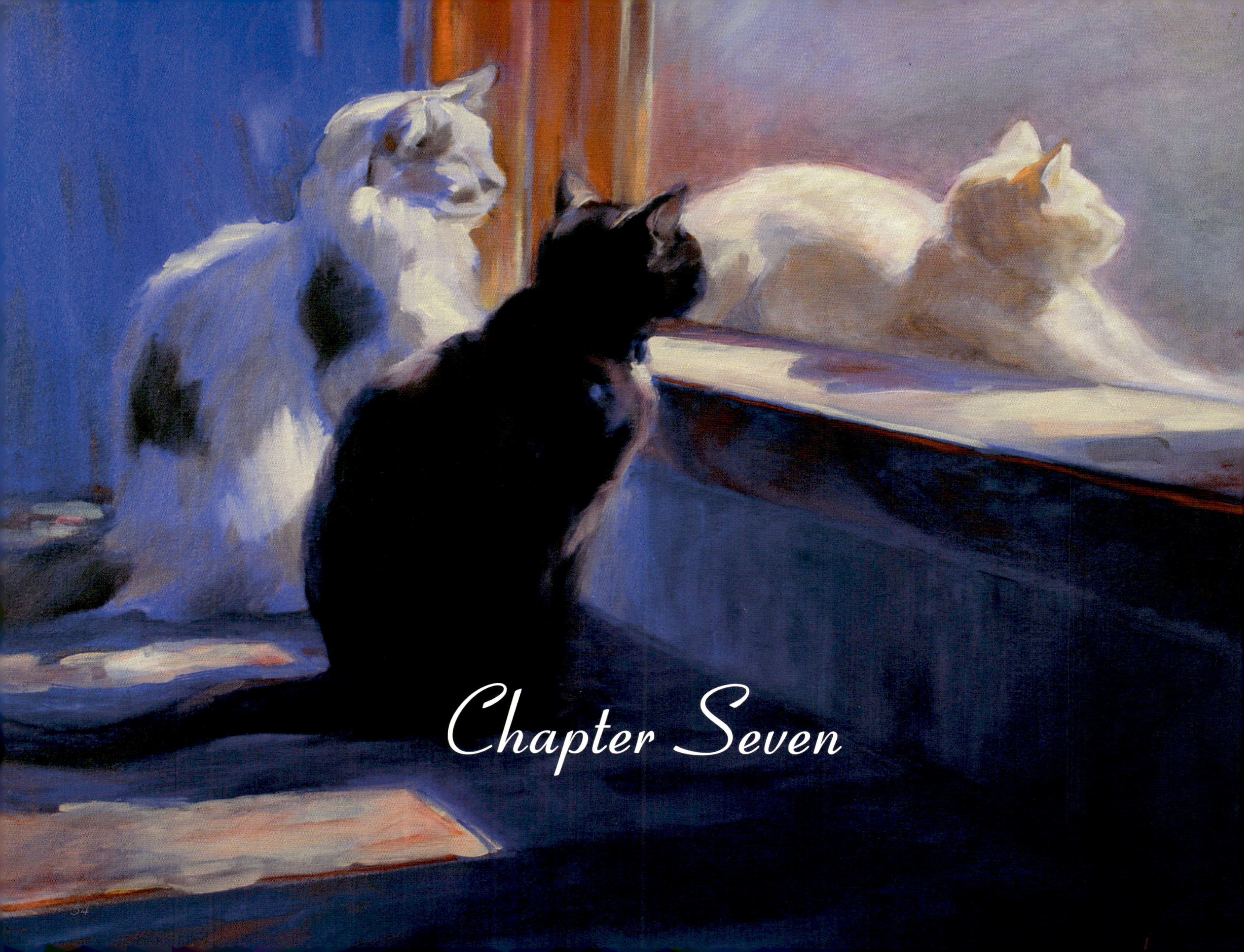

Chapter Seven

Value and the Use of Black & White

You have probably noticed that I have not mentioned black or white. Before I do, let's talk about value.

OPPOSITE:
Portion of *Three Cats* by Julie Hanson, 2005.
Acrylic-Oil on canvas, 30" × 30".

As we saw when we were on a lower rung of our ladder, value is the lightness or darkness of a color, quite separate from the color or hue. Think of a black-and-white photograph. We will use #1 to represent the darkest possible value (or black) and #10 to represent the lightest possible value (or white). You can purchase a value scale at an art supply store or make your own as I did. It is nice to have an opening next to the specific value so that when you hold it up to your subject, you can compare the two.

Now let's look at the color wheel in black and white (fig. 34).

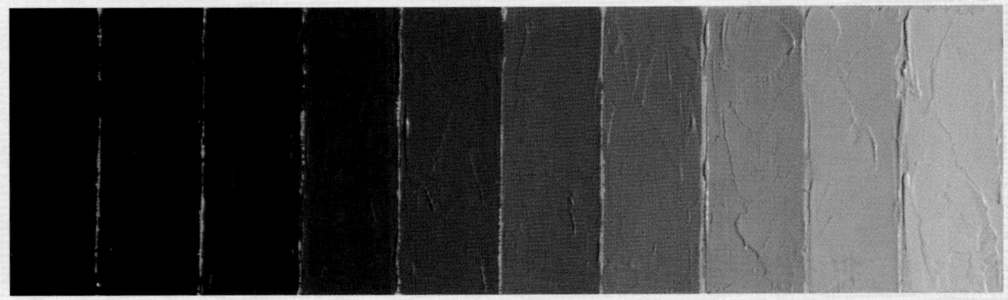

Handmade value scale.

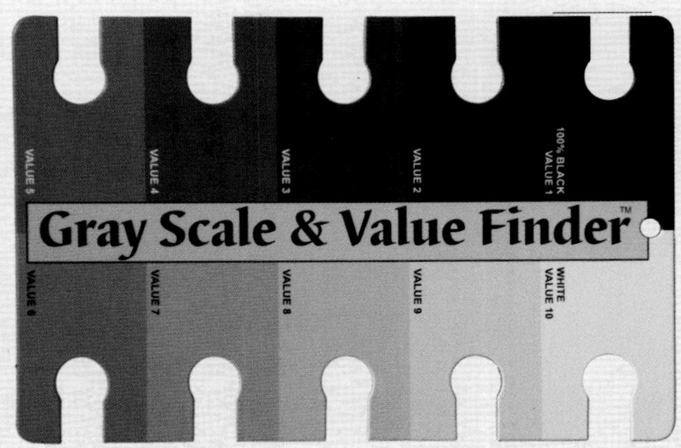

Store-bought value scale.

You can see that each of the colors has its own value, and that most of the colors have quite different values from each other. This is important, because this can be confusing for the beginning color student. If you get the color right but not the value, it will not work in your painting. This is one of the reasons instructors teach beginning painters how to do value underpaintings or studies in earth colors first. That method works out the value relationships in a painting without having to think about the color relationships until later, thereby simplifying the initial composition and the patterns of light and dark. The downside of that method is that it leaves the color until last, and I want you to learn to put the color first and do your thinking in color so that you can get magical color happening in your paintings.

To control a color (hue), you need to be able to change its value. You need to be able to lighten and darken a color in your painting. How do you do this?

In the study of light, black is the absence of color; however, in the study of paint pigments, black is actually the opposite. You can get a sort-of black by mixing all the colors together. It won't be a true black, but then remember we are working with actual pigments now, not the ideal concept of light. And actual pigments have their own strengths and weaknesses. Plus, if you add a bunch of light-value colors to that mix, it will, of course, be lighter, more brown or gray. Some would say muddy. I don't think about color that way any longer. After years of painting, what I know now is that a muddy-looking color is just a color in the wrong setting, or seated next to the wrong family member.

Note: Remember that you want to pit a warm color against a cool color to make it sparkle and create a plane change. If you don't do that successfully, your color may look muddy or flat.

If you purchase a tube of black, will that help you darken a color? Well, yes. If you add a darker color to another color, you will darken that color. But the problem for the colorist is that black is best at darkening a value. It is not as good at darkening a color. That is because black is really not a color. As we have seen, there is really no place for black on the color wheel, and when you use black to darken your colors, you are snuffing the light out of your primary colors and the luminosity you are trying to achieve by pitting warm against cool. That is not to say that black is bad. Black is a powerful value regulator, since it is one of the most extreme values possible, as you can see by looking at the value scale. Black does kill and cool color, and I want you to be able to control your values and colors without it for now, so that your focus will be on maximizing luminosity.

How do you darken, then, without the use of black? You use your darkest-value colors and sacrifice the extreme value you would get with black for strong color relationships instead. That is what we are trying to build. Refer to chapter 6 for warm darks and cool darks. We want to accentuate our warm/cool contrasts to get our colors to glow. So, we darken as best we can. It is more important for the colorist to get a warm or cool dark than a black per se.

That said, be aware that there are numerous blacks available to the artist, just as there are whites. Experiment!

Simply put: The best way for the colorist to darken a color is to add the available dark pigments. As a painter of vibrant color, remember when you do this, you will be thinking about warming or cooling your darks, not just getting their value darker.

Although the colorist usually does not keep black on their palette, white on the other hand, is essential. We usually use white to lighten a color, although remember that when white is used, it *always* cools the color. That can be a great thing when you have a lighter cool color, but when you want to warm and lighten a color, you are in trouble. You must then use a light-value pure color that has warmth to lighten a darker color, if possible, and some form of yellow is often your answer. If you look at the work of the impressionists including Monet, you will notice that yellow is often used instead of white (or added to white) because it gives warmth to something white in the sun.

Note: White doesn't ever make something warm, it makes it lighter in value and cooler. So when you paint, you need to use white to lighten the value of a color. But remember that white will always cool that color at the same time.

If you look at the previous illustration of the value scale, you'll also notice something that's important for painting in vibrant color:

Julie's Rule #3: The extreme values (1, 2, 9, 10) on either end of the value scale are powerful; they want to come forward. The middle values on the value scale recede in relationship to them because they are less powerful or noticeable.

Let's look at white in mixtures in figure 35 to understand another important point about color values and mixtures.

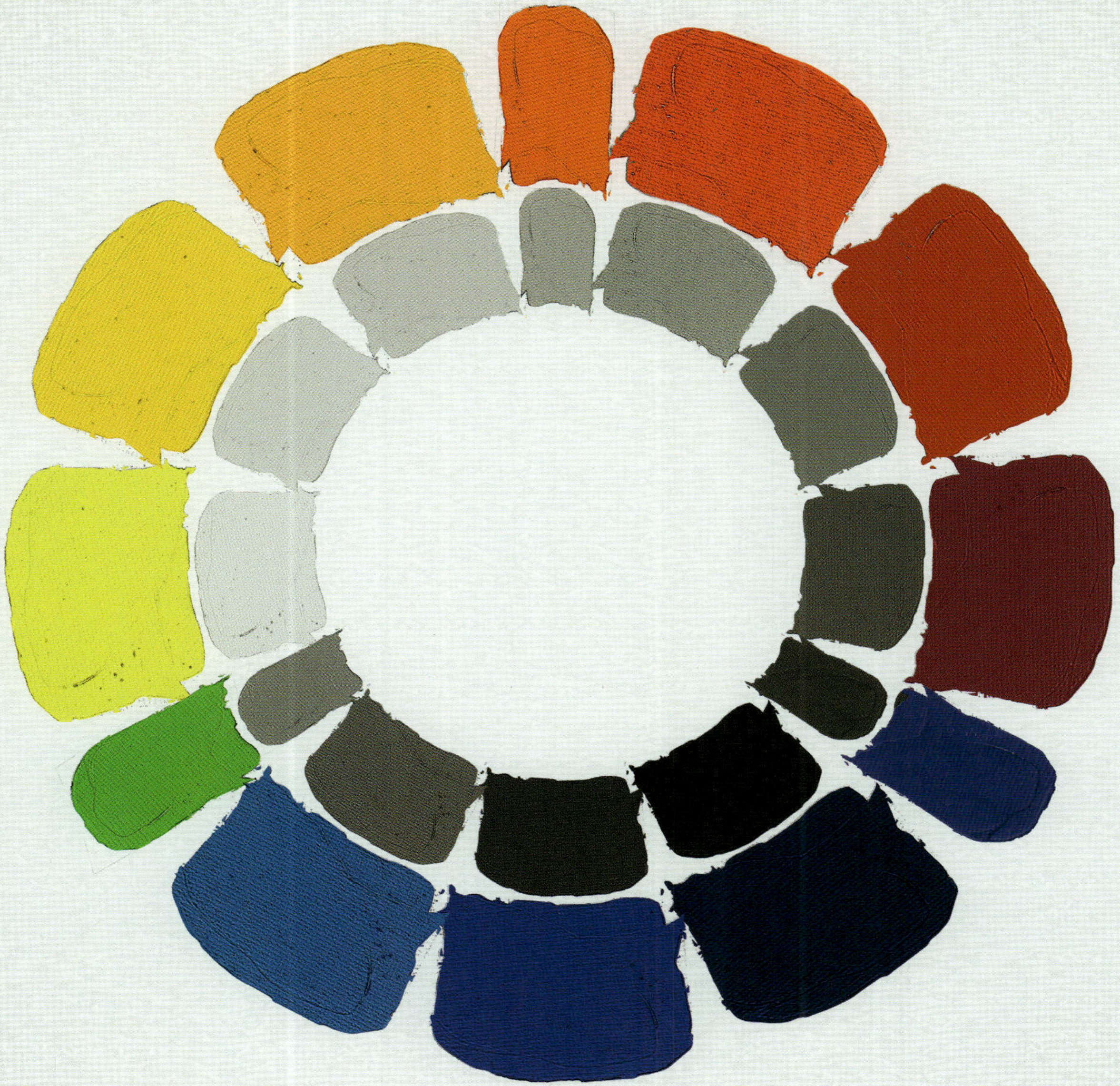

FIGURE 34.
Notice that each color of the color wheel has its own value separate from hue. The printer inks shown here may not match the actual paint colors.

This exercise teaches you how to mix color values. Remember, this chart was made with pure tube pigments. Think about the variations with all of the possible mixtures, and white to regulate value.

Look at the lightest and middle range values and see how many color choices are available in that value range. Now look at the extreme darks and see how many choices are available. Notice anything that might be a problem?

Note: This is a problem, particularly for the pastel artist, since each color pastel stick is a pre-determined color/value. There are not many dark choices, so you have to use them wisely.

The impressionist painter (or colorist) tries to work in the value ranges that give the most choices for pitting warms against cools at the same value. Can you see more clearly why black is not that important? The impressionist painter tries to work in the lighter value ranges because of the sheer number of color choices. White is glorious because there are so many subtle choices, so we minimize darks. Try this chart for yourself. There are also a variety of whites to choose from. As you recall, titanium tends to be opaque, stronger, and brighter, while zinc is a little more transparent and weaker and has just a touch of yellow.

Julie's four rules of painting:

1. **Warm colors come forward and cool colors recede in relationship to each other.**
2. **Pure colors come forward and mixed colors recede in relationship to each other.**
3. **Extreme values come forward and middle values recede in relationship to each other.**
4. **Detail comes forward and lack of detail recedes in relationship to each other.**

These are the rules I teach beginning students. You can use them to finish your paintings after doing the primary tones. They will help guide you to a successful finished painting anywhere, anytime.

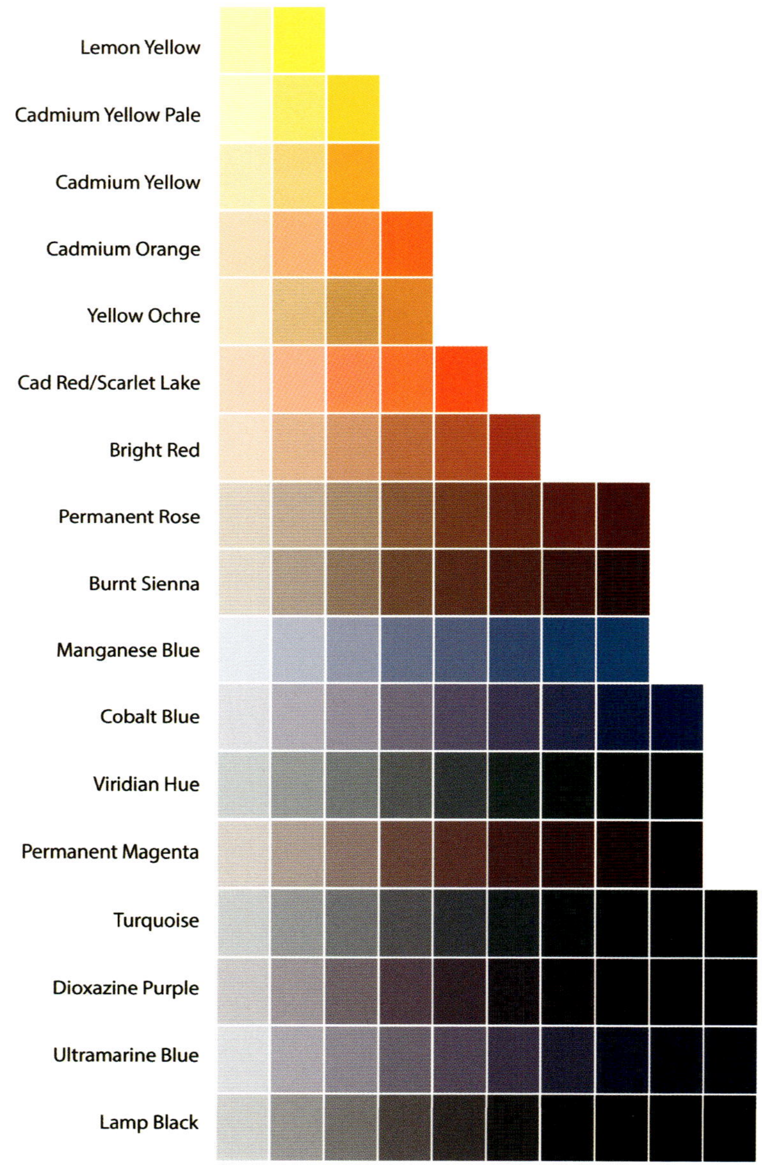

FIGURE 35.
This chart shows the different values created with the addition of white to our palette of colors. Notice what value range offers the most color choices, and the least.

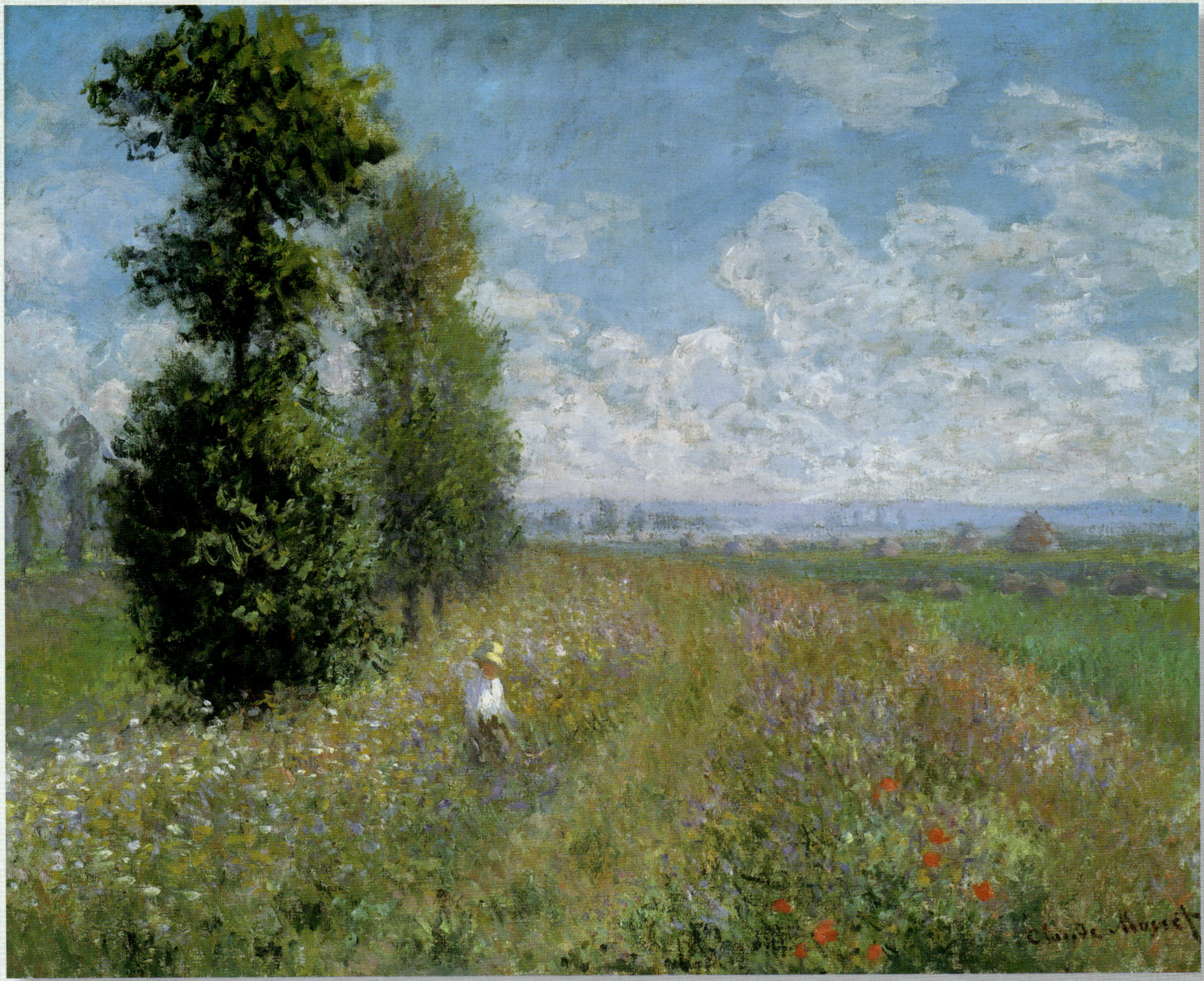

Meadow with Poplars by Claude Monet, 1875. Oil on canvas, 21.5" × 25.75". Squint and see the simplified massing in this painting. Notice that there are many colors in each of these areas, but similar values. *Courtesy of Museum of Fine Arts, Boston, Massachusetts*

Part Two

TEMPERATURE PAINTING

Part Two describes my method of painting in full color.

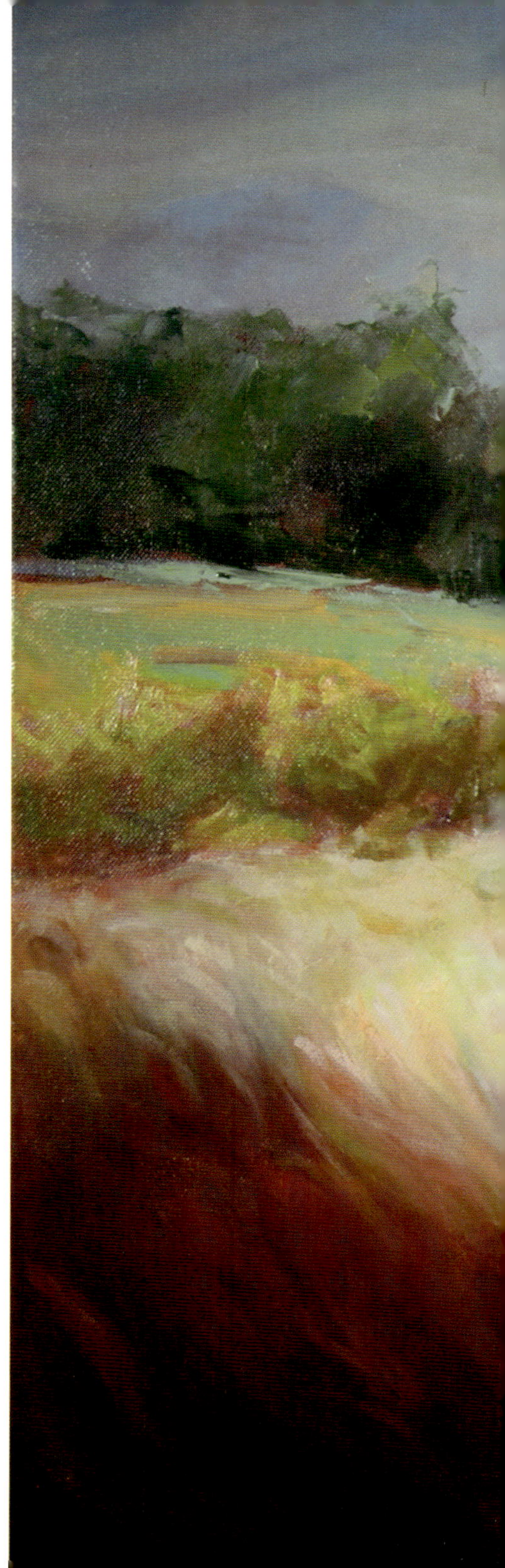

OPPOSITE:
Black Mountain Farm by Julie Hanson, 2009.
Oil on canvas, 24" × 36".

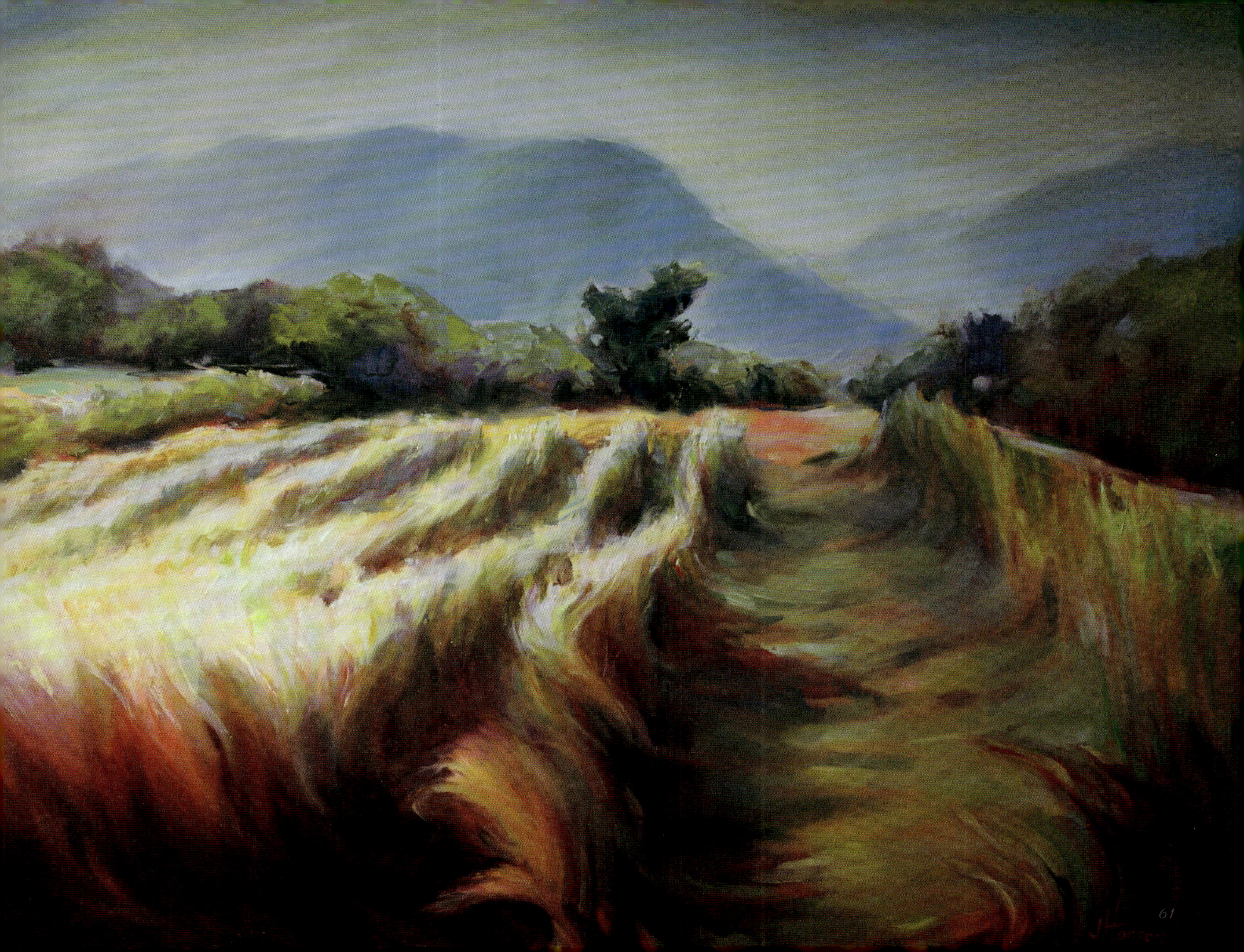

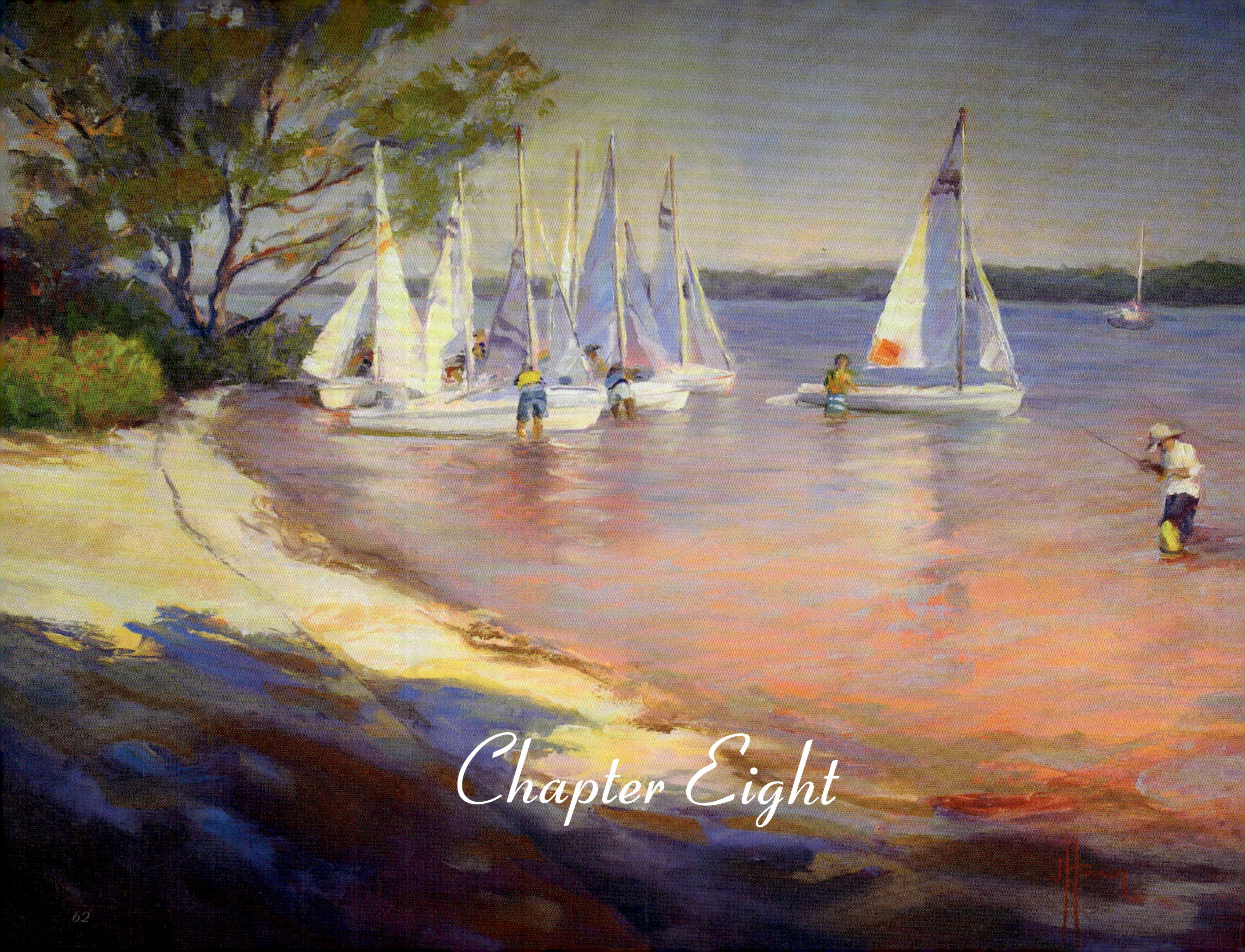

Chapter Eight

Introduction & Preparation

I was inspired by the method of painting taught by the Cape Cod School of Art in Provincetown, Massachusetts, particularly their approach to first notes. I developed a simplified method of setting up each painting by using what I call primary tones, because I wanted to bring the joy I experienced with that approach to my students. I call my approach temperature painting, in which we are looking at lights, which are most often represented by warm colors because the source of light is warm. The darks are areas in the subject that are not warmed by the sun, and are most often represented by cool colors. This method evolved out of my love of the feeling of rich, wet oil paint and working wet into wet, and the freedom of the palette knife. I use it to teach my students to see more color in their paintings and to use warm against cool to advantage.

OPPOSITE:
City Island Sailboats by Julie Hanson, 2015.
Oil on canvas, 24" × 30".

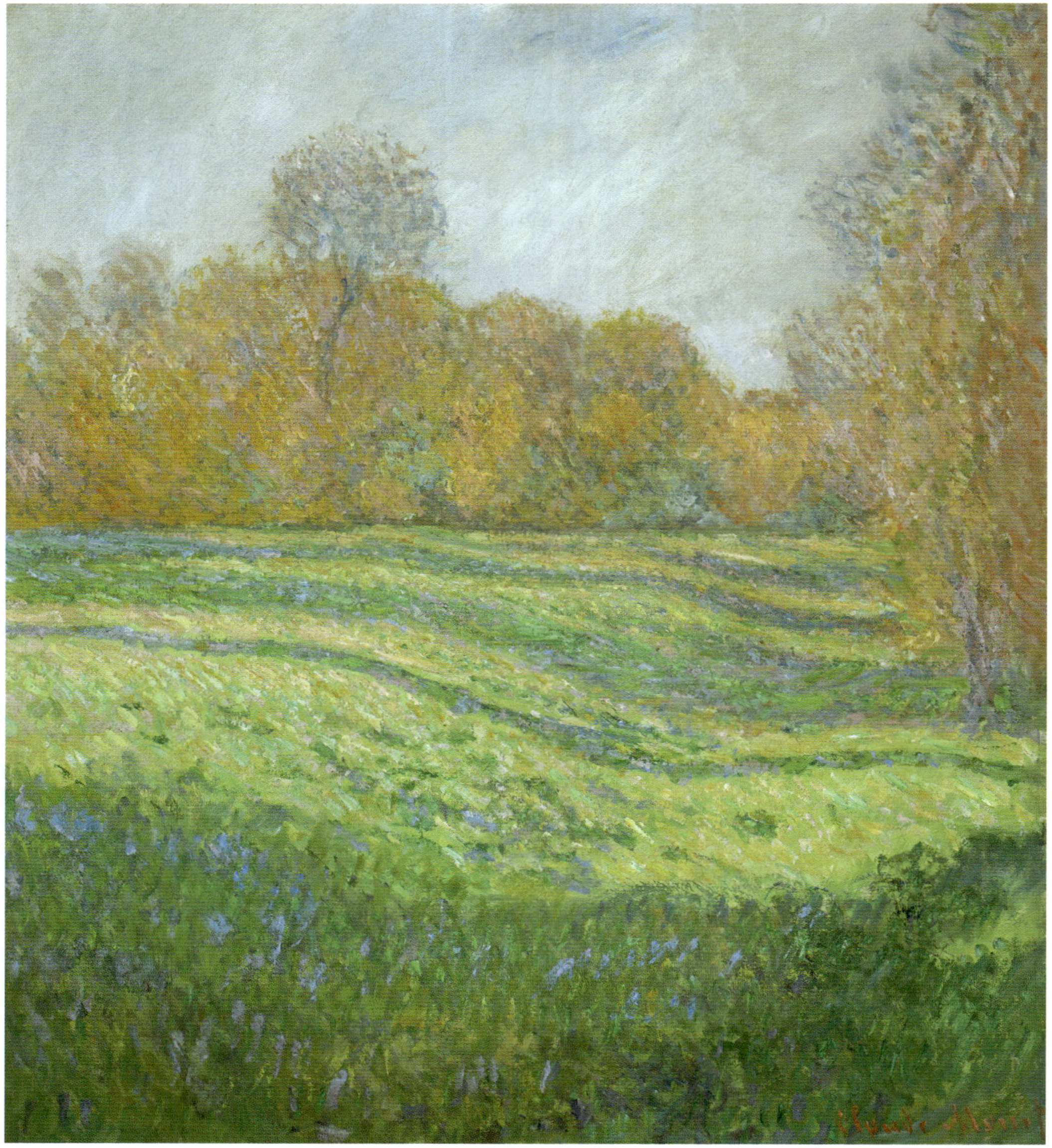

Meadow at Giverny by Claude Monet, 1886. Oil on canvas, 36.25" × 32.13". Notice how blue is holding the shadow areas while yellow and orange are holding the light. *Courtesy of Museum of Fine Arts, Boston, Massachusetts*

I remember thinking a lot about the color in shadows. We think of shadow as the absence of light, but as you'll remember from chapter 1, paint does not behave like light. Blue represents the absence of light, so I began to think about how the shadows must be shades of blue or connected to blue, and what kind of a balance there must be between the three primary colors in each subject or painting.

The object is to choose colors that will best pit against each other to create the feeling of temperature in the painting. Remember that value alone cannot create temperature. If you study the impressionist paintings you will notice that value has often been sacrificed for richer color combinations. Many different colors (hues) of the exact same value are put side by side. That is how the masses in the paintings become luminous and hold together.

My primary tones are the initial layers of paint. They represent the temperature of the subject and are applied with a palette knife. These colors are usually quite different from the subject's color in real life. Again, our goal is to best set up the temperature of the subject or the quality of the light in the scene. By using primary tones, we get this effect quickly and get luminous color in the process.

Temperature painting sets up a painting with each primary color playing its part. Not only is the white of the canvas covered completely (I try to do this quickly at the start of the painting), but these first color/value/tones or "primary tones" form an effective underpainting to set the stage with incredible visual excitement. I try to use this excitement to carry the painting to completion. With rich, wet color for me to work back into with the palette knife, more color can then be added to get the wonderful effects of wet-into-wet mixtures.

Oil and water-soluble oil are wonderful mediums for this method, as is acrylic. In acrylic, use a brush for the primary tones so that there won't be too much texture underneath when it dries. This gives the benefit of a beautiful underpainting and the excitement of the color relationships. Then use the palette knife for developing the painting further to add new, fresh color, or add in a transparent clear gloss medium to your color and apply to the primary tones underneath. I have found that working in this method improves my skills in all mediums. Remember, if you're using pastels, try to get a good value selection of colors all around the color wheel. Use the other mediums as a guide in selecting your colors (see chapter 2).

My hope is that you will explore this method in various mediums and that you will also find excitement and revelation in the hidden harmonies of color.

After numbering the light and dark sections of a composition, we choose the colors needed to develop the painting. When painting outdoors, the light is most often considered warm and shadows are cool. When your subject doesn't fit this description, you need to find a warm/cool color relationship in your primary tones that fits the situation. In the following chapters we will explore how and why colors were chosen for the primary tones by using several different subjects.

Note: I always scan my subject by carefully looking from side to side to "see" and "feel" the temperature of the subject (the lights compared to the darks), and the possible color choices that best represent that feel.

After primary tones have been applied, I choose colors, this time much closer to the actual color of the subject. Paint is again applied with the palette knife. The advantage for me is working wet into wet. This keeps my color fresh and, if done well, prevents color from over-blending and keeps me from indecision and wishy-washy painting.

Note: When I paint, I want to express an exciting interpretation of my subject. I do not want a photographic rendition. I want a successful drawing with an exciting composition and glorious color combinations that sing and sparkle, and the appropriate value relationships. Without these elements I feel a painting is incomplete, or worse, poorly done with many missed opportunities.

If you walk outside and look at your surroundings, you will see how important temperature is. There are things in the foreground that need to be kept warm so that they will come forward in your painting, and there are also objects warmed and "lit" by the sun. When something is not lit evenly, though the local color is warm, such as a red apple or an orange flower, you must make a distinction in your color choice to show that this red object is actually cool because it is not being warmed by the sun. So the first distinction made from looking at your surroundings is determining what is lit and what is not.

The next decision is where your subject is located in your painting. Is it close to you or farther away? Let's say there is a patch of lit grass at your feet and another patch in your neighbor's yard. The one farther away will need to be cooler so that it "distances." So, temperature painting is not just the distinction between what is lit and what is not, it is also distinguishing what is closer and farther away in your subject.

There is a third important aspect to temperature painting that is often overlooked. Let's say you are painting a round object like a lemon or a still life with vases, and you have noted that these objects are in the sun. You have also noted that there is a lit spot, say, on the lemon, and that part of the lemon is also in shadow. Those two elements alone will not give you what you need to make the lemon look round. You will also need to add warmth to the inside, front, or bulk of the object to make it come forward, and since the edges of the object are receding, you need to cool them down. Warm colors will bring elements forward and establish the foreground, while cool colors will pull your eye back. So, every time you paint any object, you also have to consider its temperature because there are warm and cool choices in every object you paint. You can see that temperature painting is an extremely powerful tool in developing your final painting.

Now, go and get your favorite book of post-impressionist paintings and look at them carefully. What you are likely to see is a kaleidoscope of color in one value "mass." The painter will have one value hold the mass, or large area of similar value, but this will be made up of many colors. They can be warm and cool, bright and dull, but what they have in common is that they are ***all*** the same value. Wouldn't it be better to have luminous color than a missed opportunity for color in your painting?

PREPARATION

I use the following supplies for painting in oil and set up my palette by putting out my colors in a line starting with white, lemon yellow, cadmium yellow pale, cadmium yellow medium, orange, cadmium red light, bright red, quinacridone rose, permanent magenta, dioxazine violet, ultramarine blue, cobalt blue, and manganese blue. When I lay all my colors out like that before starting to paint, I can quickly scan and see by comparison the temperatures of the colors I might need for the subject I am painting.

My optional colors are whatever I decide I will need for the painting at the time, and these might include burnt sienna, yellow ocher, or any of the earth colors and possibly greens, which might include permanent green middle, permanent green light, viridian, or turquoise.

I use the following supplies for temperature painting in oil.

Palette box and disposable palette paper pads: For mixing paint, I usually use a gray disposable twelve-by-sixteen-inch palette paper pad with tear-out sheets. I keep that in a Masterson palette box with a tight, snap-on lid that keeps my paint fresh for days to weeks.

Palette knife: I usually use just one size for painting. It is a diamond shape about two-and-a-quarter inches long and not sharp enough to be dangerous. I use this knife for everything; sometimes I even sharpen my pastel pencil with it!

Paper towels: I usually use Bounty or a better-quality towel because I don't want the paint soaking through to my fingers.

Wooden paint box: Mine is thirteen inches by seventeen inches by two-and-a-half inches deep. I keep my tubes of paint here including pastel pencils and my palette knife.

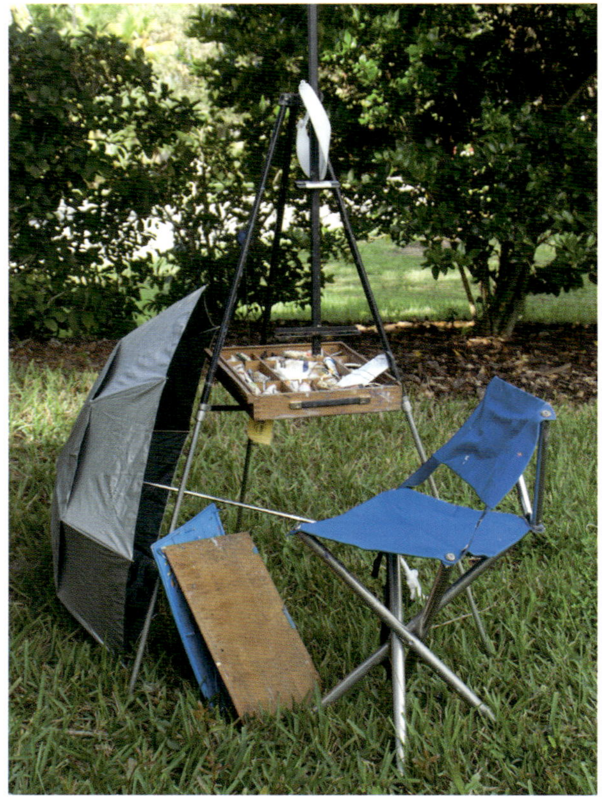

Pastel pencil: I use a pastel pencil for drawing in my compositions. Any color works if it isn't too dark, but I love red and pink the best. I prefer this to other drawing mediums because it is erasable, flexible, and even contributes color to my painting.

Support: I have painted on many types of supports over the years. I used to cut up sheets of four-by-eight-foot hardboard from a lumber company. I put several coats of gesso on them before painting. I have also stretched my own canvases, experimenting on many different fabrics. Now I buy ready-made canvases because they are convenient. I work on many different sizes but always recommend the twelve-by-sixteen-inch size for my classes. Class time is too short to try to cover a larger size, and it's also a comfortable size for the palette knife.

Canvas painting bag: I use a canvas bag to carry my painting box and other supplies. When I paint outdoors on location, all my things are put in a rolling cart.

Easel: I have tried most easels for painting outdoors, and my favorite is a simple, lightweight aluminum easel with expandable legs and a center bracket that I use as a shelf for my painting box.

Because I often paint outdoors, I carry a good visor, sunscreen, portable folding stool, and umbrella to shade me and my painting.

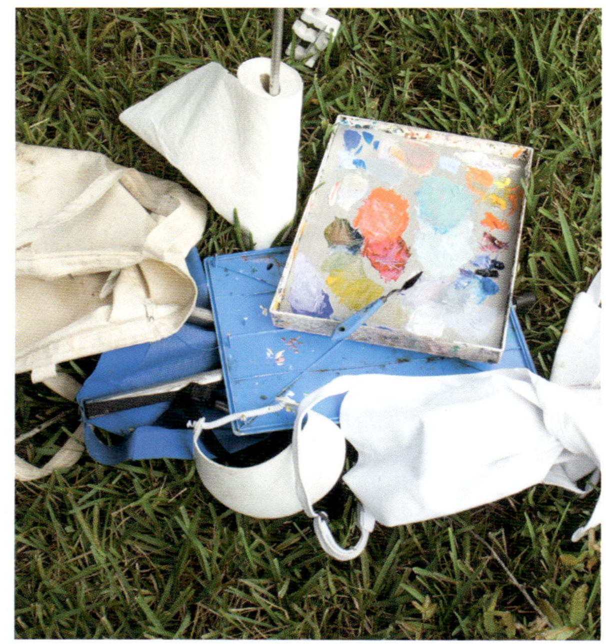

Pigment Supply Lists for Oil, Water-Soluble Oil, and Acrylic

– Oil List –

- Lemon yellow — Holbein
- Cadmium yellow pale — Windsor & Newton
- Cadmium yellow — M. Graham
- Cadmium orange — M. Graham
- Cadmium scarlet — Winsor & Newton
- Bright red — Holbein
- Permanent rose — Windsor & Newton
- Quinacridone violet (permanent magenta) — M. Graham
- Dioxazine purple — M. Graham
- Ultramarine blue — M. Graham
- Colbalt blue — M. Graham
- Manganese blue (hue) — M. Graham
- Titanium white — M. Graham

Optional:

- Permanent green light — Holbein
- Winsor emerald — Winsor & Newton
- Viridian — M. Graham
- Burnt sienna — M. Graham
- Terra rosa — M. Graham
- Yellow ochre — M. Graham
- Raw umber — M. Graham
- Turquoise — M. Graham

– Water Soluble Oil –

- Lemon yellow — Holbein
- Cadmium yellow — Holbein
- Cadmium orange — Holbein
- Cadmium red light — Winsor & Newton
- Grumbacher red — Grumbacher
- Permanent rose — Windsor & Newton
- Permanent magenta — Holbein
- Dioxazine purple — Winsor & Newton
- Ultramarine blue deep — Holbein
- Colbalt blue — Holbein
- Manganese blue nova — Holbein
- Titanium white — Holbein

Optional:

- Yellow ochre
- Burnt sienna
- Raw umber
- Yellow green
- Turquoise
- Middle green
- Viridian green

– Acrylic –

- Lemon yellow — Holbein
- Cadmium yellow medium (or deep) — Golden
- Cadmium orange — Golden
- Pyrrole red light — Golden
- Pyrrole red — Golden
- Permanent rose (quinacridone) — Winsor & Newton, or Fluid Opus hue — Golden
- Quinacridone magenta — Golden
- Dioxazine purple — Golden
- Ultramarine blue — Winsor & Newton
- Anthraquinone blue — Golden
- Colbalt blue — Golden
- Manganese blue — Golden
- Viridian — Golden
- Burnt sienna — Golden
- Titanium white — Golden
- *Zinc white

* recommended

Optional:

- Yellow ochre or raw sienna
- Raw umber
- Turquoise
- Any earth colors
- Greens

Chapter Nine

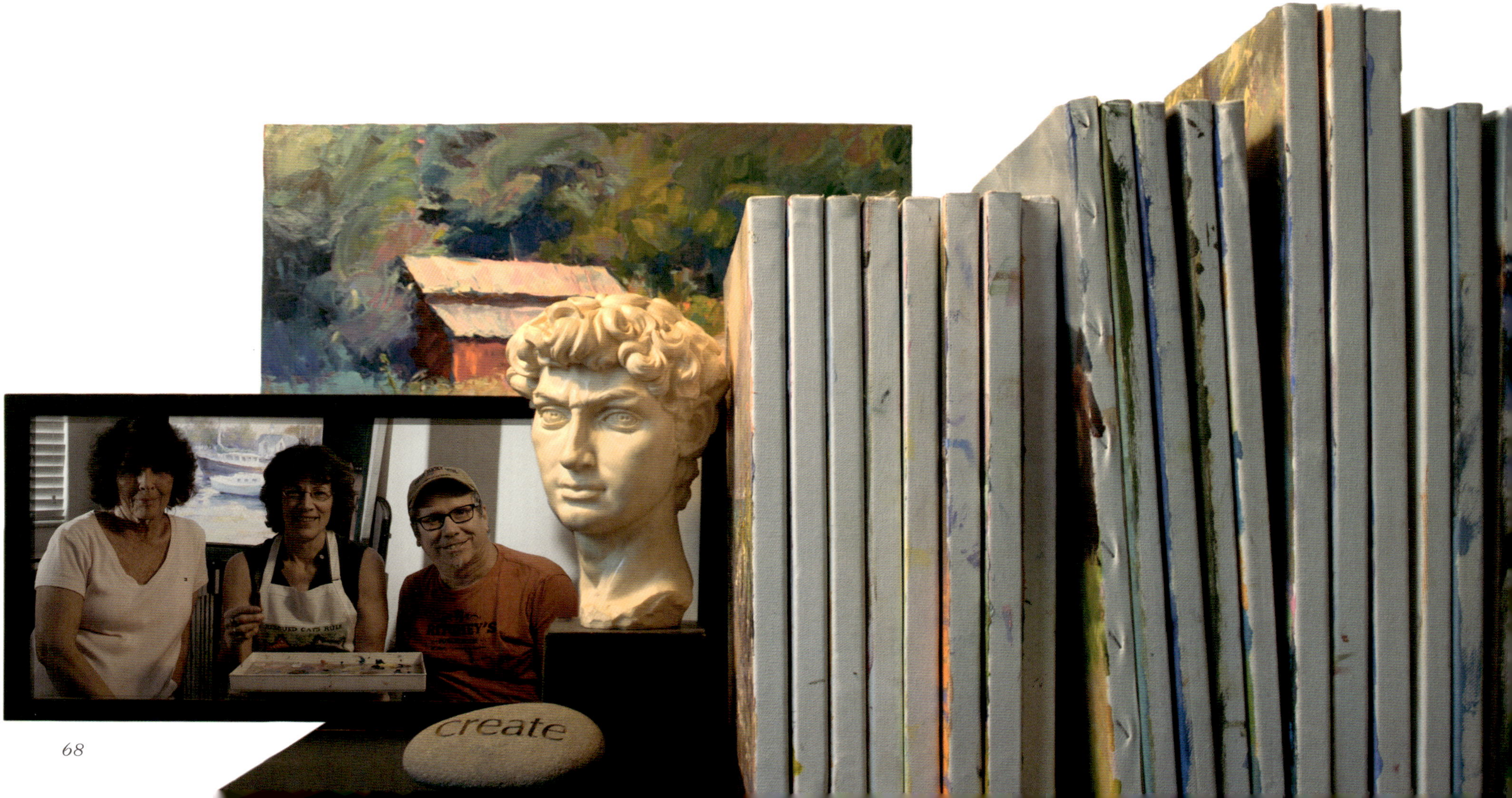

I believe art is the pathway for our inner voice.
Each of us has an artist within.
Learn the skills and find your voice.

Temperature Painting Step by Step

As I consider subject matter for a new painting, the first question I ask myself is whether I have an emotional connection to it. This is the driving force for me to start a painting and carry it to completion. My favorite subjects are ones with lots of light so that I can see the underlying patterns of dark and light clearly. This is the "grist for the mill." Subject is less important to me than the artistic elements within it. With that in mind, the most unlikely subjects can become the source of a great painting. Other important things to consider in a potential subject are a good gesture or energy, interesting shapes, enough contrast in either dark to light or warm to cool, or any other quality that speaks to me in some way.

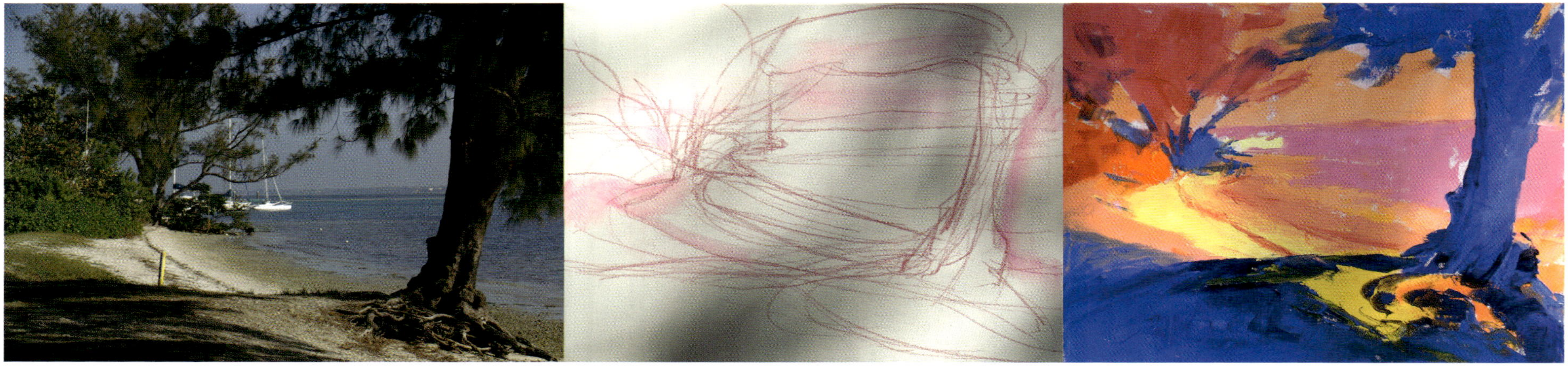

Subject. | Sketch. | Primary tones.

Once I find the right subject, I start drawing. The initial drawing is an important step in beginning my painting. This is the time I organize my thoughts by moving shapes around and deleting shapes that don't help me develop the concepts I am beginning to see. I look at the underlying forms and find a connection between them. I can make the shapes in front larger if needed to create a sense of perspective. I use the principle of overlap more than the traditional one, two, or three-point perspective. In other words, foreground shapes overlap or "take a bite out of" the shapes behind them. If you do this correctly and adjust your values and colors accordingly, you can achieve great depth in your painting. At this point I am also thinking about what colors I'm seeing and feeling in my subject and how these colors will be adjusted to move back in space.

Another essential at this stage is a good gesture drawing to represent the feeling of energy in the finished painting, with the eye able to travel through all parts of the painting. I like to keep this simple. Sometimes it's an S-curve; sometimes it's a C-curve. Sometimes it's something else, like a cloud pattern that emanates from the center of interest or the direction of waves on the water that lead your eye in some way. I also use this gesture to help me simplify the subject. Details that don't fit the gesture need not be included in the painting. For many years, I drew a small thumbnail sketch prior to drawing on my canvas. This is a helpful tool to learn how to simplify and to see what would make a good composition. Although I rarely do that now, I automatically do that in my head with the drawing on the canvas. I use a colored pastel pencil for drawing because it doesn't muddy up the background. It is fairly erasable and, if anything, the color may contribute to the end result.

When I am satisfied with my sketch, I concern myself mostly with the shapes of the lights and darks. I have given some thought to this as I've been sketching, but now I look at every object in terms of how it is lit and shadowed. I break the large areas down into smaller shapes of dark and light. These are part of the overall composition, and I can tell if some of those shapes need to be tweaked or modified to come in line with the gesture. Always look to see what direction the light is coming from before you do this. Keep your thoughts organized and your painting simplified. As a general rule, horizontal surfaces receive the light and are the lightest. Vertical surfaces are tied to shadow. The exception is when the light is coming in low and hitting those planes as well. When using my method to set up your painting, you must decide whether the vertical planes and the planes at an angle are receiving light or shade.

After making these decisions, you are ready to number your lights in sequence and alphabetize your darks in sequence. In any subject, the easiest things to see are usually the extreme lights and the extreme darks. With this in mind, your lightest light will be number one, your second lightest light number two, etc. Your darkest dark will be labeled A, your second darkest dark will be labeled B, etc. As your lights become darker, step by step (3, 4, 5 values), they will be meeting your lighter darks in the middle somewhere (E, D, C values). Because these middle values are harder to identify than the extremes, and these are the values where darks and lights meet, the numbering process helps you to get correct value relationships during set-up, rather than correcting the values later.

After numbering and lettering, we decide the colors needed to develop the painting. Generally speaking, for this method, light is considered warm and shadows are cool. When your subject doesn't fit this description, you would set up a warmer shadow color combination in your primary tones.

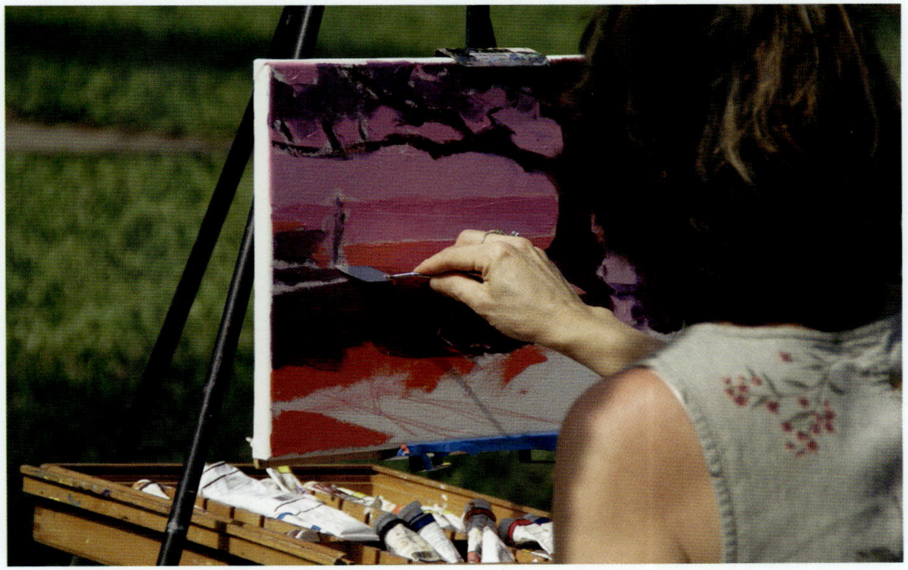

The author painting on location.

In review, here is a simplified outline of the temperature method.

1. Find your subject. Why do you want to paint this? What kind of an effect do you want to create?

2. Create a gesture drawing. Determine how to simplify your subject and find the "energy" needed to make a dynamic painting. Do a series of thumbnail sketches if you have time for them. If outdoors, you must work quickly before the light changes. Choose the best composition.

3. Determine what direction the light is coming from.

4. Look at the pattern that the light and dark make and simplify that if you can. Make your composition about that! Often, I don't draw the object itself, but rather the shape of the lit part of the object and the shape of the part in shadow.

5. Sort out the value scale of the lights in your subject. Be mindful that every object in your painting is receiving light, but it most likely has a different "local" or actual color. This means there will be multiple values represented, since each lit object's actual color also has its own unique value. The objects' values will be different depending on what part is being lit or shadowed. We are concerned with the lit areas only in this step. One of the easiest ways to simplify values in even complex subject matter is by locating the lightest light. This means the lightest possible value of your subject receiving light. We're going to designate that value with a #1 since that is the lightest possible light you can make with your paint. This primary tone would be made with mostly white pigment, but you would add one of your warm colors to make sure you've given this color warmth as well as light. Remember that white is not a color but a value regulator and should rarely, if ever, stand alone. When it stands alone, it is a cool temperature. Locate the second lightest light. We will designate that #2. You can use as many numbers as you need. I recommend, however, that you try not to number more than five, or this set-up process becomes too cumbersome and the painting suffers.

Note: Numbers represent the different values of your "lit" areas only.

6. Sort out the value scale of the areas not receiving light. These are the shadows or "darks." We do not want to number them because we will then confuse them with the lights. So instead, let's use the alphabet. I have found that the easiest way to identify the value differences in the darks is by starting with your darkest values and labeling them "A." Again, this is the extreme, or the darkest value to which everything else is compared. Then look for the next darkest dark and label it "B." Try to simplify the number of darks in your subject to keep the painting fresh. Again, I try to have no more than five designations, and less if possible.

Note: Letters are for the dark, shadow, or unlit areas only.

7. Choose your color set-up. After the entire canvas has been numbered and lettered, set up your primary colors. The simplest way to begin is to remember that light is warm and shadows are cool. Basically, you have three color varieties available to use. Blue is cool. Both red and yellow are warm. Shadows are tied to blue (a color with blue in it or a cooler color than your lights) and lights are tied to yellow (red or a warmer color than the shadows).

Remember that the addition of white to your mixtures, which is necessary to get a more diverse value range, actually cools your warm lights, so be cautious with white in your light areas. Try a purer, lighter value color instead. Adding white to your dark values is much less of a problem because they are already cool.

8. Apply your primary tones. ***Mix and paint all of your designated areas*** until the white of the canvas has been covered, taking care not to mix your lights and darks, but rather to use them to set each other off. You can leave a bit of unpainted space between them. After completing the primary tones, it is a good idea to take a break. I normally move away from the easel to change my focus. When I come back to my painting, I check to see if everything looks the way I want it to. At this step, I make adjustments, such as making shapes smaller or larger, or removing items that don't fit my concept. When I am satisfied and, hopefully, excited to continue painting, I begin to complete the painting.

9. Complete the painting. After all that preparation, it is tempting to cover all of your primary tones, but try to paint only those areas that need fixing. Introduce new colors now, taking care to ***match the value of the underlying primary tones.*** I am pretty certain that some of your primary tones work well the way they are. And if it ain't broke . . . don't fix it!

Note: You must match the value of the underlying primary tones. Also, remember Julie's 4 rules of painting from Part One:

1. *Warm colors come forward and cool colors recede in relationship to each other.*
2. *Pure colors come forward and mixed colors recede in relationship to each other.*
3. *Extreme values come forward and middle values recede in relationship to each other.*
4. *Detail comes forward and lack of detail recedes in relationship to each other.*

If you are an experienced painter, you are well aware of the many variables that go into a successful painting. Temperature painting helps to organize those variables into a system that moves the painting along and keeps you from getting stuck later. Much of the hard work is done up front. You have a good gesture. You have kept your drawing simple. You have identified the source of light. You have defined form somewhat by dividing your subject into lit and unlit areas. Those shapes help to define three-dimensional form. You have identified your important value relationships and put down underlying color, which is the foundation of an exciting painting. These steps will lead you to the finished painting, whether you are a realist or an impressionist or your own "ist."

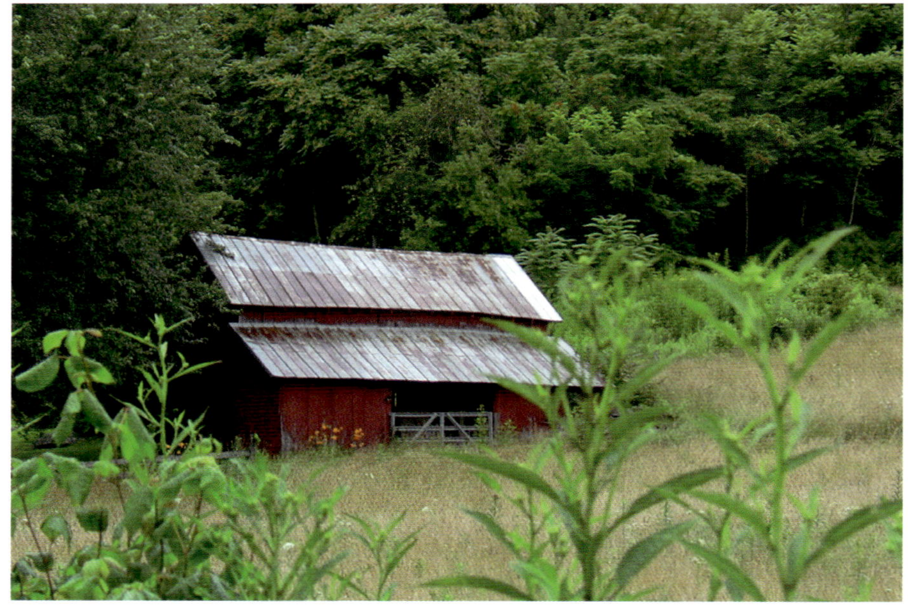

FIGURE 36.
On location.

Let's study these steps by looking at actual subjects painted from photographs, which is the next best thing to being on location. I photographed the North Carolina barn in figure 36 with the idea of painting it someday. I chose it for the first subject because it is wonderfully simple, containing only the center of interest, which is the barn, in a fairly organic and forgiving background and foreground. I liked the gesture very much, as the eye sweeps in from the bottom right, goes to the barn, and then sort of sweeps up to the upper right corner. There is a wonderful C curve in the composition. I also liked the color balance. This one had a high chance of becoming a successful painting because the field in the foreground is warm and lit, while the shadows are cooler and sit farther back. All of this helps to create a successful painting. The other thing that's significant is that there is a clear sense of light coming from above and slightly right. There are a variety of greens to play with, and they set off the values and colors of the barn and foreground field beautifully. So, all of the elements that I look for are present—a good source of light, nice gesture or flow, beautiful color, and a subject I connect to emotionally. The next step is to create a drawing that best represents the gesture.

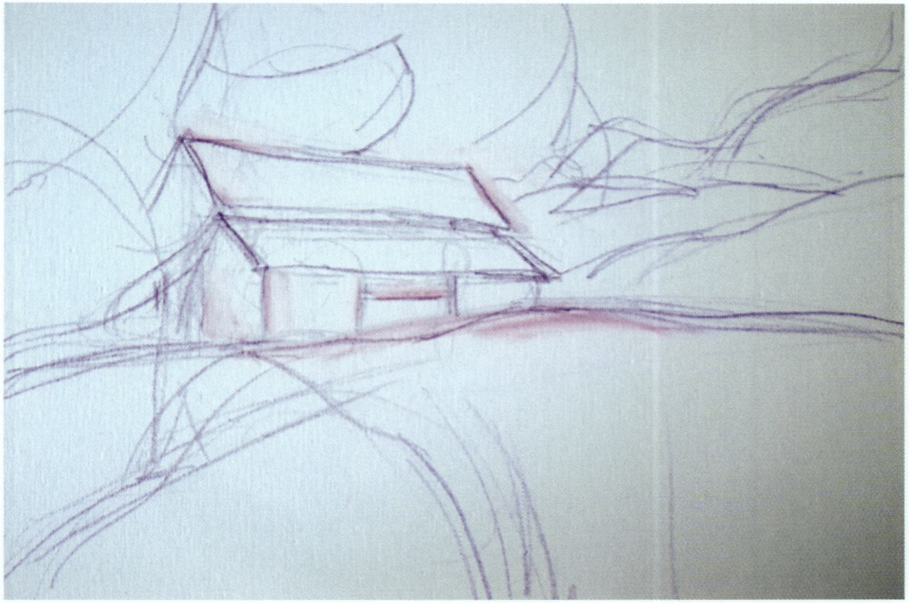

FIGURE 37.
Sketch.

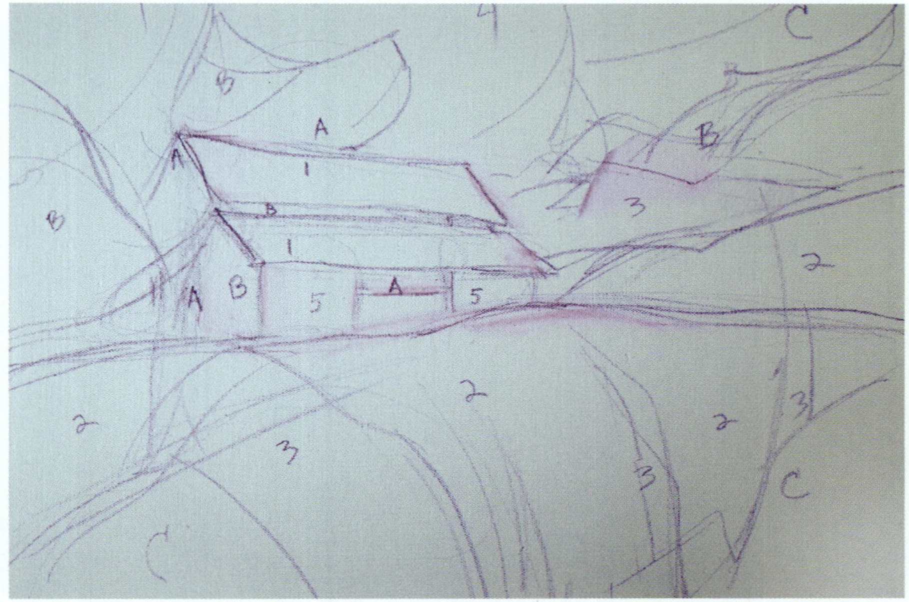

FIGURE 38.
Numbered sketch.

In the sketch (fig. 37), I tried to accentuate the foreground to lead the eye to the barn. I let the field shape on the right “take a bite” out of the barn to create perspective and push the barn back. This is called overlapping shapes and is a great way to push something back into space in your painting. I nestled the barn into shapes that will hold it and left an opening above and to the right of the barn to carry the eye up and away toward the right. All in all, I think this is a wonderful, fresh composition. Now let’s identify, as simply as possible, the lit and shadowed values.

I usually start by identifying my lightest light. Sometimes this isn’t easy to do, particularly when you work from photographs. Most camera lenses cannot get accuracy when viewing something extremely light next to something extremely dark. The camera chooses what it thinks is more important. That means that the other is misrepresented on the photograph. When I work from a photograph, I often view this inaccuracy as an opportunity to decide where I would like my lightest lights or my darkest darks (fig. 38). That way, some thought can be given to where they should be placed in my painting before I start to paint. In this subject, the lightest lights are clearly in the reflected surface of the metal roof. There is really nothing else as light as this or that I really want to be as light as this in the painting, so I numbered it 1. The second lightest light is the field and the grasses to the right of the barn, so they are numbered 2. Sometimes I will simplify a large shape of multiple values into just one value for my primary tones to keep the subject simple. This is a wonderful trick if you happen to be an abstract artist, because these simplified shapes make a beautiful abstract.

The next light is in the lit grasses in the front and the lighter area to the right of the barn, so they are numbered 3. It is very helpful, when deciding on your values, to squint. Squinting helps to simplify. It takes out the details and lets you see a generalized value to represent a larger mass. The next lightest areas I numbered 4. This is mostly the tops of the trees in back. The darkest-value light in the photograph is the lit front of the barn. There may be other lights throughout, but remember to keep it simple. Squint and try to reduce the number of lights to larger areas only and consolidate when possible. Small bits of light can be put in as details toward the end. I call this adding sparkle.

Now you have to stop numbering, because the darks, while also in value sequence, need to be represented with letters, not numbers, so there is no confusion. Start with the darkest dark, which is usually the easiest to identify. The darkest darks in this subject are on the barn and in the tree shadows behind the barn, so I labeled them A. Now we are looking for the lesser darks, primarily on the left side of the barn, in the greenery around the left side of the barn, and off to the right. These are labeled B. Other lighter unlit areas are labeled C. These are areas not receiving light but they are not terribly dark, either. Sometimes you have to make a judgment call. With the numbering and lettering process complete, it is time to choose colors.

Figure 39 shows just the application of the lit primary tones, and you can see that I chose reds and pinks for the light. Remember that the lights must come from the warm side of the palette. I chose these colors for a number of reasons. The first is because there are some fairly dark lights. If I had chosen yellow for the light instead of red as my warm color, it would have been difficult to darken yellow, since yellow is a light value. Dark yellow is really either orange or green, if you remember to move to either of the other two primary colors to darken yellow. That made red a better choice. The other reason I wanted red to represent my lights is because the photograph, with the exception of the barn, is lacking a lot of red since most of the actual color is green. This means that as the subject is painted, and if I am true to the realistic colors of the scene, my balance of red, yellow, and blue will be weakened with the absence of red.

Remember from Part One that every painting must represent red, yellow, and blue. If one of those colors is missing or weak, your painting will suffer. So in a way, I am anticipating the weakness and making sure I have included red in the underpainting. I chose a very light value of permanent rose for my #1, the roof. My thinking was that the cool red would best represent the lit, yet cool silver roof. I chose permanent rose for #2, the field, because I didn't want strong heat in the field area. I wanted to keep that soft. For the other area #2, I chose a slightly cooler color, permanent magenta. I chose a warmer red for #3 because I wanted more heat in the greens, even though I knew I would have to handle the addition of green later, carefully, when adding it to its complement, red. For #4, I used permanent magenta. This is a wonderful color to mix in with the cooler greens that need to recede in this painting and yet tie them to the light source.

I often find myself going back and forth between rule number one and rule number two. It's true that warm colors come forward and look lit, but if you overmix them as you are putting your next colors on, you might mix it to the point where it will recede. Another way of saying it is that you'll get "snagged" by rule number two. The darkest lit value is a #5. I painted that with bright red, the actual color of the barn.

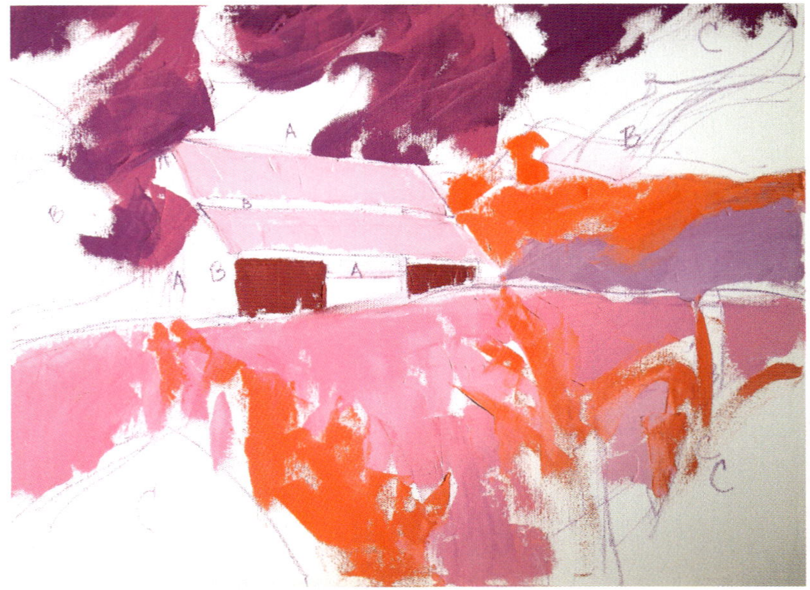

FIGURE 39.
Light primary tones.

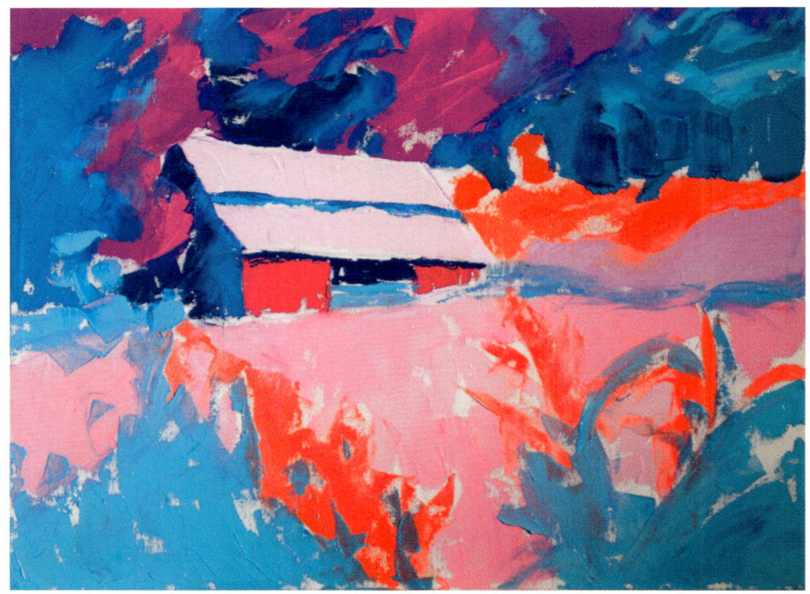

FIGURE 40.
Light and dark primary tones.

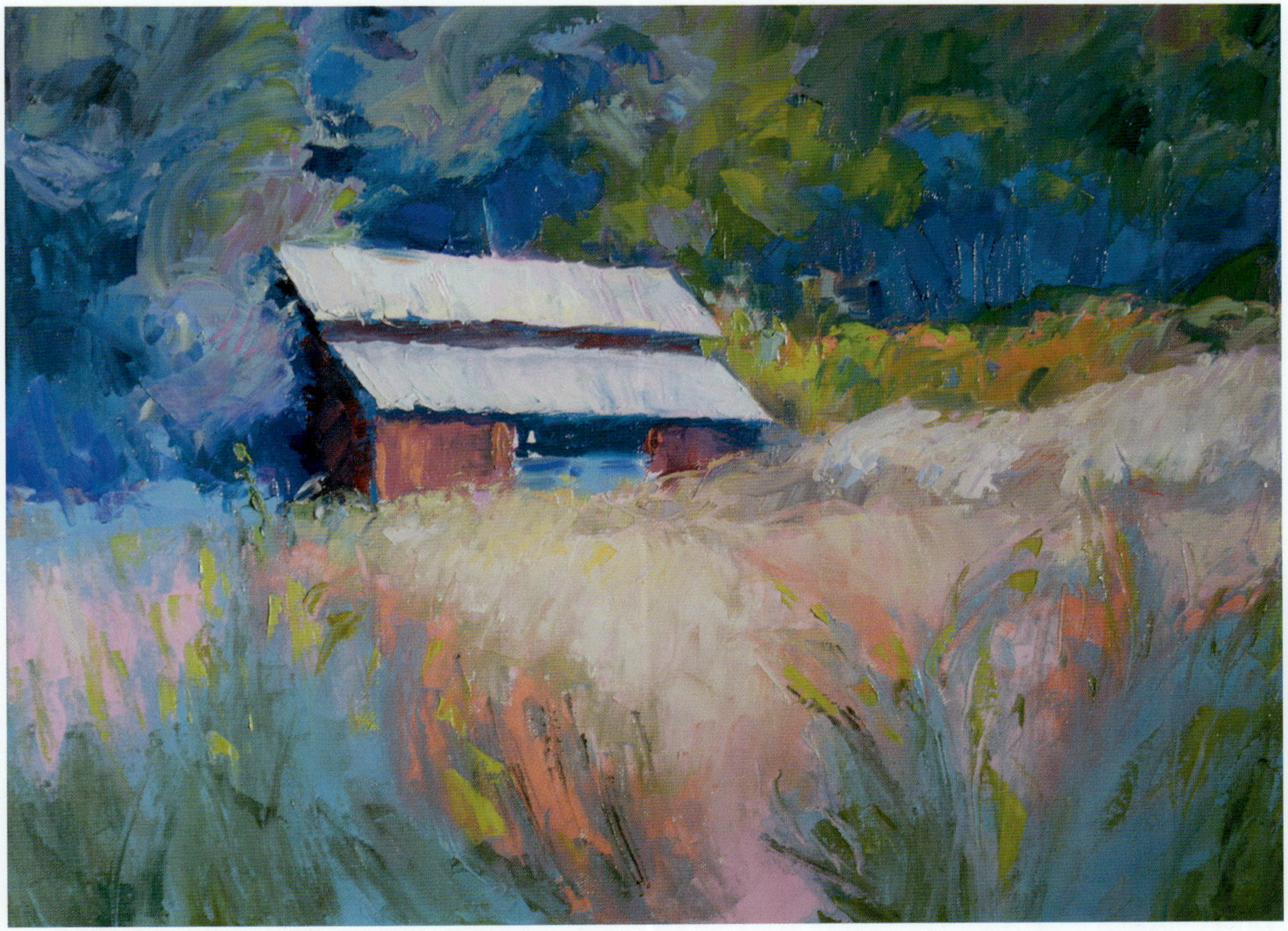

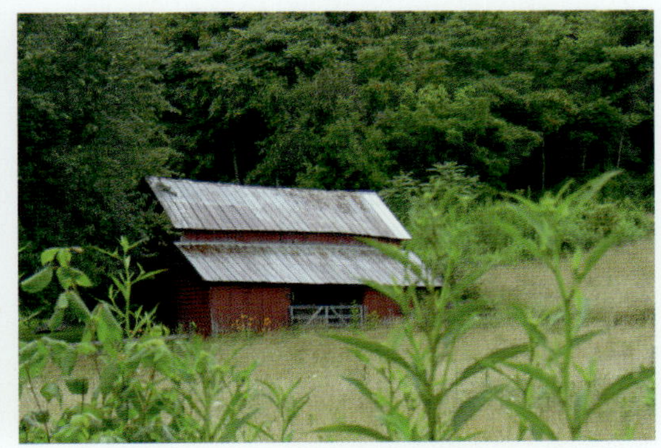

FIGURE 41.
Finished painting.

When it came time to fill in the darks, I chose ultramarine blue for my darkest dark or A (fig. 40). I did that because of its rich, dark value and the contrast it sets up with the red and pinks (better than dioxazine violet, our only other super dark, which also contains red). I then added a bit of white to lift the value so that the color would not look black. I also chose ultramarine blue because I anticipated a rich, dark green for shadows. For B, I added a little more white to A. B needs to set back behind the barn, and since blue is a cool color and when you add white it becomes even cooler, this was a good choice. For C, I wanted a slightly warmer blue but a lighter value, so I chose manganese blue (with white).

After the primary tones are in place, I look to see what's missing. Because I no longer want to be a realist, but rather to enjoy the way color plays in my paintings, I look to see what color needs to be put in first. In this painting, I needed to see the green as quickly as possible since I wanted to showcase the red barn. I often start in the background, because when working wet into wet it's easier to lay down the paint on objects in front of something than it is to do the background after the object is done.

I began with the shadow greens or B. I made the color with cobalt blue plus a small amount of cadmium yellow medium and white to match the value of B. I then mixed the green for the lit areas in the background by mixing lemon yellow with cobalt blue and adding white. As the green was applied over the primary tones in the underpainting, the pink tones in the #4 area helped to neutralize the green, so I carefully let them mix just a little. I mixed up a warmer green, over the lit areas to the right of the barn and in the foreground, from cadmium yellow medium and manganese blue with a small amount of white to match the value underneath. In the process, I let some warm red show through the primary tones.

For the lit areas in the roof, I mixed lemon yellow with a touch of bright red and added white. I liked the spontaneity in this painting and decided to quit before over-rendering it. I went back and put a little more detail on the barn, being careful not to cover the primary tones completely, and tried to show some texture and directional strokes that would help to form the structure of the barn. I also cooled the rooftop by adding a touch of violet (in the value of #1) to the lemon-yellow and white mixture so that it would look silvery.

There's a touch of warm darker green in the foreground to help ground and pull those areas forward. That color is a mix of cobalt blue and cadmium yellow medium with a toothpick amount of cadmium red light in the green to give it heat and pull it forward, while avoiding muddying it.

I love to see a painting that has not had all of the life rendered out of it, and for this reason, I consider this painting successful (fig. 41).

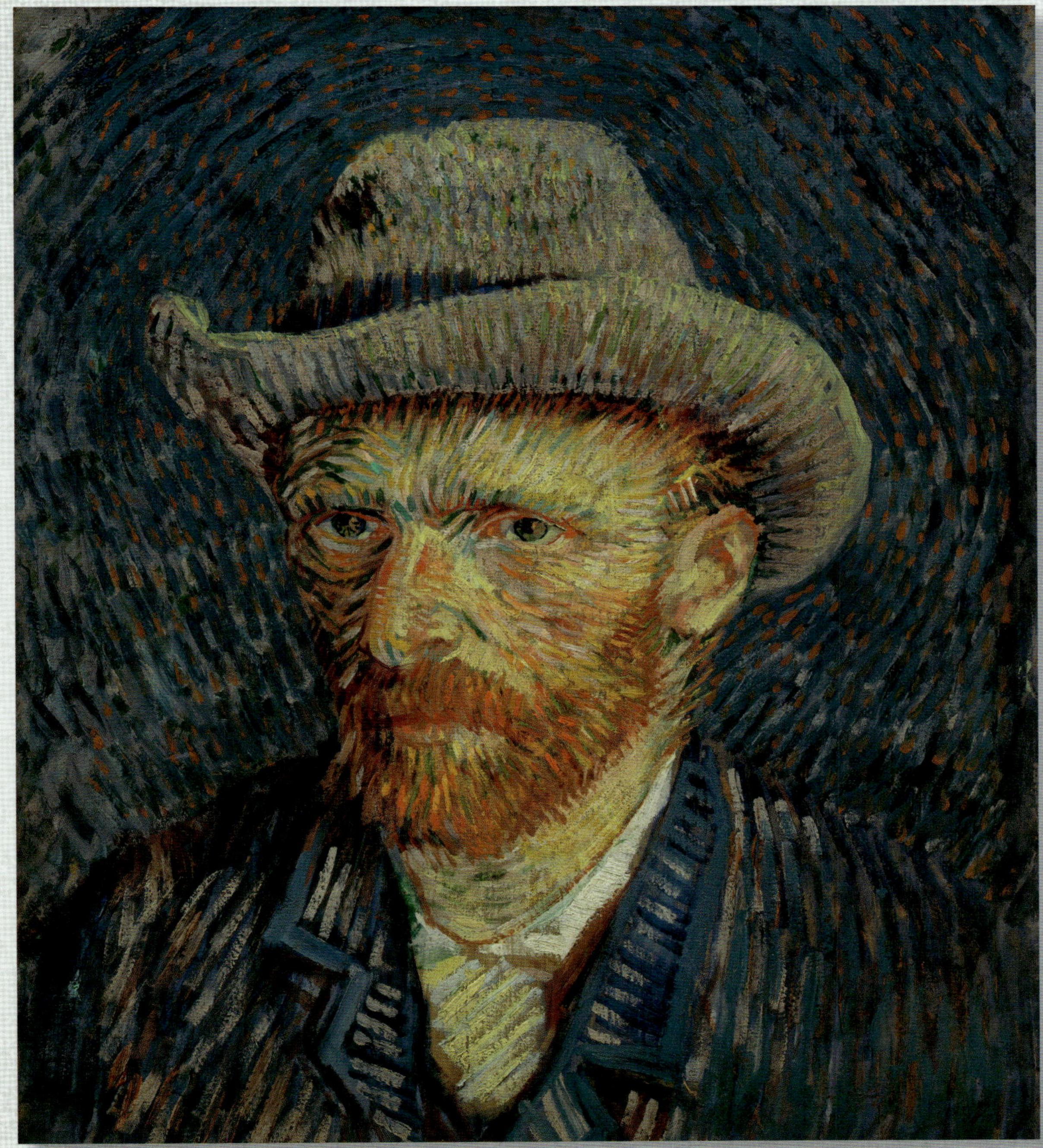

Self Portrait with Grey Felt Hat by Van Gogh, 1887. Oil on canvas, 44.5 cm x 37.2 cm. *Courtesy of Van Gogh Museum, Amsterdam*. Here is a painting that has not had the life rendered out of it. You can see fresh color in every stroke.

Now let's go step by step through the process of painting several different subjects with me and two other artists. Jim has quite a bit of art experience but is new to oil. Mary, a beginner with a keen sense of color, was working in acrylic.

I took the photograph in figure 42 at one of my workshops in Taos, New Mexico. I chose it because of the light and the shapes, and the way the light travels from front to back. The light shapes in the foreground push into the distance and the light from the upper right sky sweeps from the back toward the front. I see a C curve, similar to the red barn painting. The difficulties I see in advance are getting the patio and the wall to feel like stone. And as it sweeps across the middle of the painting, the wall creates a stop or an obstacle. The light in the front and the back of the painting needs to be unified so that the wall doesn't break the C curve and prevent the viewer's eye from traveling beyond the canvas. This photograph was taken in the morning, so there is strong light coming from the left.

As you can see, by our sketches, we all decided on a horizontal composition. I struggled with my drawing because I wanted to get the wall to make a turn and recede. In my first drawing, it was too large. I used a red pastel pencil and you can see my erasures. Jim drew his with pencil and Mary used a light color pastel pencil. There is a lot of detail in this photograph, and it was a challenge to keep it simple. The first sketch shows the basic composition and location of horizon line, stone table, etc.

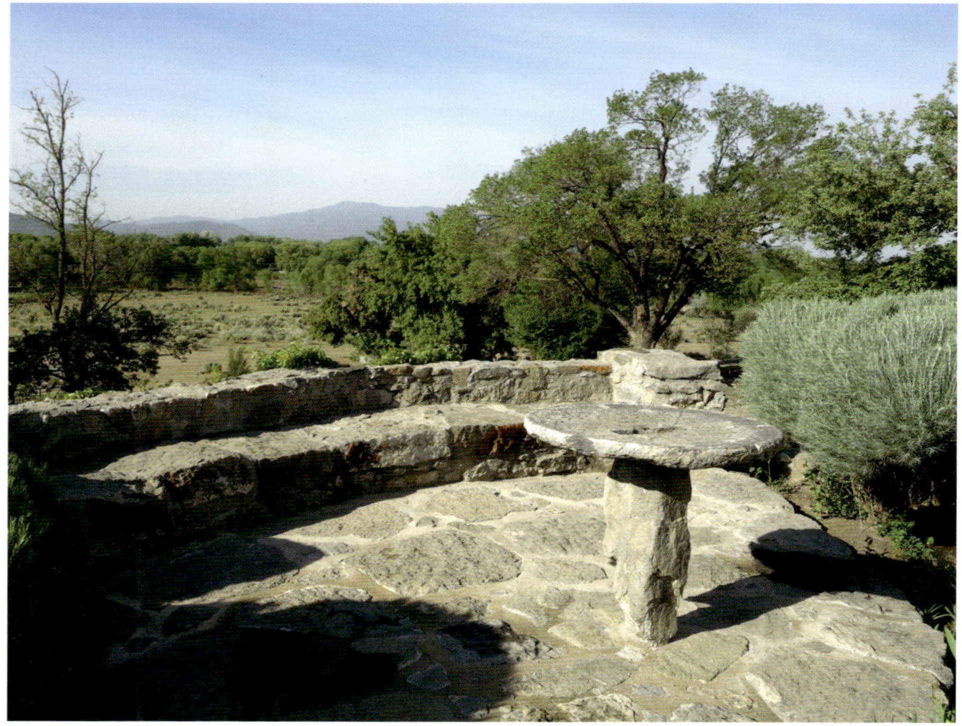

FIGURE 42.
On location.

After the initial sketch, we added more information to define the shapes of the shadowed areas and the shapes of what is receiving light. Figure 43 is my numbered sketch. If you look carefully, you can see that the lightest lights are numbered one and are mostly on the stone table edge. This is because the light is coming in from the left and not the top. The second lightest light is the top plane of the bench area behind the stone table and the lit edge on the back wall of the stone bench. There is also some of that value in the distant sky.

The third lightest light is the patio floor toward the front and on the front edge of the top of the table. The fourth lightest light is the distant ground beyond the rock wall. There is also some of that value up in the higher sky. Since that part of the sky is closer to us and darker, that change in value will help us establish the

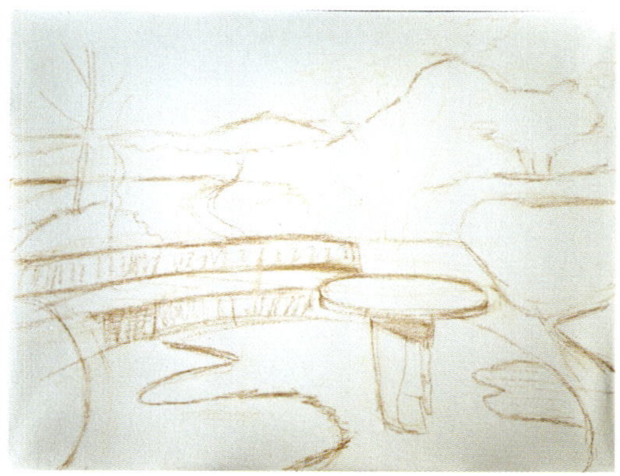

Mary's sketch.

Jim's sketch.

sky coming forward overhead. The fifth lightest light is the lit sage grass in the front to the right. And we're also seeing some darker lights in the distant tree area and in the middle area of the lit portion of the trees right behind the wall, which is a warm, "dark" light. We are representing the light in this subject with seven lit areas.

This is a lot, and it is possible to simplify this further, but for the sake of instruction, let's leave all seven. When you are actually on location, and can read the values and colors more fully, it is easier to make these decisions. The photograph is convenient, of course, and with it there is a much larger margin for modifying these value relationships.

The darkest darks are mostly in the foreground, and that works. Those darks will be used to set off the warm lights. A generalization is that your darkest darks will most likely be in the bottom third of the painting. Your second darkest darks will be in the middle area of the painting or middle third, and your lighter darks will be in the distant parts of your painting or top third. This is because of **Rule #3: Extreme values come forward, middle values recede.** That is how we have set up the value changes in this subject. Sometimes in your subject, there are multiple lights lying alongside each other, as in this situation. The lit areas of ground behind the wall and the lit tops of the trees behind that, along with the lit mountain in the distance and the lit distant sky, are all near each other. The shadowed horizon line of the trees in the distance provides the only break. We made the decision to treat the mountains as a shadow, not a light. This sets up a beautiful, clean, clear cool to help set off a warm, light distant sky and the lit treetops in the distance.

The light in this subject is so warm, and the feeling of a summer morning is so strong, that we decided on cadmium to carry the heat (figs. 44–46). For #1, we used lemon yellow and white; for #2, it was darkened one value by adding less white and

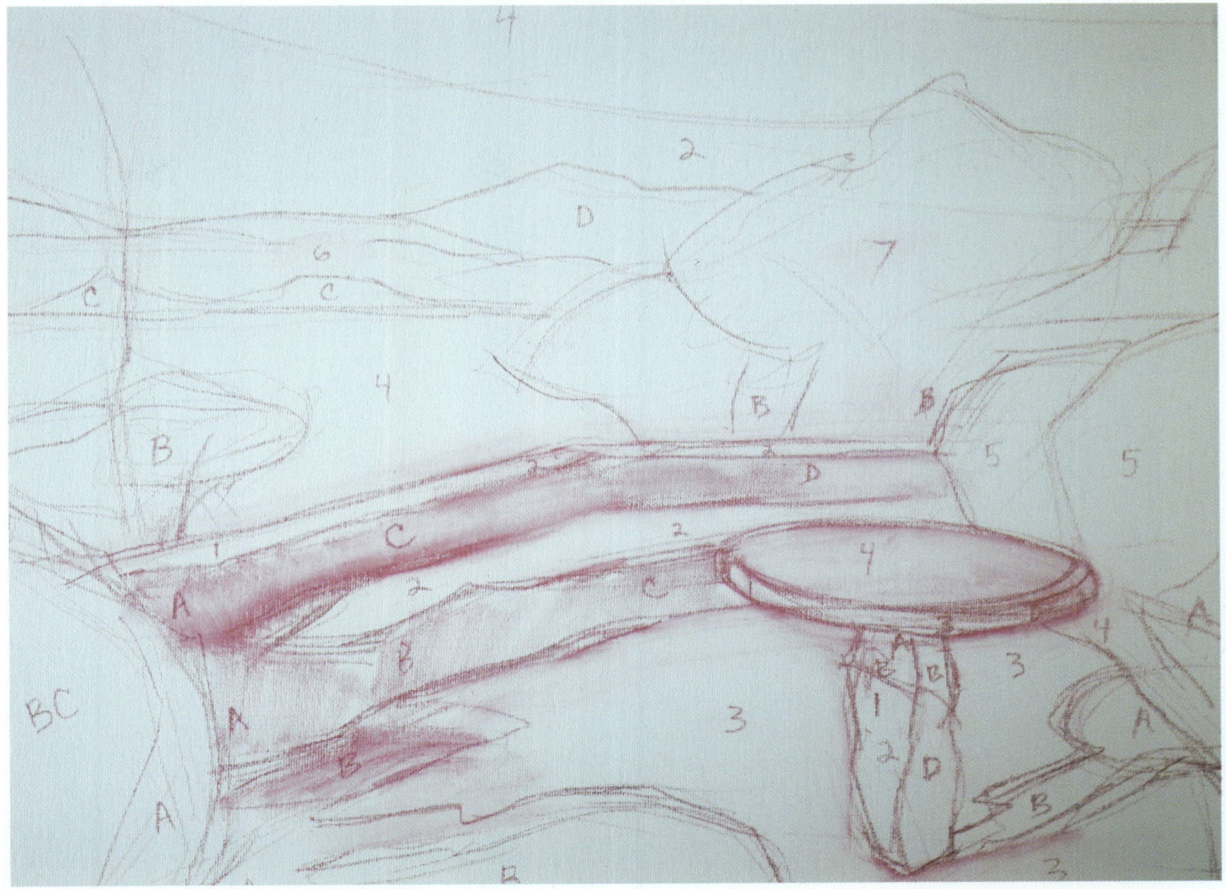

FIGURE 43.
Julie's numbered sketch.

beginning to move toward cadmium yellow. For #3 it was cadmium yellow medium straight out of the tube for me. You can see that Jim and Mary were beginning to push their values a little faster towards orange with more heat. For #4, I began to use cadmium orange, Mary was pushing toward permanent rose, and Jim was adding even more heat. I used cadmium red light with white for #5. For #6, I used bright red with white to adjust the value. And for #7 we all used permanent rose with a small amount of white. We needed to add white to permanent rose to make sure our lit values were getting darker step by step. Most quinacridone roses are too dark out of the tube for our value #7, so white must be added to keep this color from becoming a dark.

We started A with a touch of violet added to ultramarine blue. This is our darkest dark and we need it where it will have the most power. Here it is in the front where it will oppose the strong, warm light coming in. The other A's are on the bottom left behind the shrub and on the left of the bottom of the wall. The B's are also ultramarine blue but we added white to lighten their value in contrast to A. We set up the C's with manganese blue with white. And for the mountains, a D value, we went back to our A mixture and added even more white. Violet helps in the distance to set off the warmer colors in the sky and lit trees, and violet with a lot of white recedes beautifully. Primary tones are done, and the blue is a good choice because it is the complement of orange and will set off the fire power of orange.

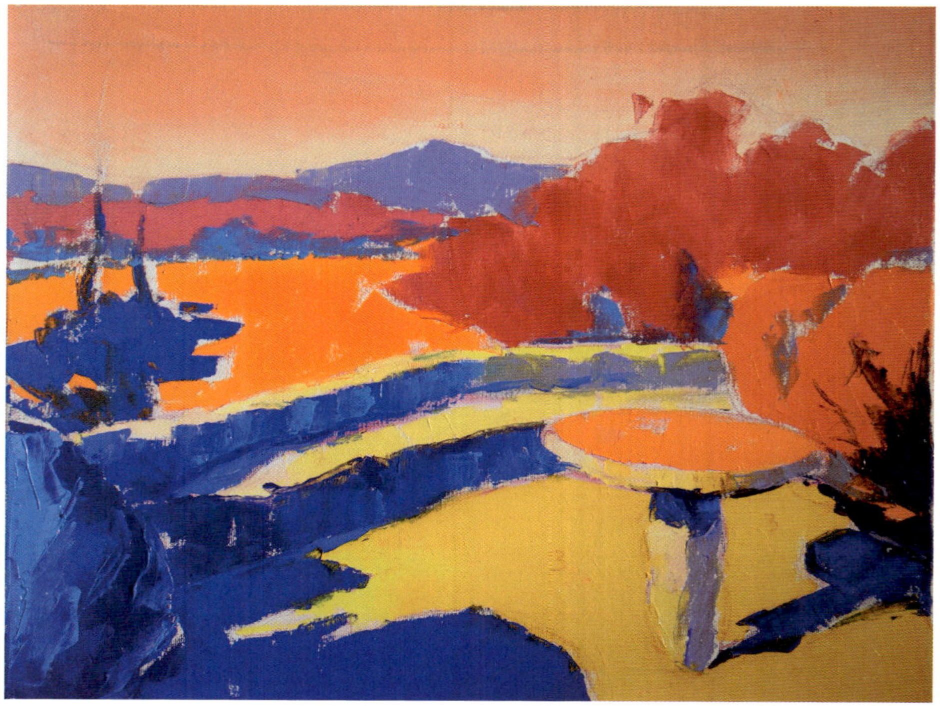

FIGURE 44.
Julie's primary tones.

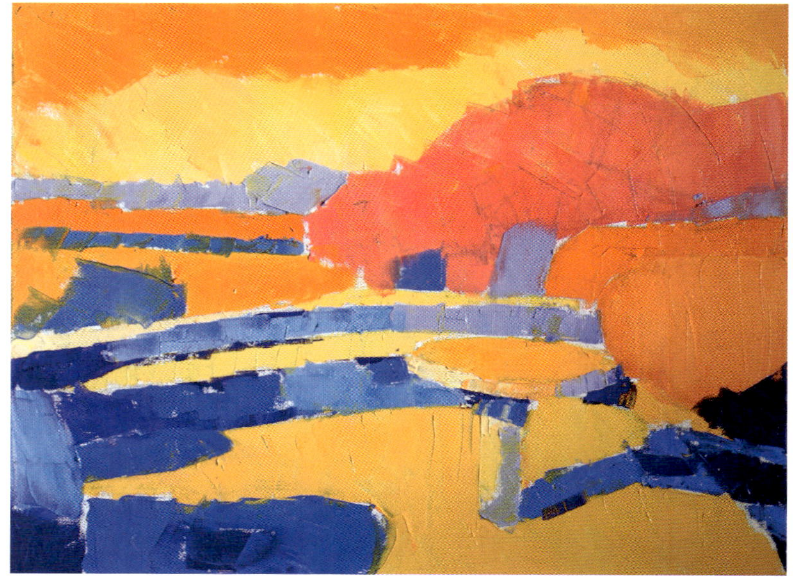

FIGURE 45.
Jim's primary tones.

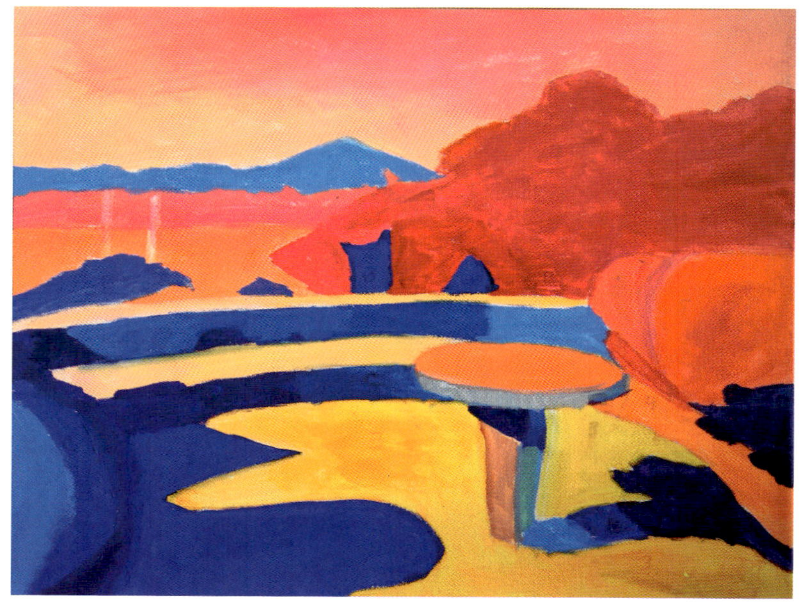

FIGURE 45.
Mary's primary tones.

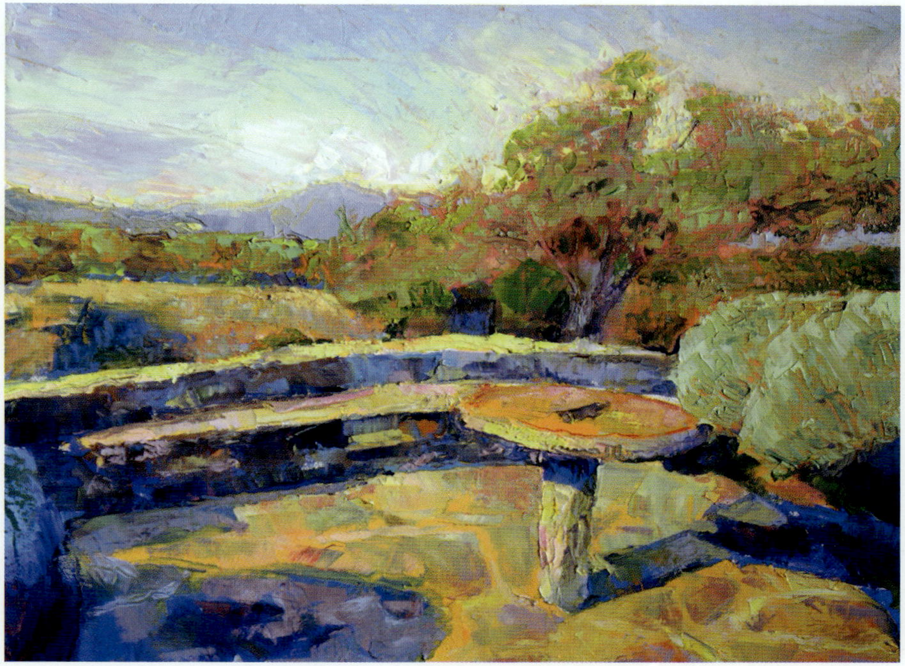

Jim's finished painting.

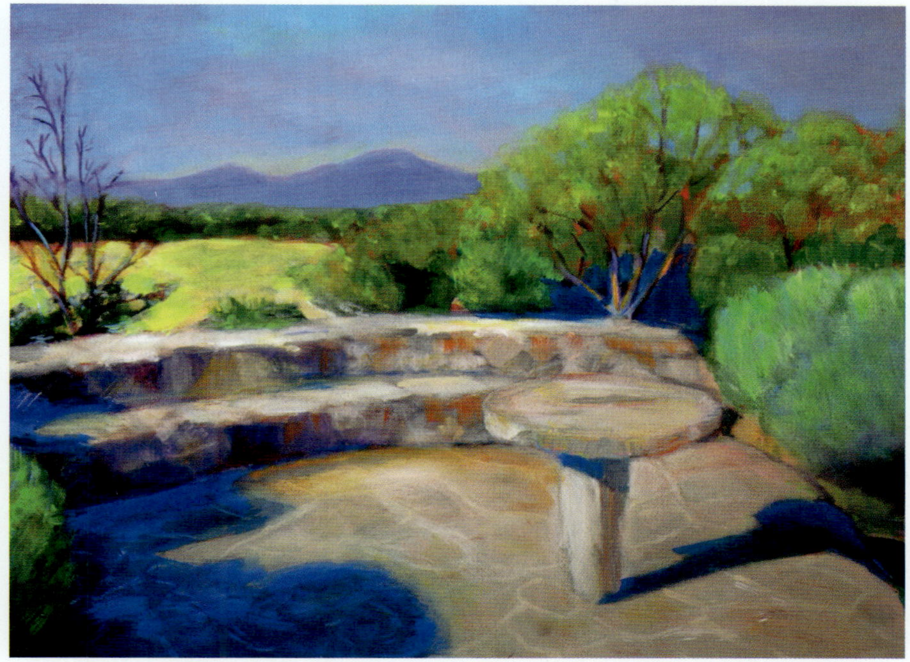

Mary's finished painting.

My biggest struggle in this painting was pushing back the strong heat of the orange value #4 light in the ground area beyond the wall. Although cadmium orange was the right value for that area in the primary tones and expressed extreme heat, it overpowered the cadmium yellow medium in the foreground. I struggled to knock that back, and when I did, I lost the strong heat I wanted. Jim kept the heat in the foreground, which I really like. And he's got great lights in the sky and a gorgeous color for the mountain. Mary, who loves color, got some wonderful blues and greens in her foliage. In critique of these paintings, I would like to see more heat in my foreground patio and possibly a little more color in my shadow area. I also lost a lot of heat in the trees beyond the wall and didn't get the exact feeling of the lit sage green for the grasses on the right. While Jim kept the heat, his shadow areas are a little too broken up and in places are too light in value. Mary has a sunnier feeling in her painting of a summer day, but a little less feel of a desert than either Jim or I. I think this is because she is working in acrylic and her blues and greens are so vibrant. I would like to see her wall end less abruptly and the pink color in the shadow area be less prominent.

You can see that no one paints the same as anyone else. The temperature painting method sets up the basic relationships in the underpainting, but there is a great range of interpretation in the rendering. Remember, as you try for appropriate colors to complete the painting, you must match the value of the primary tones below them.

Let's talk about some of the color mixtures used to complete these paintings. Both manganese and ultramarine blue mixtures were used in the sky. For the very distant sky we added lemon yellow to the mixtures with the correct value to match value #2 underneath. A wonderful mixture to help the sky recede into the distance is also lemon yellow added to a little bit of violet with lots of white. Jim did this successfully.

I often make a middle green for foliage and then make mixtures to either warm it up or cool it down. This mixture is made with cobalt blue and cadmium yellow medium or cadmium yellow pale (my middle yellow). This creates a middle value green which can be cooled down by adding ultramarine blue or lemon yellow and more white. To warm it up, I frequently push manganese blue into the mixture and limit the amount of cadmium yellow medium, adding

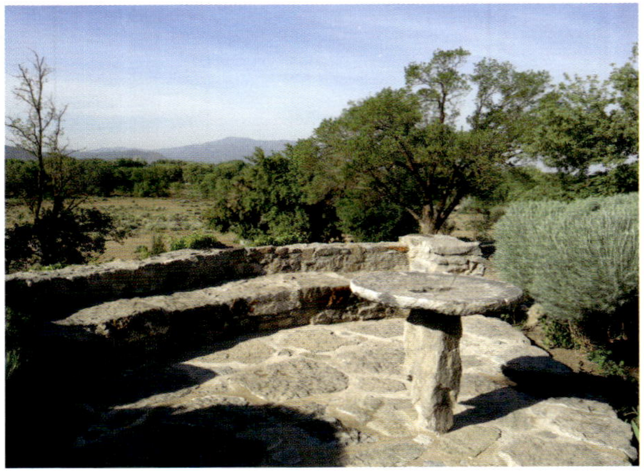

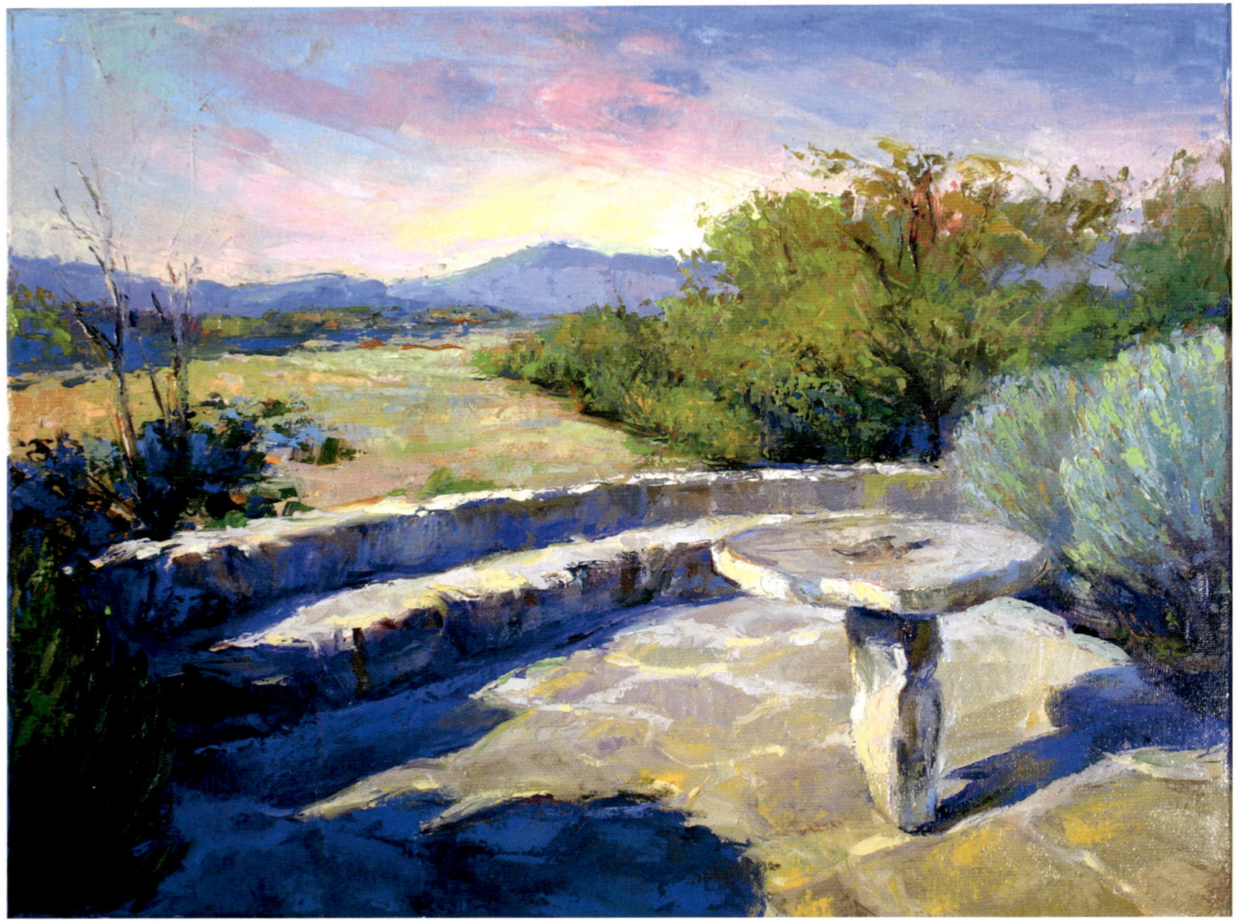

Julie's finished painting.

more lemon yellow. In this circumstance, manganese blue and lemon yellow make a purer green than manganese blue and cadmium yellow medium, although cadmium yellow medium is warm and lemon yellow is considered the cool yellow. This is where Rule #1 and Rule #2 conflict, and the reason you get a muddy green and lose the power of warm. Heavily mixed colors can create muddiness. When you mix cadmium yellow medium with manganese blue, cadmium yellow medium is beginning to bring red into the mix and the colors now begin to be heavily mixed instead of having the purity of manganese blue with lemon yellow. Rule #2 says that mixed color recedes while pure color comes forward.

Sage green for the shrubs on the right is made by mixing cobalt blue with a touch of lemon yellow and white. I used a variety of blues in my shadows. These ranged from ultramarine blue mixed with permanent rose for a cool purplish shadow, to cobalt blue mixed with cadmium red light or bright red (a toothpick amount) for a warm shadow. I also used all three blues mixed with cadmium orange and white for the grays in the stonework. I tweaked a little permanent magenta into cadmium yellow medium with white to cool the lit stone area of the patio slightly, and also a bit of cadmium orange to warm it slightly. The greens in the trees behind the wall had a wonderful permanent rose primary tone to work into, and that helped push the greens back. In doing that, however, I lost some of the heat. I used several of the green mixtures to make the greens for the trees. To make the light pop, one of the last touches I used was a bit of cadmium yellow and white on the stone floor, making it a tiny bit lighter in value than the main light values there. All in all, this has been a wonderful learning experience.

I took the photograph in figure 47 in Door County, Wisconsin, when I was teaching a workshop there. I was attracted to the large field in the front and the gesture of the diagonal coming from the bottom right and moving up to the far left. I also liked the weight of the trees there, the simplified shapes, and the way they lead the eye to the barn. I would have loved to have put in the red tractor, but it was too small and I didn't want the painting to be about the tractor. I wanted to have the feel of the Midwest in this painting and I wanted to feature the barn.

Since I grew up in Minnesota, this subject resonated with me. I also thought about what cadmium red light would do for the field. I imagined cadmium red light (with white) for the entire mass. I could anticipate how the cadmium red light would dominate and push everything else back and would "hold" the foreground, and how the other colors would look in relationship. Although the roof of the barn is lit, this is not a bright day, and I wanted the initial values to be dark enough to have full saturation of color. On a bright day, the lights would be lighter and the darks would be darker. The light appears to be coming from above and left.

Wanting to make the most of the foreground, I decided on a square format for this piece. Mary liked the square format, too, and Jim went with a horizontal fourteen-by-eighteen-inch canvas. We all sketched in our compositions. In Jim's numbered and lettered sketch (fig. 48), you can see that he called the clouds the lightest light, the roofs of the barn and silo the second lightest light, the sky the third value light. The field is slightly darker, and it darkens two more times toward the front, where the fifth and sixth light values lie.

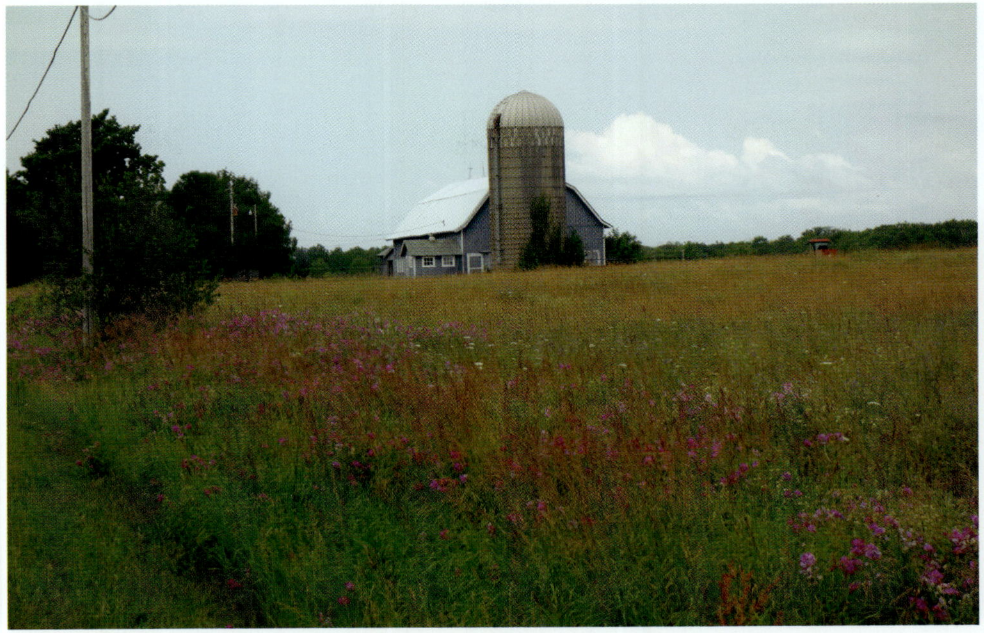

FIGURE 47.
On location.

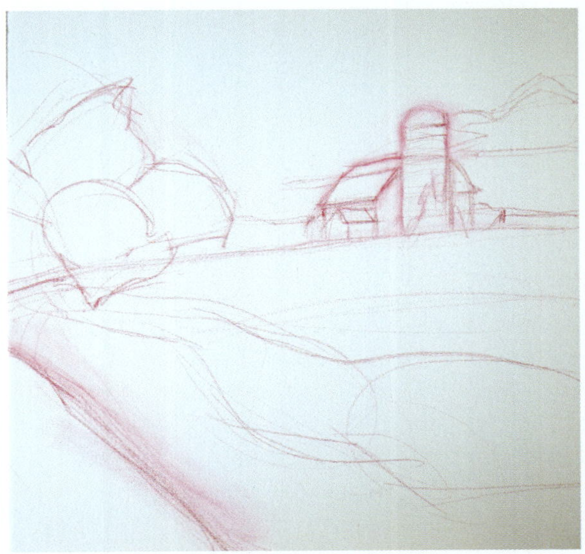

Julie's sketch.

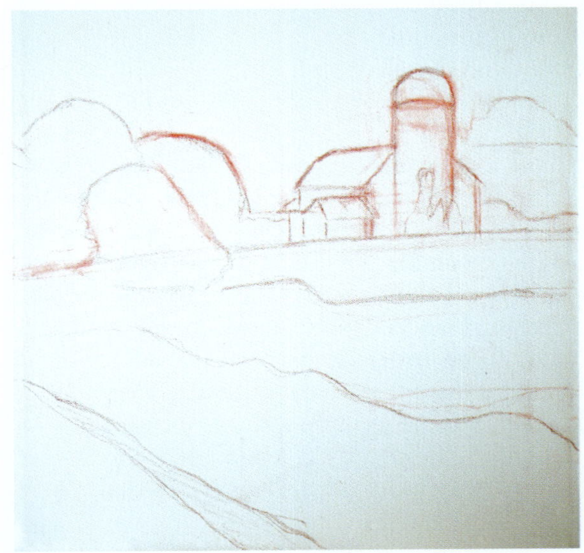

Mary's sketch.

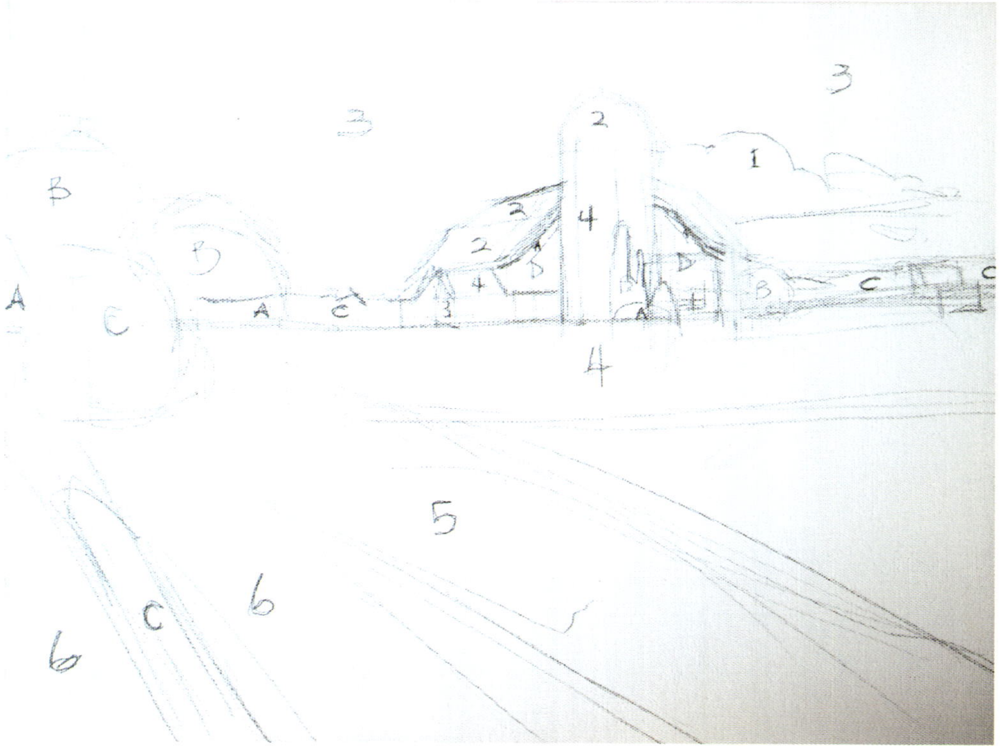

FIGURE 48.
Jim's numbered sketch.

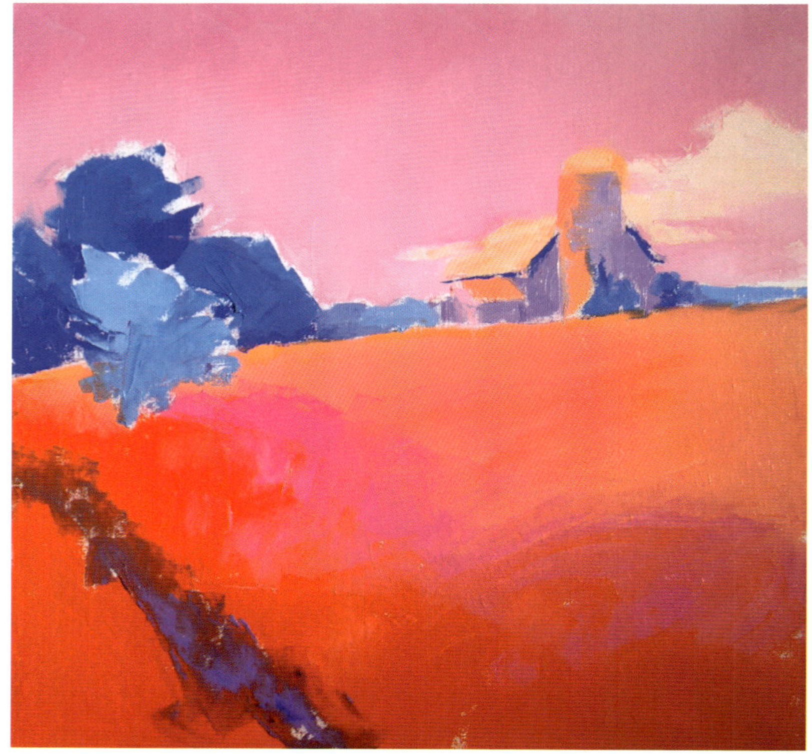

Julie's primary tones.

The trees are really the darkest areas, and there is very little of that, but you can see the A's for the extreme darks, the Bs, the Cs, and even D, our lightest dark, represented by the shadow side of the barn.

I thought about starting the lights with yellow, but because of the overcast feeling of the day, I decided to go with the cooler permanent rose for #1. Since this is the lightest light, I mixed quite a bit of white into the permanent rose. I added a little heat for the roof, value #2, and found that cadmium yellow and/or cadmium orange with lots of white did a good job there. Permanent rose made a great choice for value #3 because of its cool nature for the sky and yet its position as a "warm" on the color wheel. The entire sky is the light source in the photograph because the sun is overhead. You can see that Jim chose cadmium orange, while Mary and I chose cadmium red light. We stayed with the reds for all six of the lit values, alternating cadmium red light with permanent rose at each of the lit value changes. At this stage, the painting is already taking shape.

For A, our darkest dark, we chose ultramarine blue; for B, cobalt; and for C, manganese blue. For our lightest dark or D, we chose violet with much white. Remember that with every shadow color you must add enough white to each letter to differentiate it from the value before. Remember too, that white cools colors as well as lightening them. I chose violet for D because the blues in this photograph are moving into a pink sky. Violet begins to push blue toward red on the color wheel.

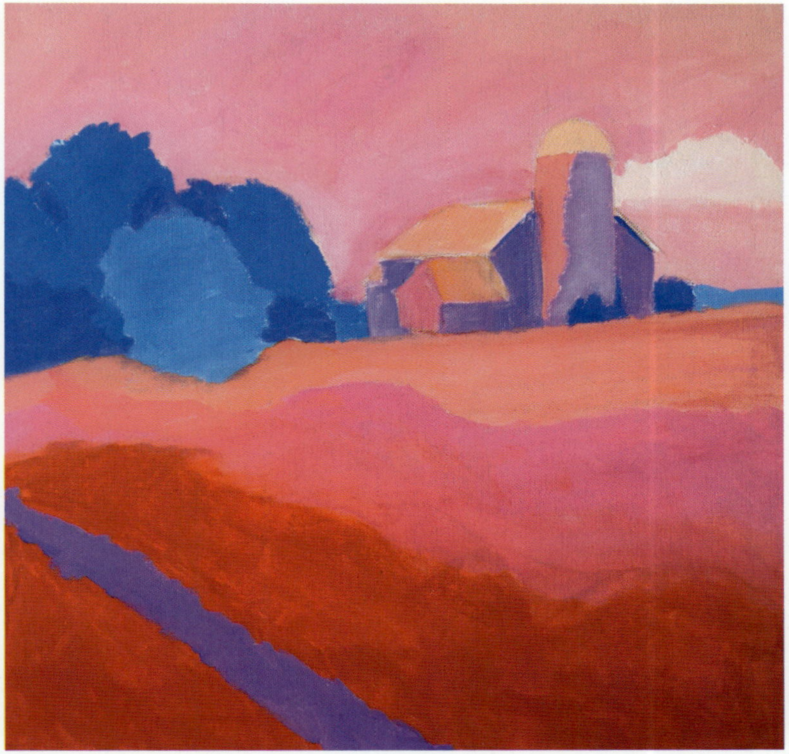

Mary's primary tones.

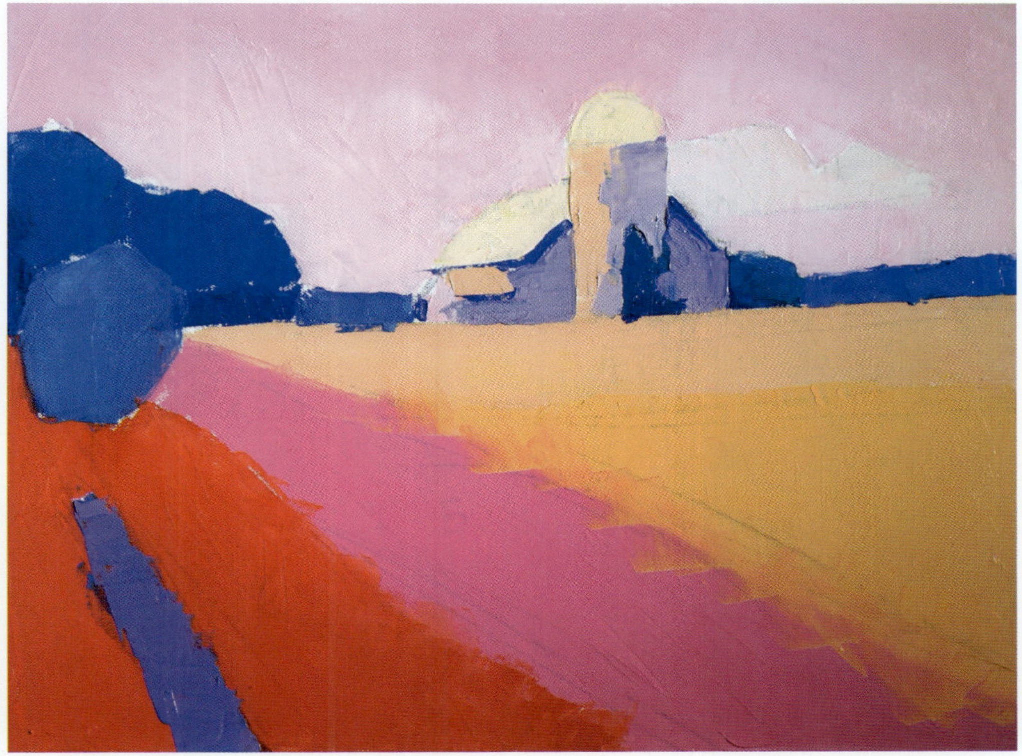

Jim's primary tones.

With the primary tones complete, it was time to work this painting! For the finished painting, we are showcasing Jim's. He did a great job of keeping the Midwestern feel. The colors are more muted than both Mary's and mine and this feels so Midwestern to me. I like the open feeling and the subtle changes in the meadow. The cloud stays behind the silo beautifully, the barn roof has just the right amount of warmth and light, and the field is luminous. Remember that the goal of putting paint over the primary tones is to hold true to the same value as what's underneath. When the impressionists did this, it enabled them to put many colors alongside each other without the large areas being broken up, as long as each color sets off the colors next to it. So, for the sky, Jim mixed a small amount of ultramarine blue with white and matched the value underneath. He also added lemon yellow and white to the clouds and distant sky. He kept his greens for the trees clean. The darks are cobalt blue and middle yellow. The lights have more yellow (and white) added to that mix. The additional colors added to the field are very similar to the primary tones, but they push the field a little more yellow in the distance. There are beautiful bits of red showing through from underneath, and while I think the foreground field needs a little more detail and even more warmth, the entire mass holds together and the painting is beautiful.

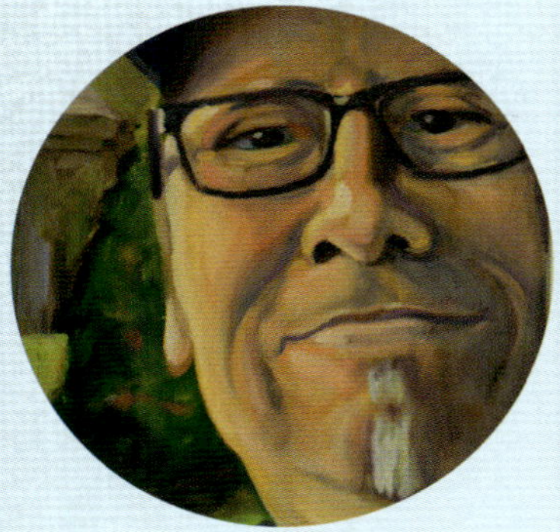

A self-taught artist, Jim Karell has had a career in video production and graphic design. His true passion, however, has always been fine arts, where he excels in portraiture and acrylics. Jim used the author's palette knife technique to produce the paintings in this book.

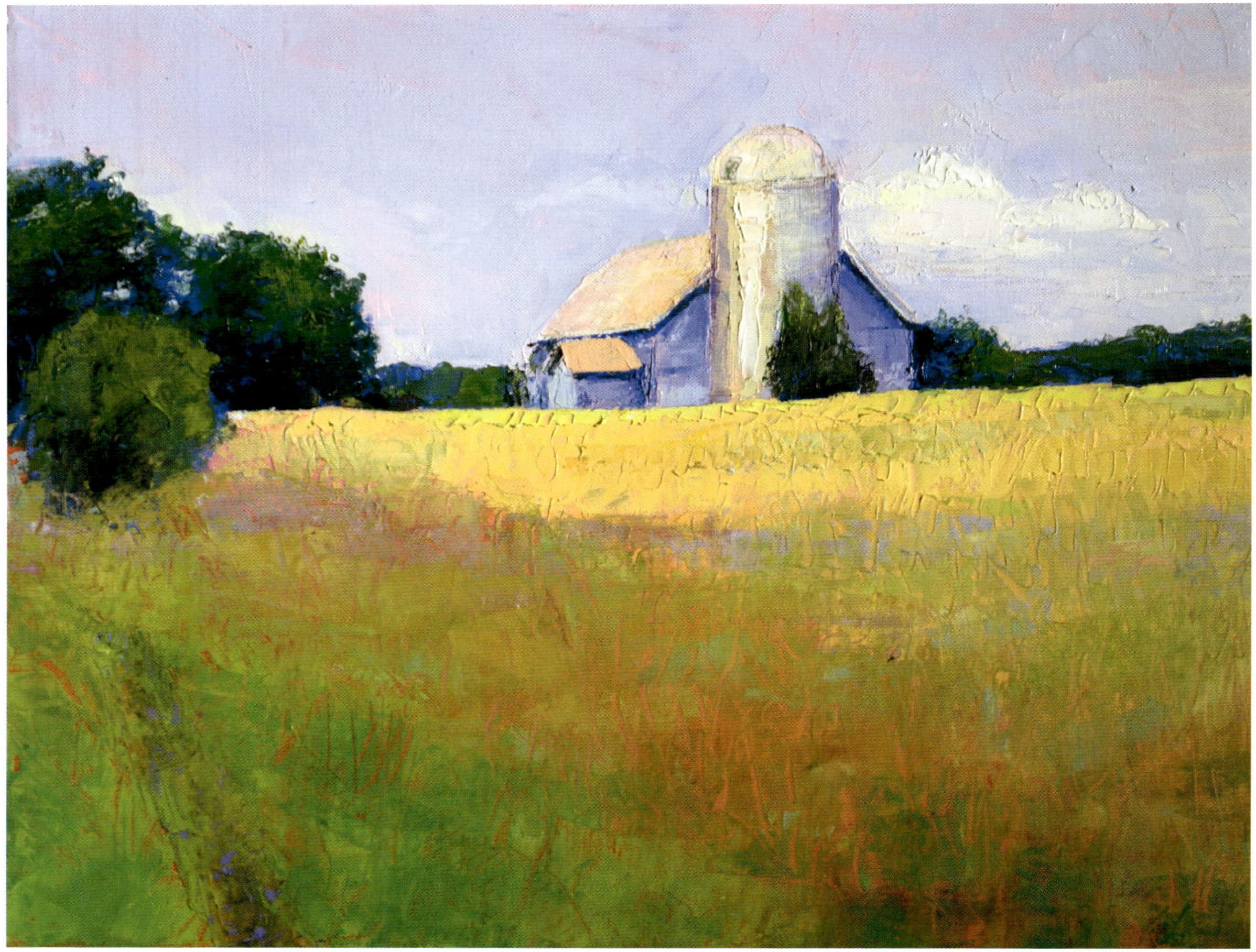

Jim's finished painting.

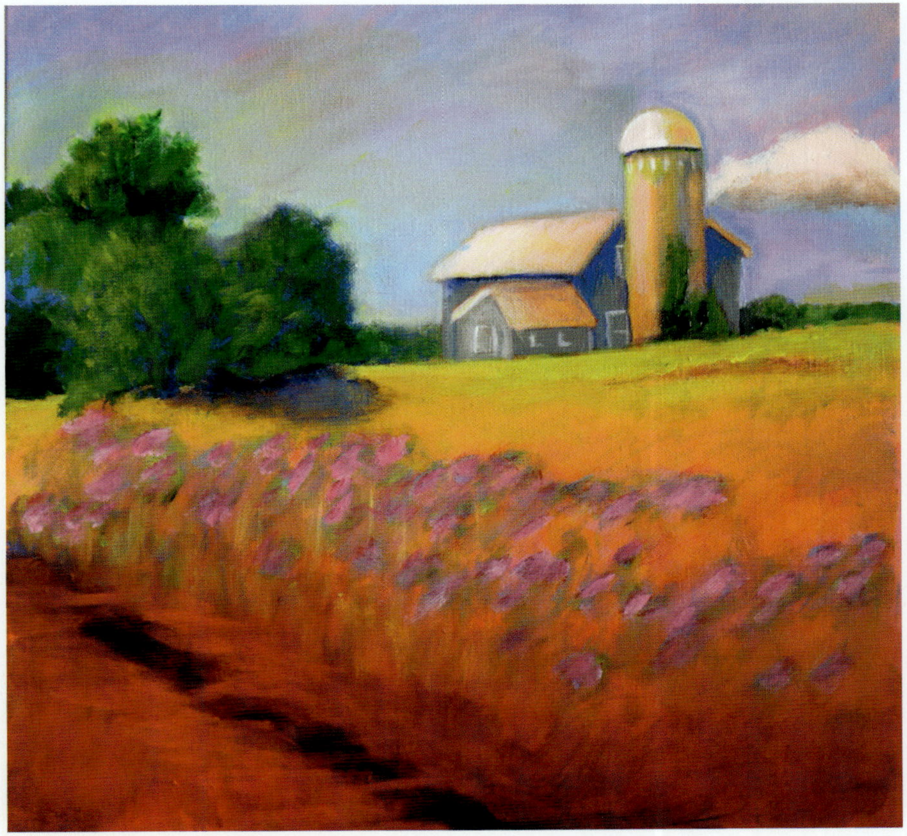

Mary's finished painting.

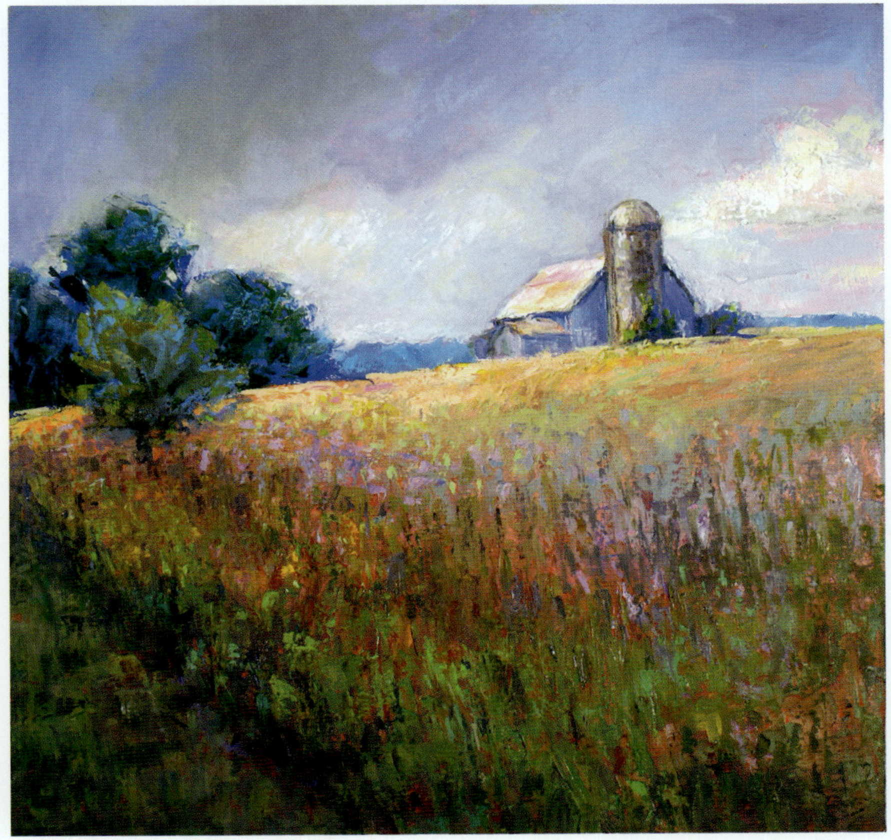

Julie's finished painting.

In Mary's finished painting, once more, the color is luminous. By putting in more details of the flowers in the foreground, she is pushing the field back toward the barn and still getting away with gorgeous color. Mary struggled with perspective on the building itself, but the field pushes it into the distance successfully. Once again, Mary is portraying a sunny day by keeping her colors clean. I would like Mary to do a little more work on the foreground by putting some darks under her flowers and by correcting the perspective on the barn.

On my painting, I found I needed to make the barn smaller. In my initial sketch, the barn was too large and too important. I like the manganese blue in the distant tree line. I left that alone. I like that the greens favor blue in the trees on the left, but I too, struggled with the foreground and wish I had done a better job of keeping it simple and putting in fewer and larger strokes. The square canvas seemed like a good idea at the time, but as I painted, I found it difficult to keep the large area simplified.

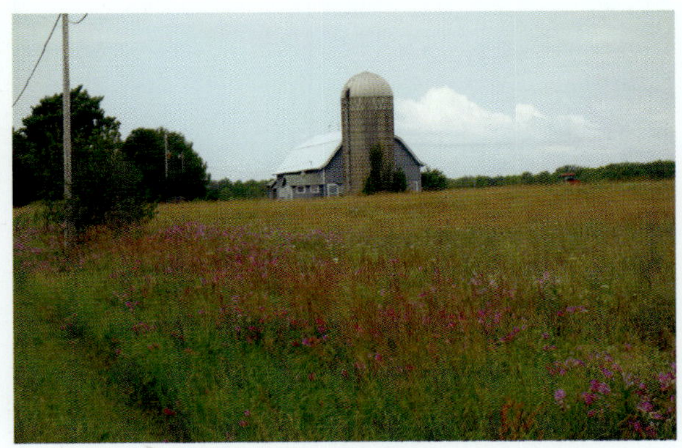

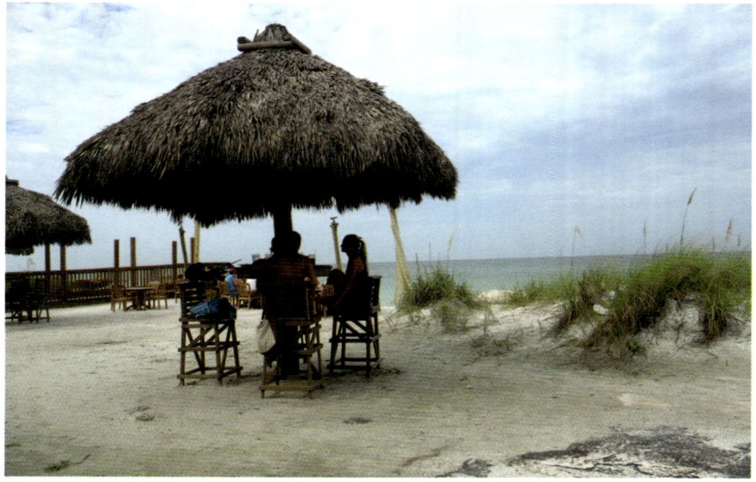

FIGURE 49.
On location.

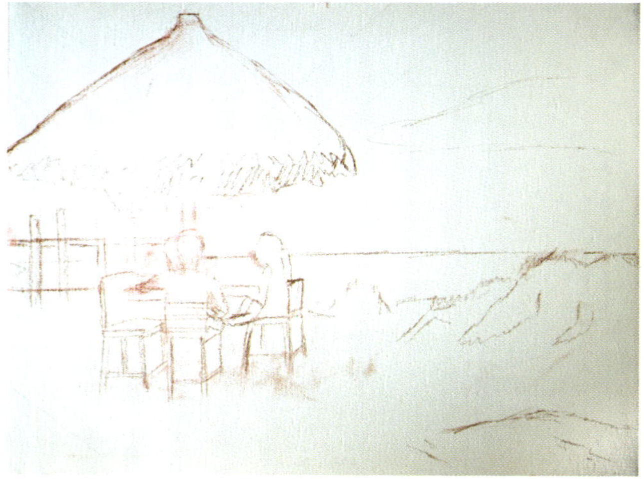

Mary's sketch.

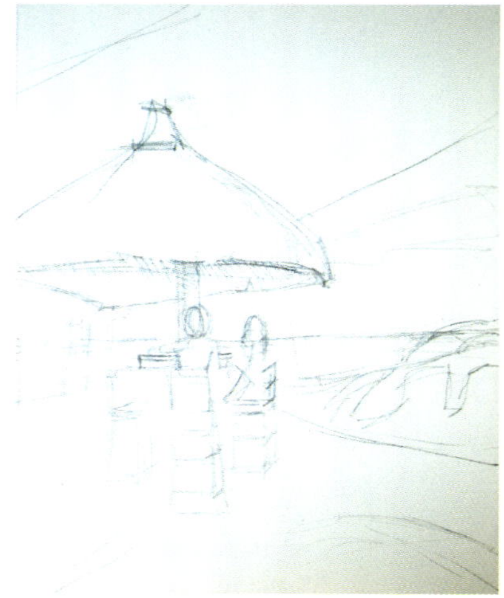

Jim's sketch.

I chose to paint the tiki hut photograph because of the atmosphere (fig. 49). I liked the simplicity of the silhouetted figures under the roof and the way the foreground leads to it and then lifts up into a lighter sky. There was a second corner of another tiki hut to the left of this main one and all three of us cropped that out as we set up the drawing. This is because that area led us to the extreme left edge and we didn't want the emphasis to be there. We also cropped off the left edge of the main tiki hut because it is such a large mass in the painting and an isolated form with its super-dark shadow. We didn't want it to look so massive. Again, I looked for a subject that appealed to me, a diverse range of values, and an arrangement that would make a good composition. The goal is to improve every photograph without necessarily copying it. Always look at your subject and decide if it would be best oriented horizontally or vertically, and select the canvas that works best.

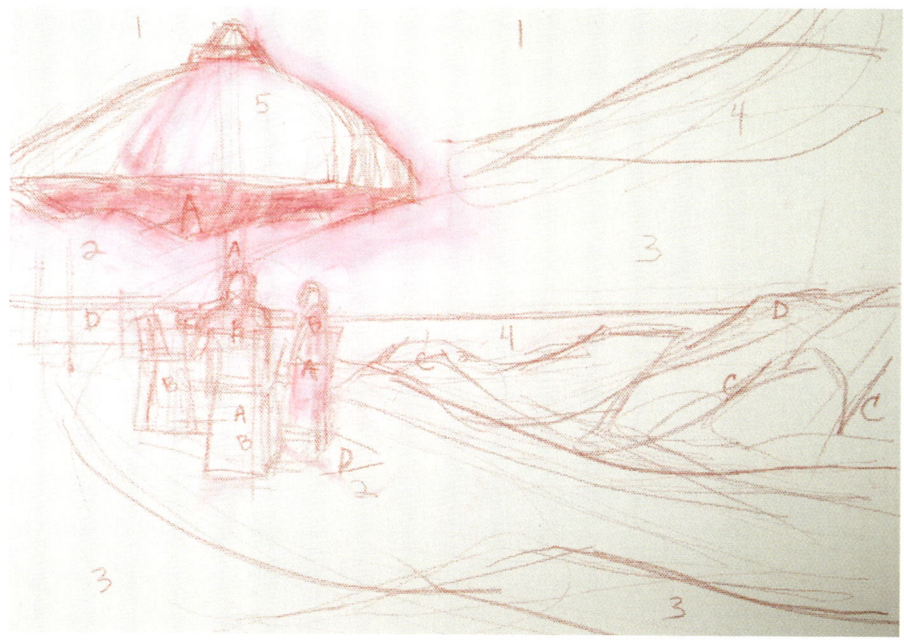

FIGURE 50.
Julie's numbered sketch.

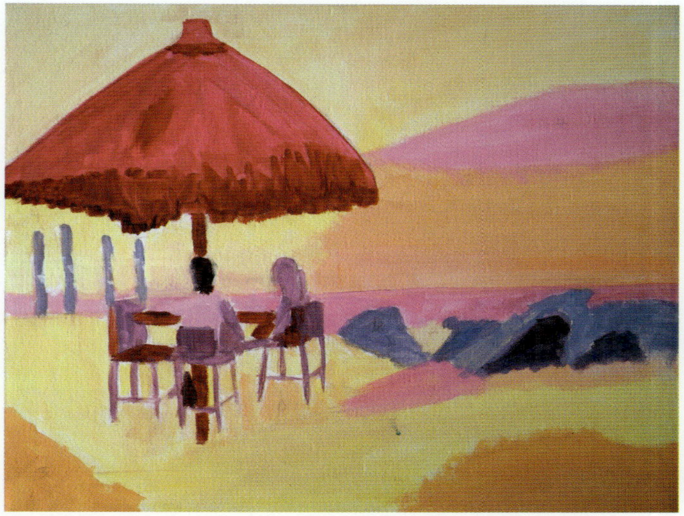

Mary's primary tones.

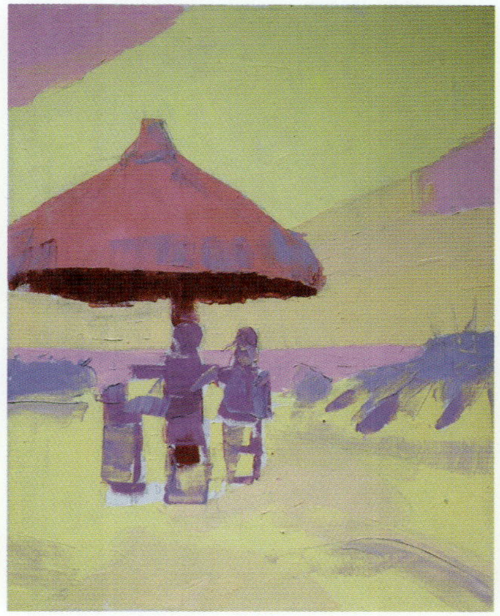

Jim's primary tones.

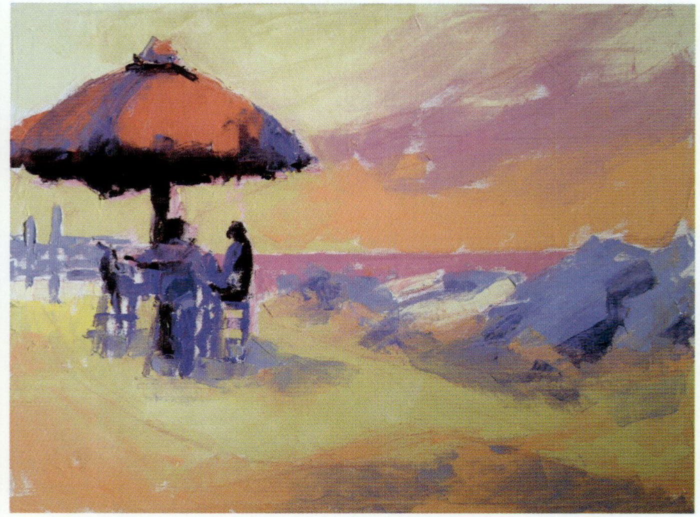

FIGURE 51.
Julie's primary tones.

In the numbered sketch (fig. 50), the lightest light is clearly the sky. We decided that areas of the lit sand were the second lightest light, along with the sky on the extreme left under the roof. Because the sky is to play such an important part in this painting, we gave the distant sky a #3. We also decided that the generally lit sand areas, not the extreme lit areas, would also be represented by value #3. When I squinted and looked out toward the horizon in the photograph, the cloud to the right of the roof and the water looked very close in value, so I gave them #4. Although a fairly dark value, the roof itself is lit and I made that #5. When you look at the grasses to the right in the photograph, notice that they are receiving light and parts of them are in shadow. The subject has so many lights that I decided to paint the grasses using mostly shadow primary tones. This was a judgment call anticipating what would be needed to set off the lights.

The darkest dark, A, is under the roof and in the silhouette of the figures. There are also lesser darks there and these are lettered B. There are tiny bits of B darks in the dune and the grass also, but I didn't want to make them that dark, because I wanted the focus to be on the tiki hut and figures, so I labeled the shadows C and the top part D. I labeled a couple more light darks D as well.

The next step was to choose our colors. There is a reason why I choose certain colors for my primary tones. Sometimes I choose a slightly darker, warmer color so that as it is developed further, it will help to pop the lighter, brighter colors added on top. For this subject, I was concerned about getting enough value contrast in the sky to represent the atmosphere of the day, so I decided on cadmium red light or cadmium orange for #1. This would give me a base to add other colors. It has a fair amount of power, but at that value, it's easy to work with. So for #2, I used cadmium orange. That is a light value and a lot of white is needed. I was not afraid of it being too warm for the job. I again went with cadmium orange for the same reasons for #3. I switched to permanent rose for the #4s so that I could begin cooling the temperature for both the clouds and the water, even though the water contains some light. I used bright red with white for the roof. That color has a strong enough presence, can be cooled with white, and still looks lit at that value.

I debated the darks carefully. Although in the photograph they look super-dark and super-cool, rich darks like those work better on an extremely sunny day when there would be much higher contrast between lights and darks. Also, if I used that dark color/value there, the tiki hut would not recede. I decided on permanent magenta. That color sets up a slightly warmer dark, which you would see on a day that is not very bright. I used the same color with the addition of more white and a bit of cobalt blue for B and C, with even more white in the mix. I wanted a cool D, so used violet plus more white.

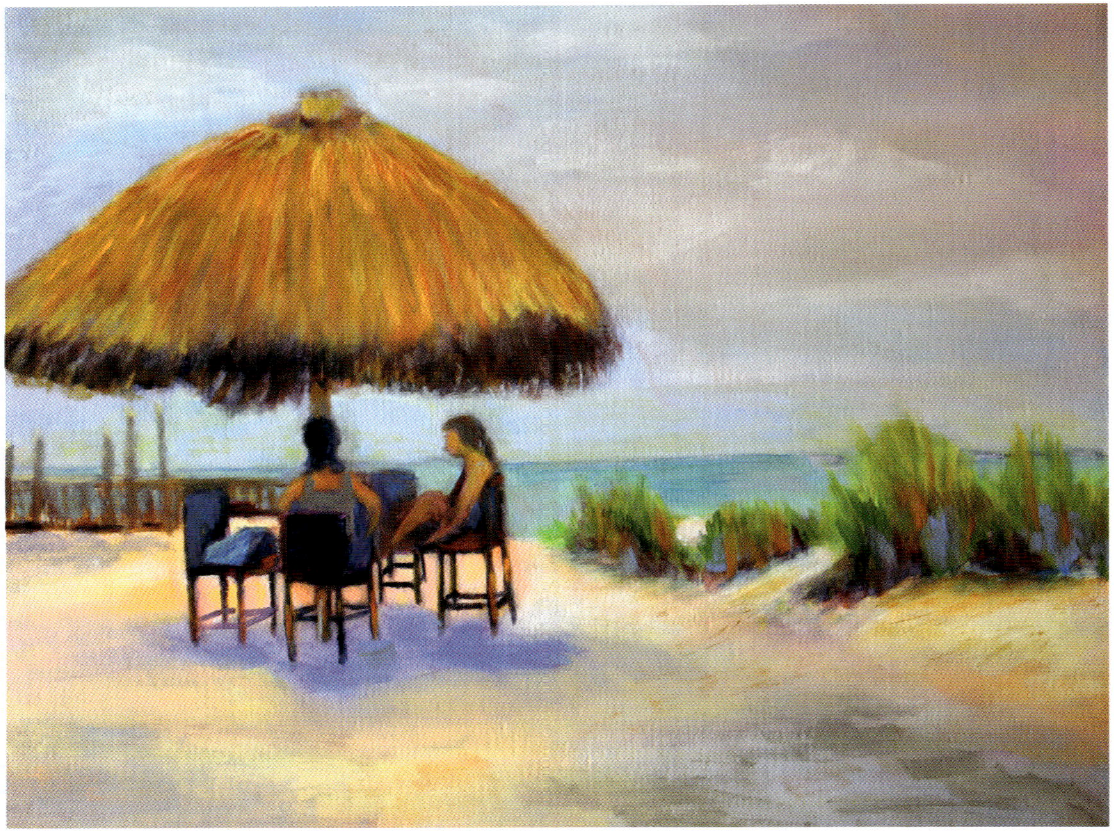

FIGURE 52.
Mary's finished painting.

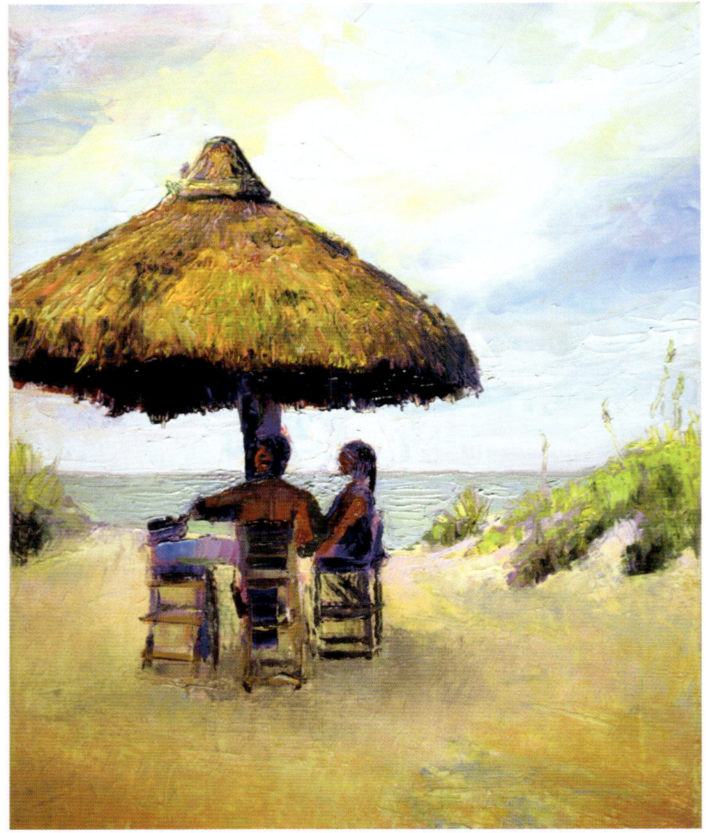

FIGURE 53.
Jim's finished painting.

I liked the way this painting worked at this stage, particularly the atmosphere created by the warm colors in the sky and the cool shadows (fig. 51). Now the foreground needed warming up and pulling forward, so I made a warm shadow with bright red and cobalt blue and white. A few more darks were needed in the bottom right along the base of the grasses than I had in the primary tones. For this darker area, I mixed manganese blue and cadmium yellow pale (warm green) into permanent magenta. A variety of blue grays were mixed for the sky. In the center I used manganese blue with white to put over my value #1. The warm lights of the sky were cooled down. I added warmer grays to the cooler clouds. A light sand color highlight was made by using a touch of warm yellow with permanent rose and white. I also added a bit of ultramarine blue to the light sky behind the umbrella.

Mary, once again, kept her colors pure and bright (fig. 52). I like the glow around the sand area in her painting and the color of the water. Her "day" is not as overcast as mine, which she achieved by keeping the sky more blue. Her chairs are convincing, though her figures need a little more work.

Jim also portrayed a beautiful sunny day with his lemon yellow in the sky and the wonderful roof (fig. 53). The roof is my favorite part, as I feel you can reach right out and touch it. Note the way he kept the color of the water in the distance soft. I would like to see Mary and Jim's paintings developed further with a warmer foreground to pull the front forward and push the subject area back into the scene. A little more work will make the figures more believable. You can see how each of us changed the atmosphere to suit.

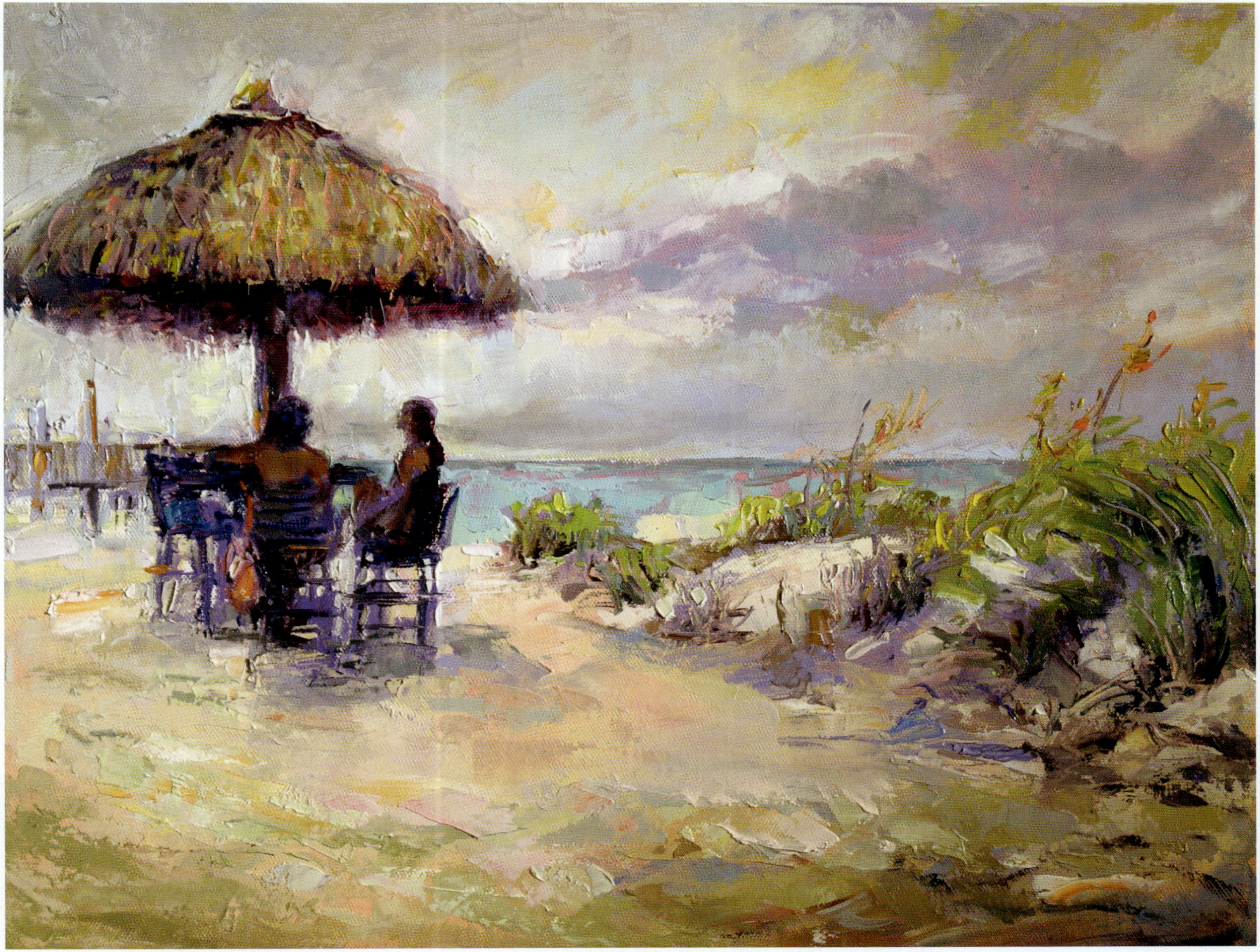

Julie's finished painting.

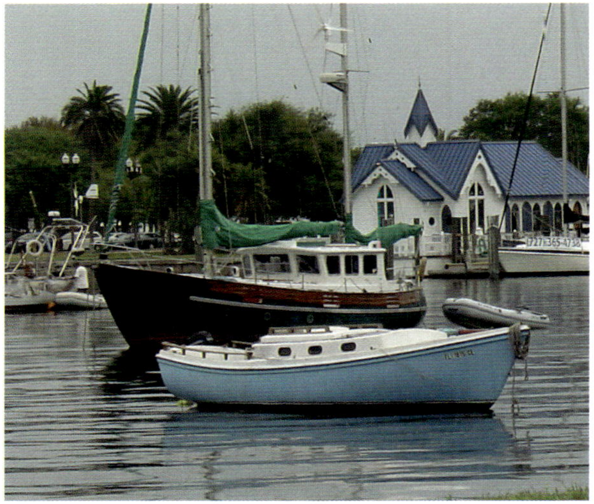

FIGURE 54.
On location.

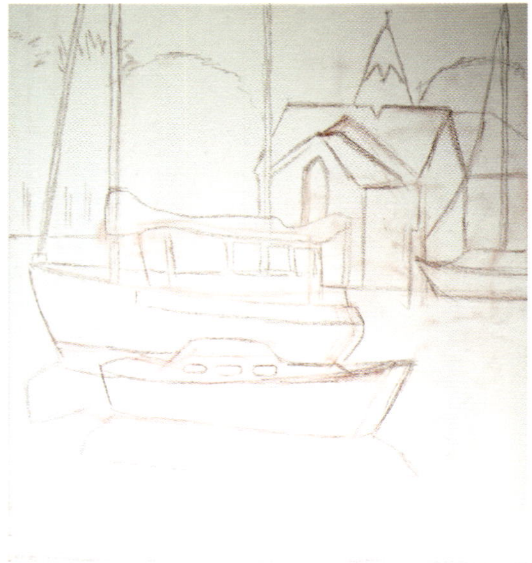

Mary's sketch.

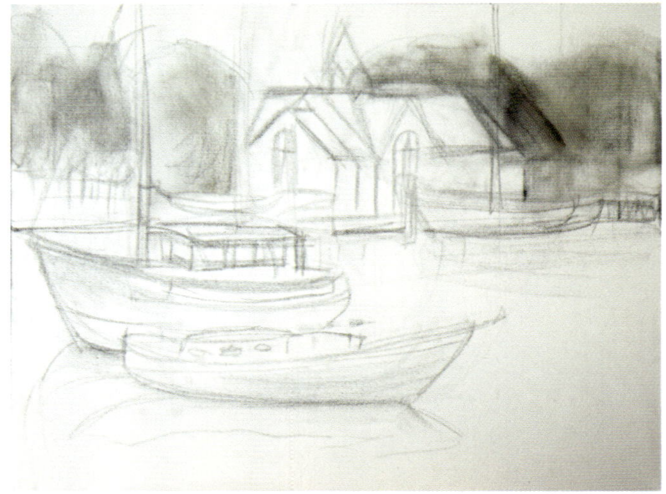

Jim's sketch.

I took the photograph in figure 54 at the bay front in St. Petersburg, Florida. The photograph included a lot more information, but all of us zeroed in on the two boats and the building behind them. This cropped composition offered a variety of subject matter including water, and I liked the way the light came from the right and lit up the front planes on the boat and house. One of the difficulties of this picture is that the boats and the building are similar in size and are centered in the composition. Each of us tried a different size canvas in hopes that we could make the composition work. I was hoping that I could start by sweeping in from the front bottom right corner through the boats, capture that dark front of the second boat and a dark to the left of it, and then swing the eye to the right, above the building and out the sky on the upper right. Water can be a daunting subject for beginners, but this method makes it much easier. In the photograph, there's a contrast of light and shadow on the water. If you set up the proper relationship of those two with the temperature painting method, it isn't as difficult to paint water as you might think. I chose a square composition just because I like working on square canvases. The challenge would be to extend the shadow of the leading boat down to the right to eliminate an empty space on the bottom. I intended to eliminate the grass and sidewalk.

This is early morning light, so it is clean and warm. Our lightest lights are on the right side of both boats and the building behind. I wanted the boat in front to hold the front position; therefore, only that boat is a #1 (thinking of Rule #3). I sacrificed the second boat and the building slightly and labeled those lights #2. The sky came in next at #3, the foreground water was #4, and the lit part of the roof was assigned #5. The darkest light appears to be the lit side of the middle boat and the tops of the distant trees, #6. There are quite a few details in this photograph, and it was tempting to number them all, but this is when restraint is needed and we stopped numbering the lights at #6.

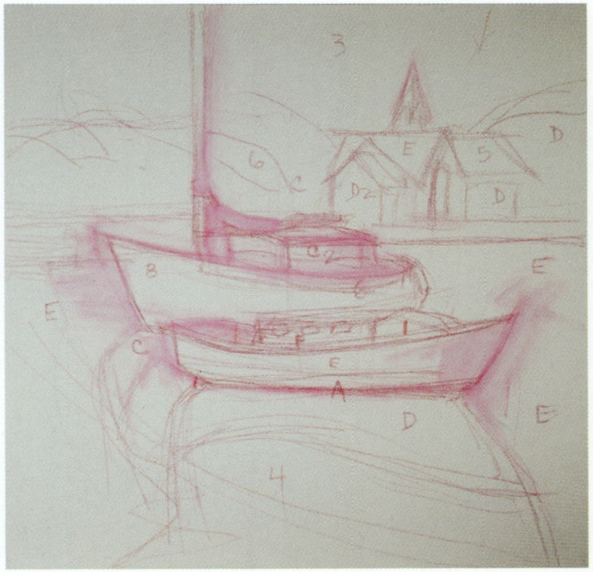

Julie's numbered sketch.

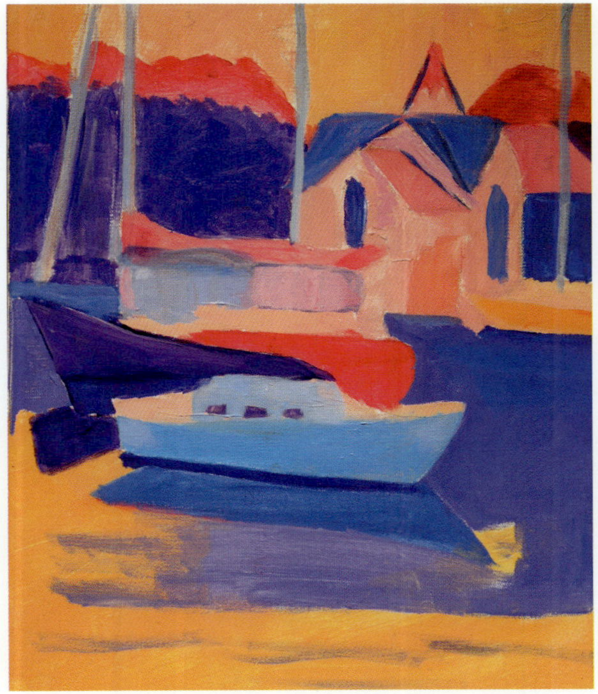

Mary's primary tones.

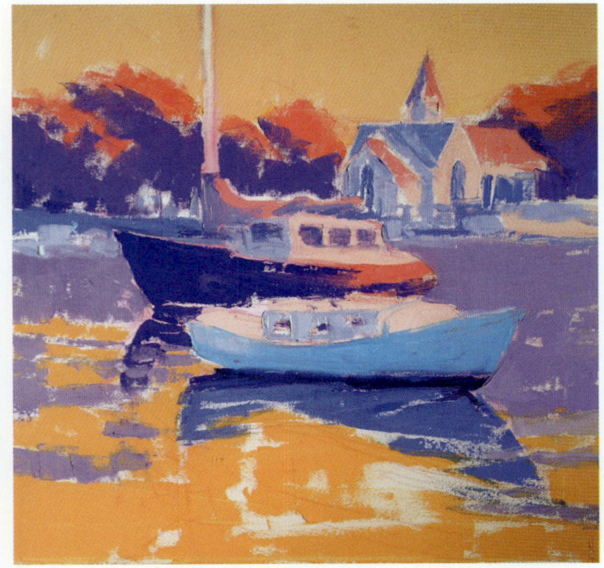

FIGURE 55.
Julie's primary tones.

While the darkest dark seems to be on the left front of the second boat, I put the darkest dark at the base of the leading boat, (again Rule #3), so that is A (fig. 55). B is the front of the second boat. This was painted from a photograph and not the actual scene, and therefore contains inaccurate values. I made the value decisions based on what I know and what I see. My guess is that if we were there in person painting the scene live, we would see exactly the values I am calling. To capture the warm lighting and emphasize the water, I decided to lighten the darks as they go behind the two boats. So the dark windows in the boat and the darks in the trees on the shore are labeled C. I like the light-value non-lit areas in this picture most of all, and that led to distinguishing between several more lesser darks, even though it is a lot. The D label was assigned to the darkened windows in the building, along with the reflection of the front boat in the water. I gave an E to the non-lit side of the building roof, the reflections in the distant water, and the front of the blue boat. And finally I gave an F to the front shadow side of the white area of the front boat. This is the highest number of labels I am comfortable with.

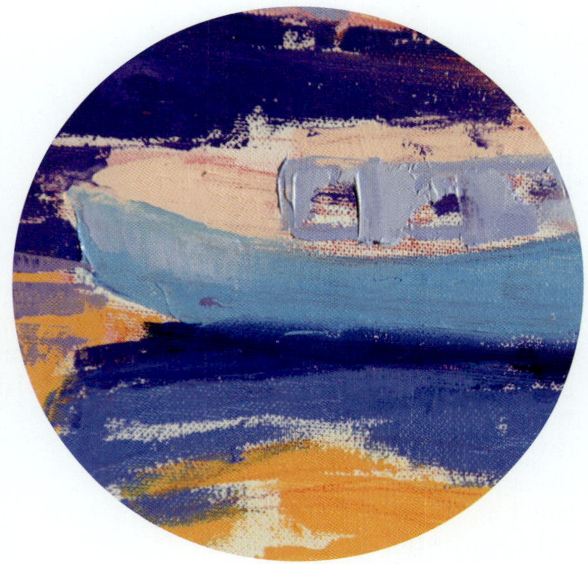

Julie's close-up.

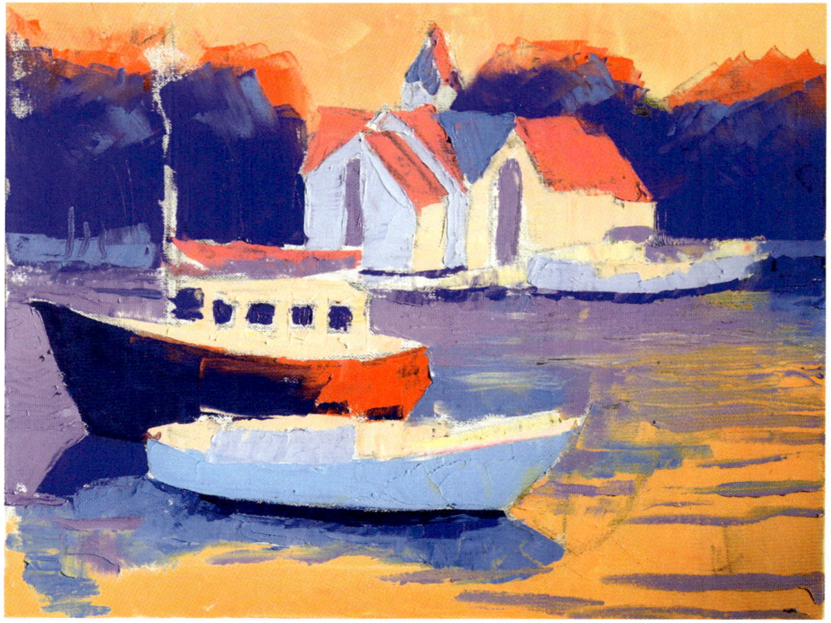

Jim's primary tones.

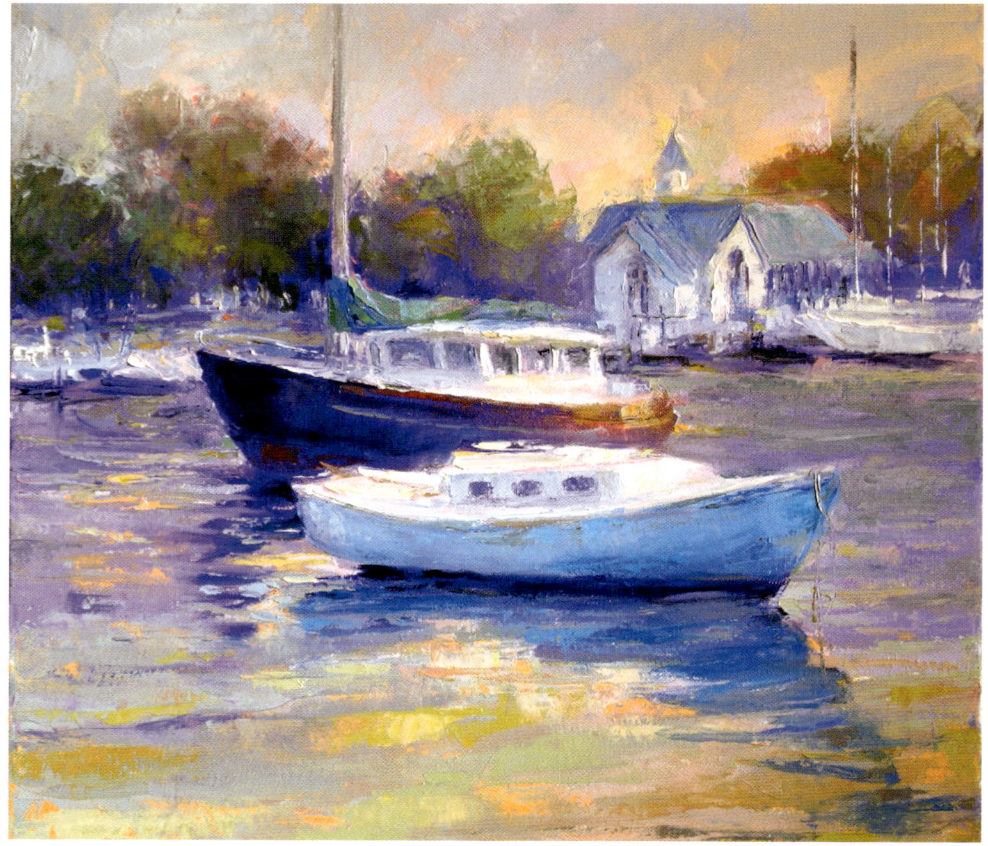

Julie's finished painting.

The golden look to the light called for yellow to represent our lights. There are a lot of lit areas here, and as you darken yellow you must do it with either blue or red. Blue is not a good choice since it represents shadow. Therefore, I used lemon yellow for #1 and cadmium orange for #2. Cadmium orange gives a little more golden color than yellow does, and the color is kept light enough to represent the #2 value because there is a lot of white added. The addition of white keeps the orange cooler.

For #3, you can mix lemon yellow with a small amount of permanent rose. This makes a slightly cooler sky color and will help the sky recede. Number 4 was cadmium yellow deep, or cadmium orange with less white than #3. We wanted this color to represent warm light and pull the foreground forward, so warm and bright is good. It provided a wonderful base for the final color. The next two values, #5 and #6, are a deep or dark light, so I moved to cadmium red light and added white to both, letting #6 get even darker with the addition of a small amount of permanent rose.

I used ultramarine blue for A, cobalt blue for B, and dioxazine violet added to my B color for C (plus white, of course). D was manganese blue added to my C color, plus white to lighten. E was manganese blue and white for the boat front, and because I wanted to showcase that, the color of E for the background water was changed to a lighter shade of my violet mixture—same value, different hue. F was ultramarine blue and lots of white.

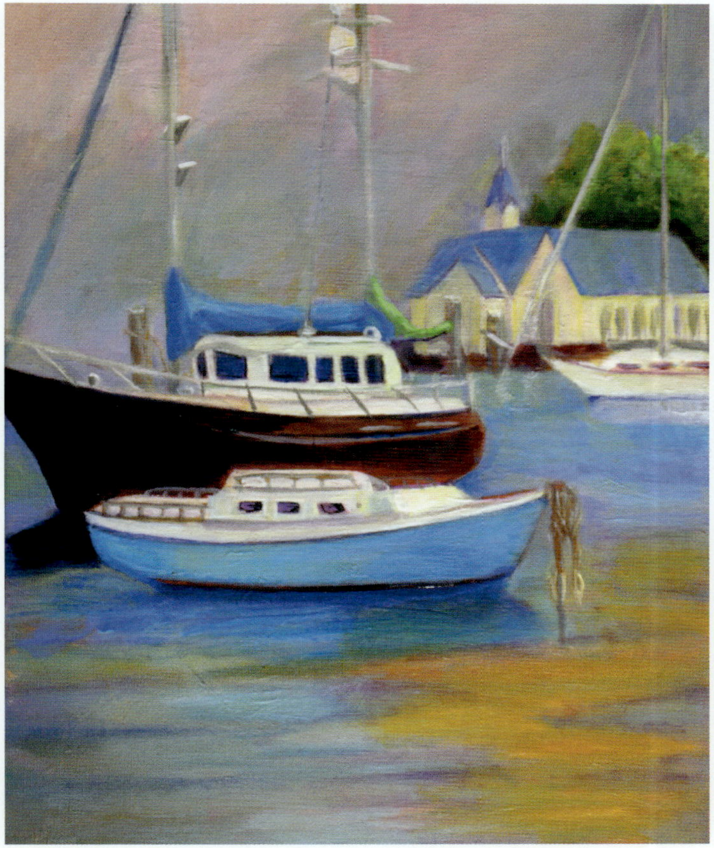

Mary's finished painting.

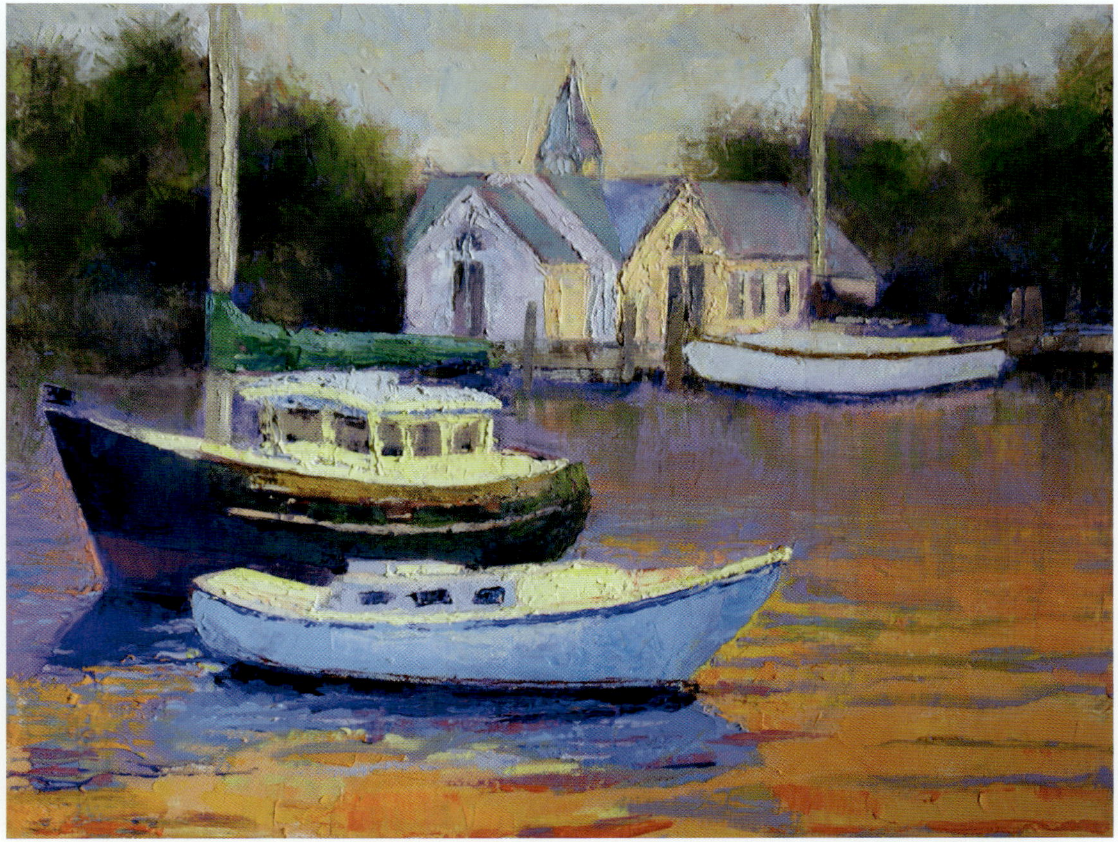

Jim's finished painting.

We all loved our paintings in the primary tones and wondered if we were actually going to be able to improve them by adding more color! But we charged on fearlessly. At this stage, Jim appeared to have made the best decision with his composition. Mary realized her building was too large and I was worried about the foreground in mine. Did I leave too much space there or would I be able to work it out in the end? We ran out of working time then, so we took them home and worked on them solo. I added greens to mine first and realized that my building was also too large, so I pared it down a bit. I added blues to the sky, matching the value to the primary tones, but tried to keep them warm. I added some details on the bank left of the boat and worked on the boats. Just as I expected, the first notes set up a wonderful feeling of water, shadow, and light. We loved the golden light that Jim got in his painting, his strong foreground color, and the color in his shadow water. We loved the detail that Mary got in her boats, and the impressionistic look of my painting. I ran out of time and didn't finish the bottom right in my painting. I think that if I had put a little more detail where the shadow meets the light, I could have pulled out a better composition. Look at these examples carefully and notice how the primary tones are showing underneath. See how they establish the relationships in the painting and give the painting unity.

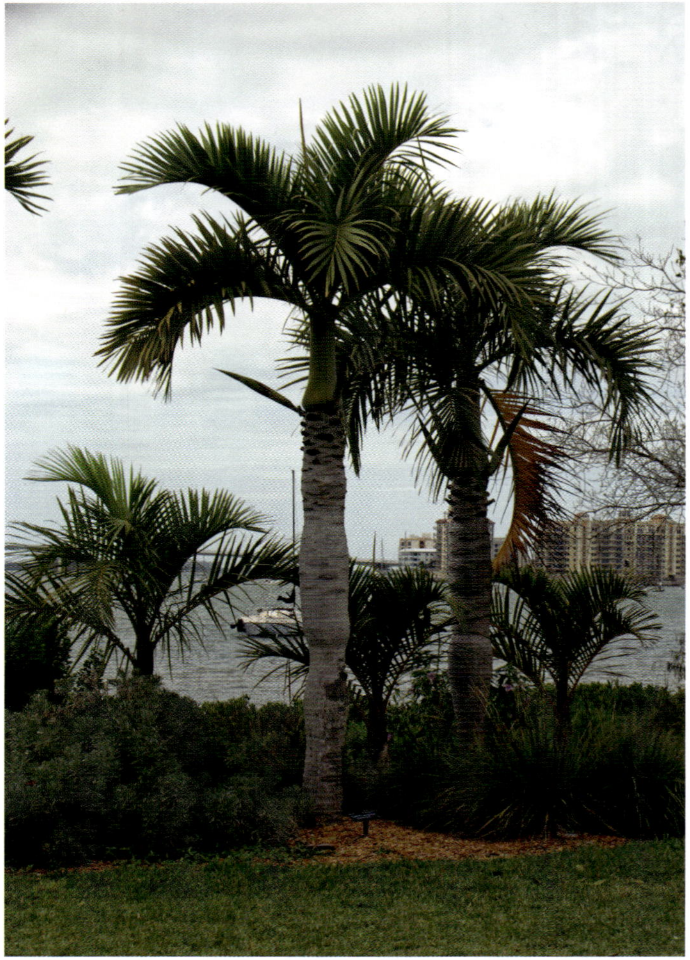

FIGURE 56.
On location.

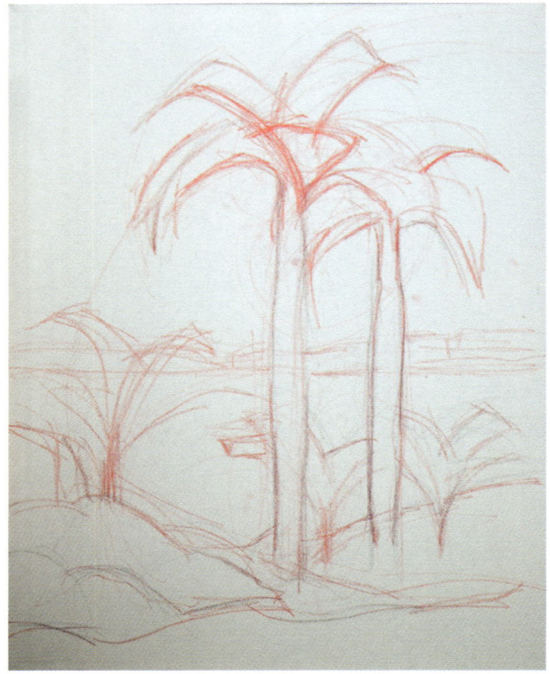

Julie's sketch.

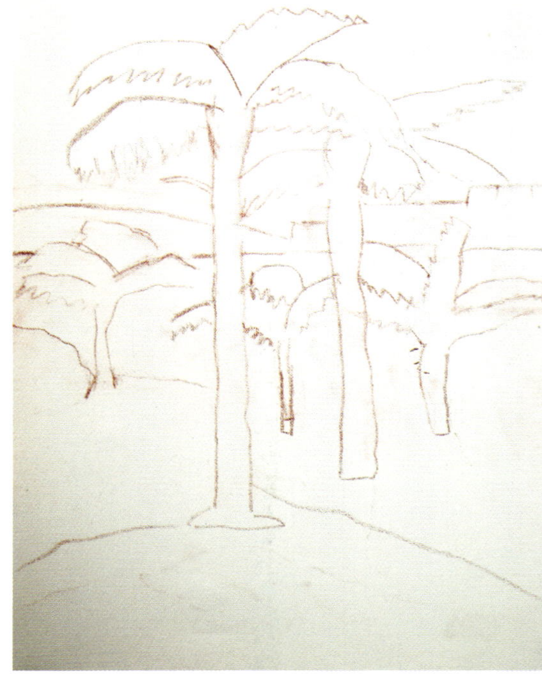

Mary's sketch.

The photograph in figure 56 was taken looking across the bay from Selby Gardens in Sarasota. I liked it because of the design of the palm branches against the sky and the little bit of a view of the bridge behind them. The trick with this photograph is to provide an opening to look beyond the palms and have a bit of view. Otherwise the foreground blocks out the background. I also chose this subject because of its gray-day look. That seemed like the perfect vehicle to show off what this method can do. As far as composition, I looked for how the eye could move through this subject and tried to use the negative shapes to tell the story.

Problems to sort out included the fact that the foreground stopped the eye from traveling back, more variety was needed in the greens, and the boat needed to be pushed back so it wouldn't attach itself to the edge of the palm. I was particularly interested to see where Jim would take his composition.

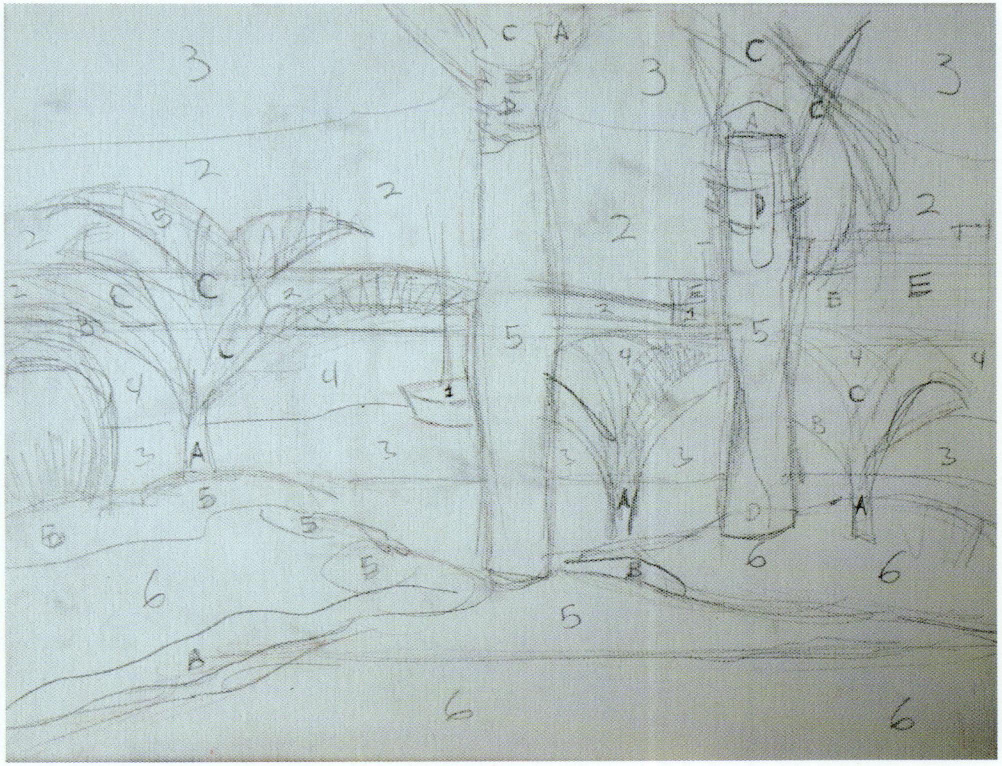

FIGURE 57.
Jim's numbered sketch.

On Jim's numbered sketch, you can see that the sailboat is number one (fig. 57). Because it is the only white object in the photograph, it's important that it be the lightest value; however, it is such a small spot that it can be treated as a detail and added at the end. But the #1 holds that value position and lets us set up our value relationships properly. Number 2 is the distant sky. Because there is a lot of sky, we gave the upper sky a #3 to prevent monotony. That will help create distance, because we can warm and darken the top sky and it will pull toward us. Number 4 is the water because it is reflecting the sky. It's not the source of light; therefore, it needs to be one value darker than the sky. Number 5 is the next darkest light, and you can see that in the foreground mulch area and the palm trunks. It is also the number for the top of the palm leaves. The trunks of the palms are a judgment call. Because they are silhouetted against the light sky, they would be better called a shadow, though the edges are certainly receiving light. The darkest light is the grass in the front and some of the greens, and we called that #6.

The darkest darks in this photograph are under the greenery in the front along the ground, and possibly also at the top of the trunks before the branches spread out. B is also located in the palm fronds and trunks and in some of the bushes as they move away from the front of the painting. Cs are mostly in the palm frond greens. There are Ds in the palm trunks, and finally Es in the buildings across the water.

Because the day is overcast, we chose cooler lights. The lit boat, which was #1, was given a touch of permanent rose and white to hold the value. The #2 position was also permanent rose, but with less white. The #3 light would need to be warmer, so we used bright red with white. There was a small amount of value #3 at the leading edge of the water, but we chose to use permanent rose and white there instead of the bright red, because we wanted that water to recede behind the leading edge of the greens in the foreground. The #4 lit value is the water farther away, and for that we darkened with permanent rose. We made the #5s bright red so they would definitely hold front position and provide a warm base to work back into. Even though this color has a lot of heat and we don't want heat in the trunks, we will work other colors into the red to cool it down in the final painting. The darkest light, #6, was made by adding permanent rose to #5 and using less white. Although the photograph does not contain this much heat, it is recommended in temperature painting to help the foreground push everything else back. If you can get a strong foreground, you can get better distance. It is just one of our tools.

We used dioxazine violet or ultramarine blue for our As. We used cobalt blue and added white for our Bs, and a lighter version of that for our Cs. Or manganese blue could be used for our Cs. Ds were violet with more white, and E, which represented the distant buildings, was created with permanent magenta plus more white.

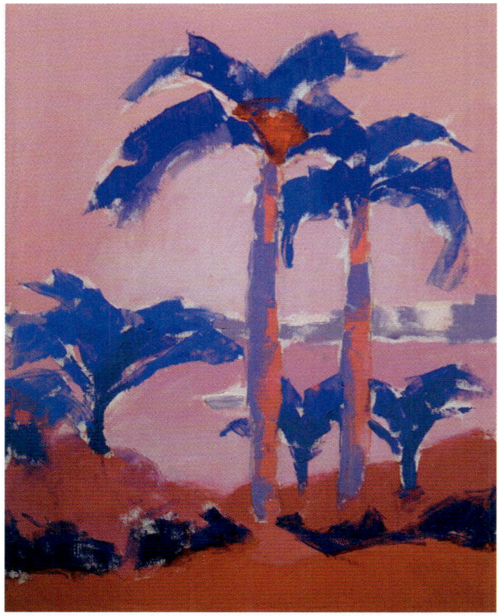

Julie's primary tones.

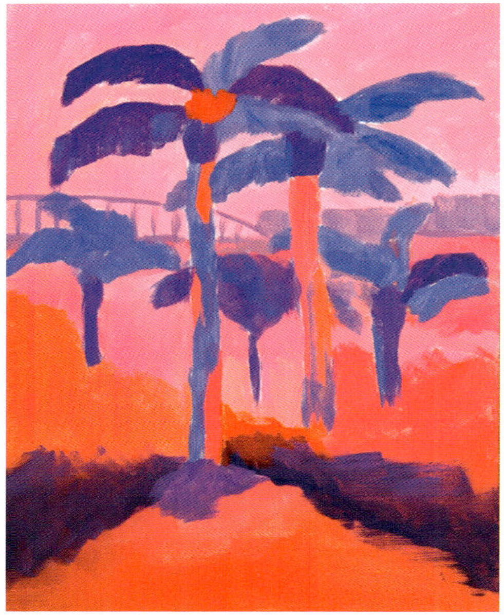

Mary's primary tones.

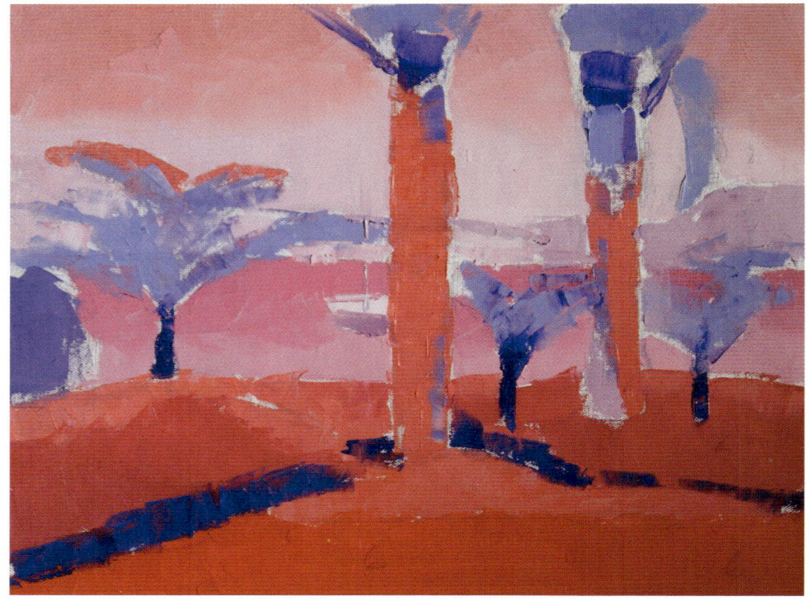

Jim's primary tones.

After our primary tones were complete, we worked on the paintings separately and brought them back a day or two later. It was fun to see how each of us interpreted our painting. We are showcasing Jim's finished painting here because he found a unique take on it (fig. 58). I love the unusual composition and the rules he broke, such as putting a palm trunk in the middle. While other people think the tops of the palm trees are interesting, Jim made the subject about the trunks and the light and the feeling cf the water and the bay. I love the way he developed the trunks. You can see that he calmed the red, but also that the red is still giving strength to the finished color. Most likely, without the red underneath, the colors would not be singing as loudly. Jim's greens are luminous because the reds are helping them from underneath. I particularly like the bits of yellow in Jim's painting, and my favorite part, besides the trunks, is that bit of green palm frond on the left palm tree. He left the shape loose, suggested, not defined.

As for mine (fig. 60), I wanted to play with the shapes of the palm fronds and had fun adding a variety of colors to them. I added orange and white into the sky next to the main trunk and put cooler blues loaded with white to match the value of the primary tone over the upper sky. I enjoy painting palms because it's a challenge to get the shapes to work without them becoming stiff and over rendered. My favorite color choice on my completed painting is the manganese blue and the greens mixed with it. It comes alive with so much of the underpainting in pink tones.

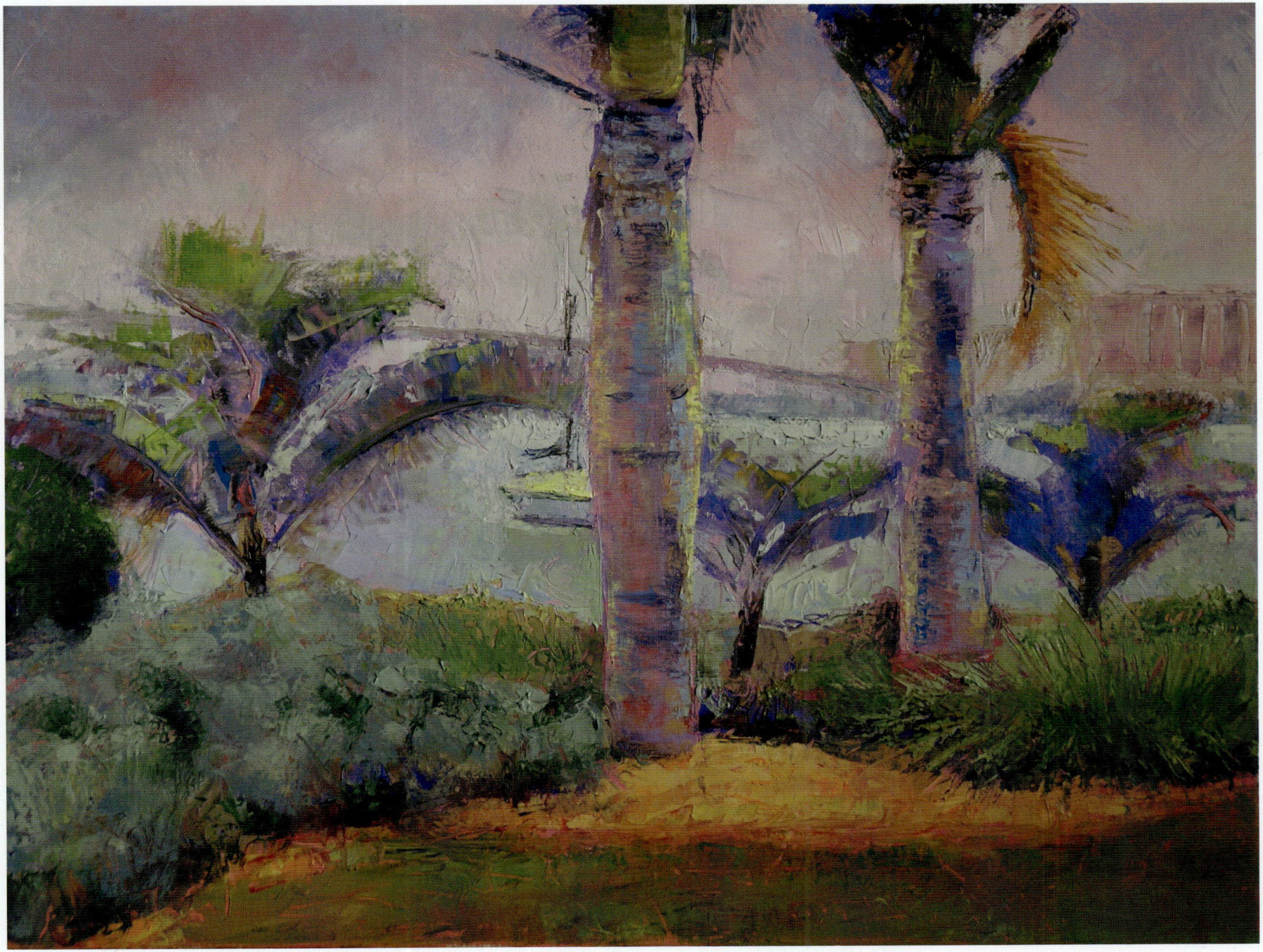

FIGURE 58.
Jim's finished painting.

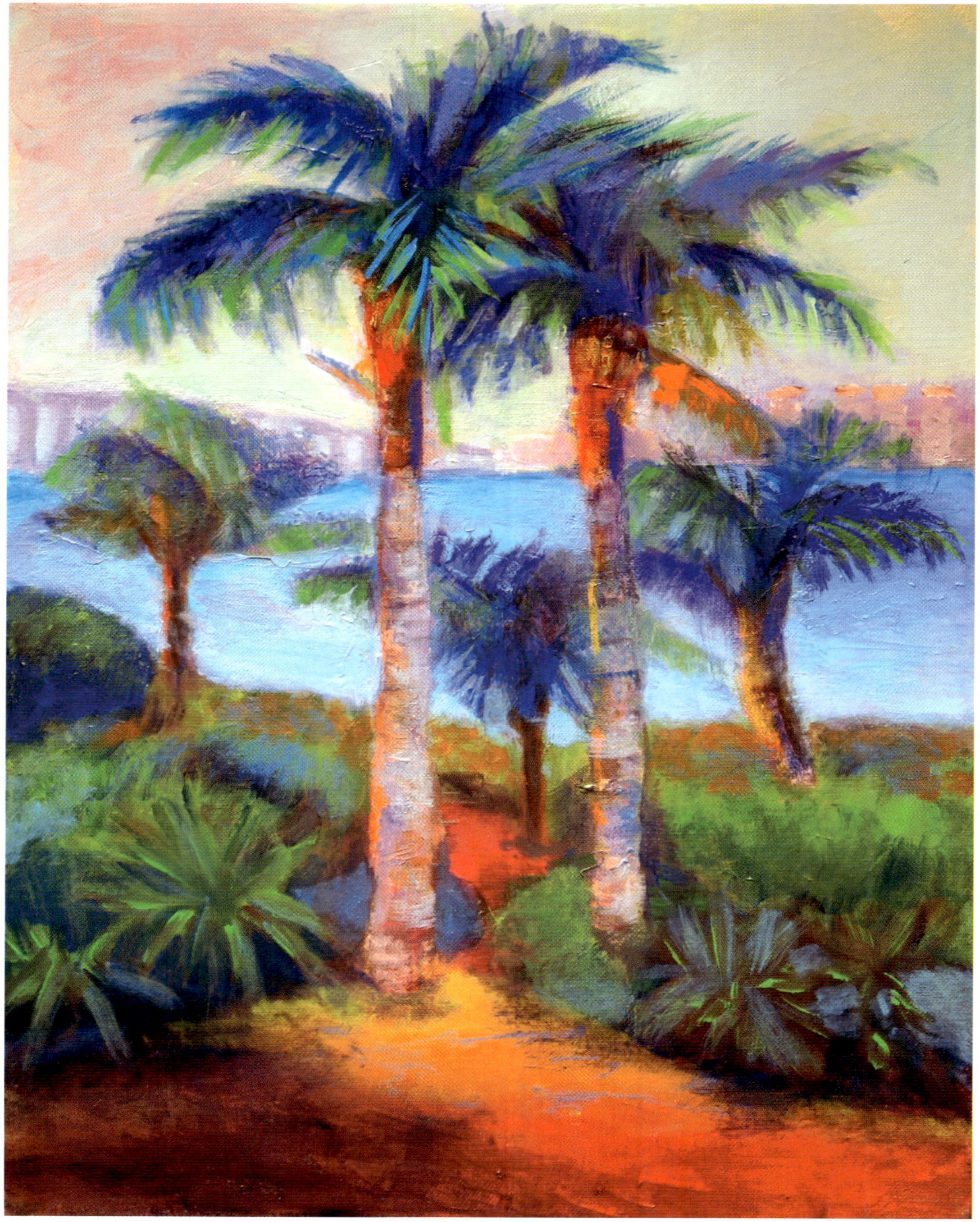

Mary's painting is full of color (fig. 60). Her use of stronger and more vibrant color in the greens along the shore helped to "pop" the palm trunks. There are some amazing color choices in the trunks of the two main palms. This is what color does when it is used to advantage. These paintings, with their multiple choices of colors added after the primary tones were painted, show what is possible when you're looking to create exciting color. Although the photograph portrayed a gray day, there are many colors that will get even gray to glow.

FIGURE 59.
Mary's finished painting.

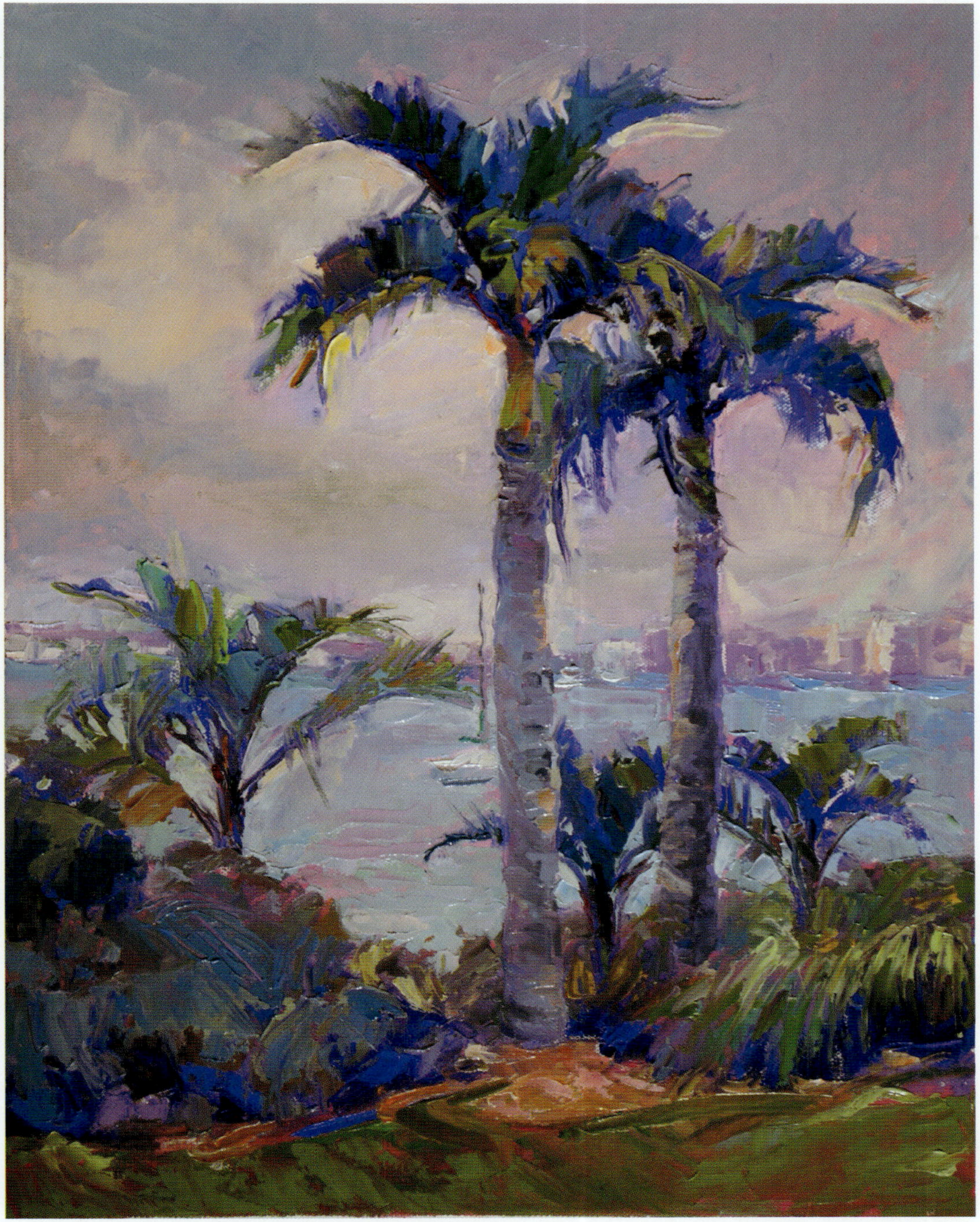

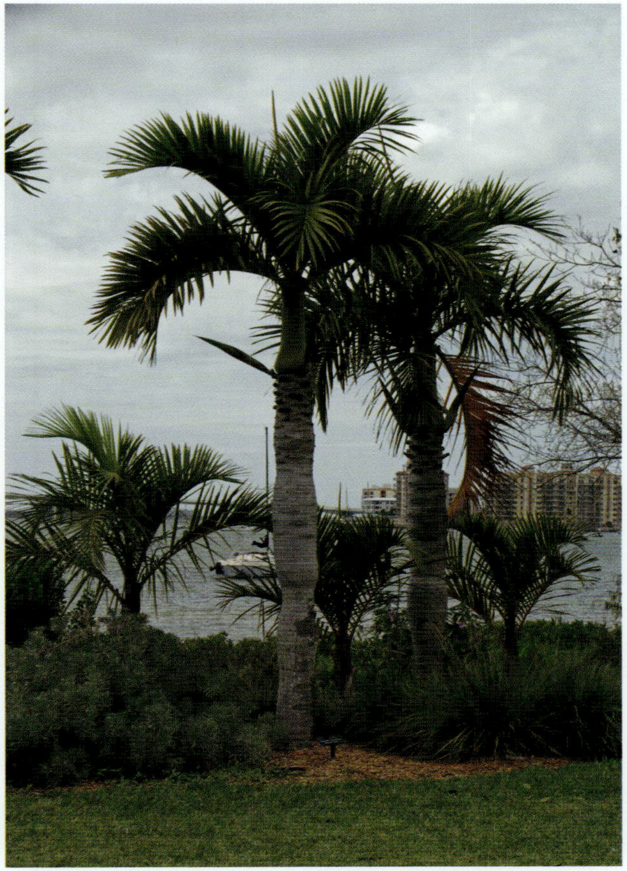

FIGURE 60.
Julie's finished painting.

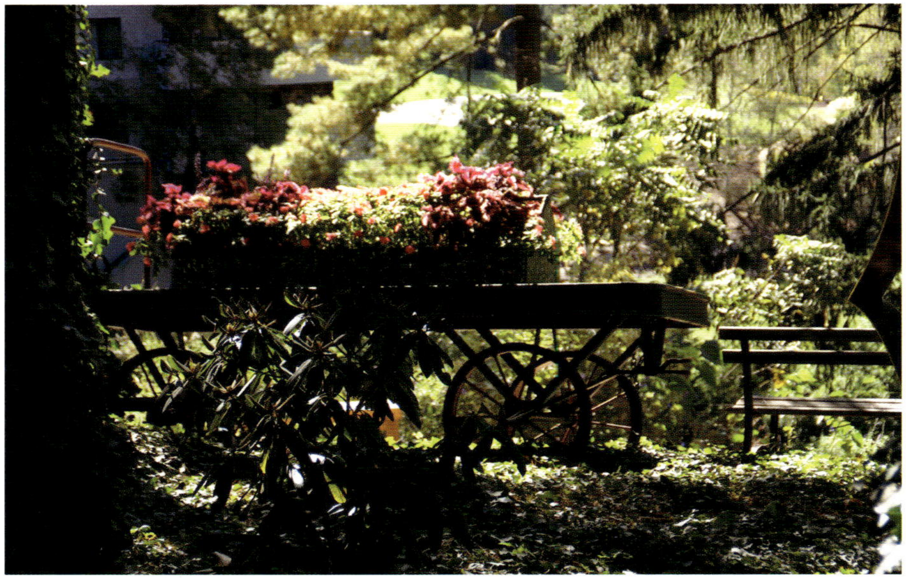

FIGURE 61.
On location.

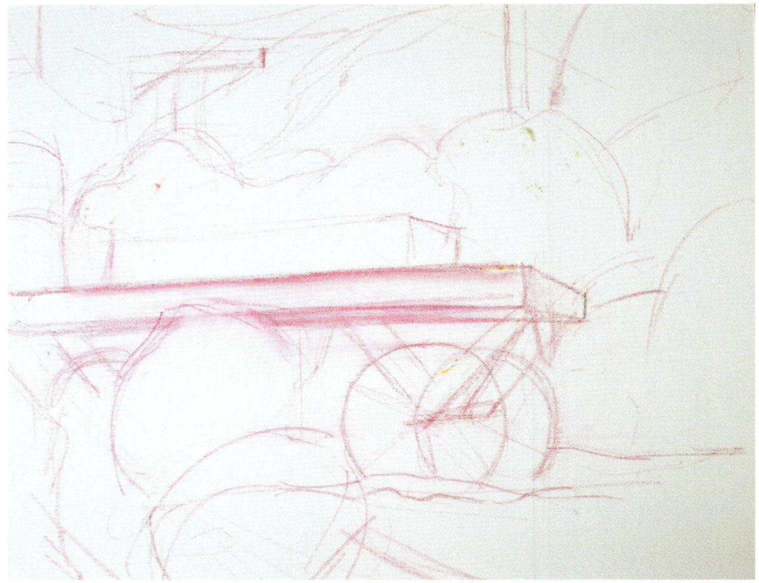

FIGURE 62.
Julie's sketch.

This photograph of a flower cart has been a favorite of mine since I took it a few years ago (fig 61). Look at the pattern of the light against dark and the way the light shines through the wagon. When I squint, I see the light sweeping across the foreground from the left. Notice how the lighter-value unlit areas act as neutrals to showcase the super-lights and the super-darks.

One of the biggest challenges in setting up this composition was finding a way to simplify it. The easiest way to do that is to squint until a visual pattern emerges. You can let this pattern guide you, or modify it to make a more exciting composition. I tried to do just that in my drawing by keeping larger and stronger shapes in the foreground (fig. 62). When you can identify the main shapes of the different values, the method can do a great job with setting up an exciting underpainting to capture the effect you're looking for. We found our lightest light in the center of the flower area and gave it a #1 (fig. 63). The #2s represent the light from behind in the hill area. These lights will set off some of the lights in the flowers and the foreground if we make them #2 rather than #1, allowing the lit flowers on the cart to be our center of interest. Our #3s are higher and farther away from our center of interest, and also behind the cart wheels and on the ground to the right of the cart. Our #4 value represents the lit flowers and a few darker, less important lights.

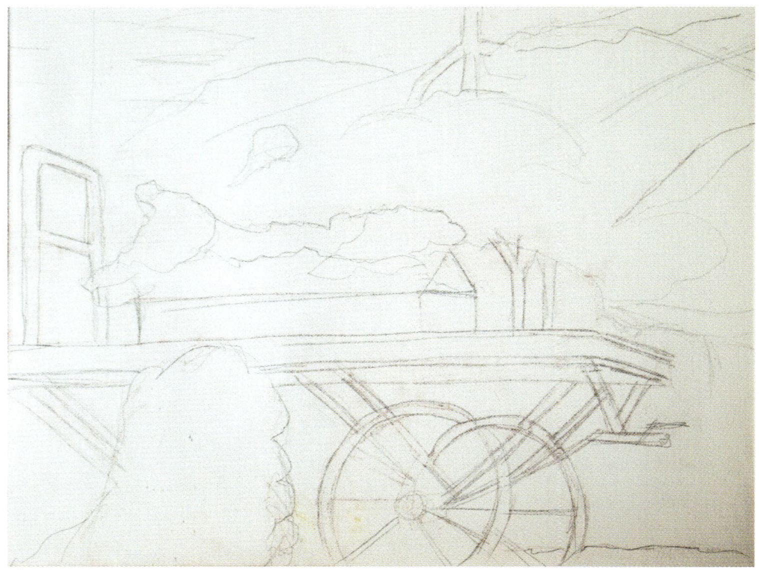

Jim's sketch.

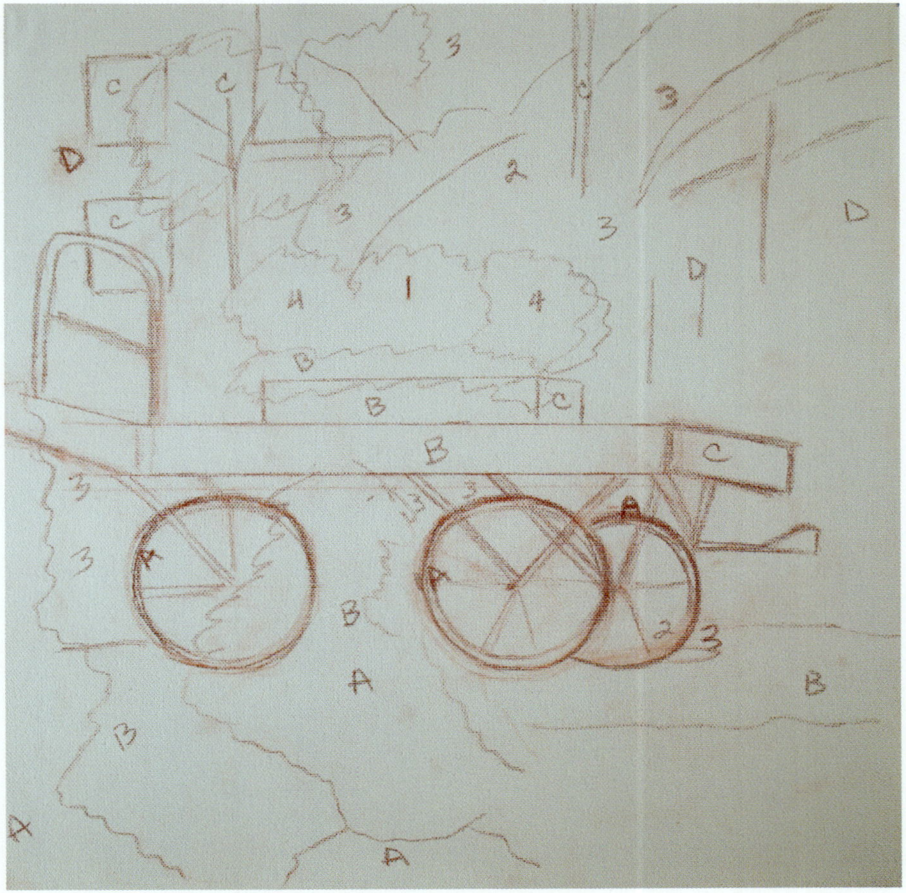

FIGURE 63.
Mary's numbered sketch.

The darkest darks are in the bottom front under the bush area, in the bottom left corner, in the wheels themselves, and the underside of the cart. These we label A. The Bs are primarily on the front side of the cart, the shadowy areas in the foreground, and in the front greens. As the front side of the cart turns, its back plane and the flower box are C, as are some of the darks on the building to the upper left. There are some lesser unlit (dark) areas behind the cart and some in the upper left corner. These we label D.

Because this photograph's center of interest is the red flowers, I chose my lights in values of pink and red (fig. 64). I thought about getting a glow out of the red flowers and figured they would be helped more by bits of pink light rather than yellow. The yellows representing light can be put on top of the pink later. The challenge in this photograph is that there are very few reds in places other than the flowers, and I didn't want the red to be isolated. Yellow greens can easily be added as needed to mix with those super-light reds to create the feeling of light. Number 1 was permanent rose and white, #2 permanent rose and less white, #3 bright red and white for a little more warmth, and #4 bright red with white, the flowers' actual color.

For the darkest dark or A, I mixed a small bit of dioxazine violet into manganese blue to darken it. B was cobalt blue and white. C was ultramarine blue and white and D was dioxazine violet and white. These primary tones are visually exciting and tell the story before a single touch of green has been added. When you think about the color wheel and the use of red, yellow, and blue, you can see that this is now the perfect stage set for yellow and the mixtures containing yellow, such as green.

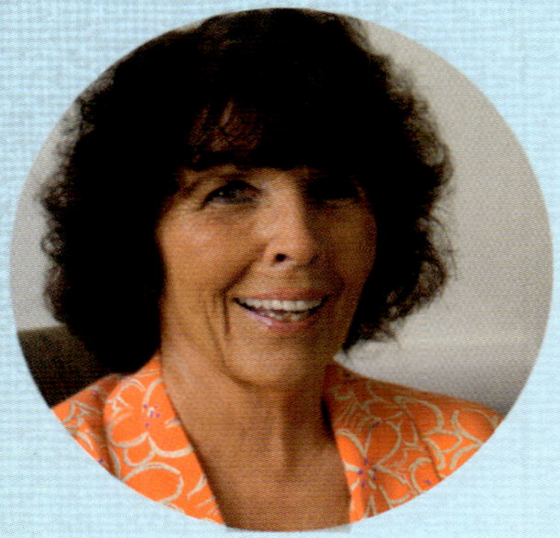

Mary started painting in oil over twenty years ago but never had formal instruction. A career in nursing management and a busy New York life left little time to continue. She recently started to paint again, this time in acrylic. Although she considers herself a beginner, she says temperature painting has inspired her to paint more fearlessly in rich, bold color.

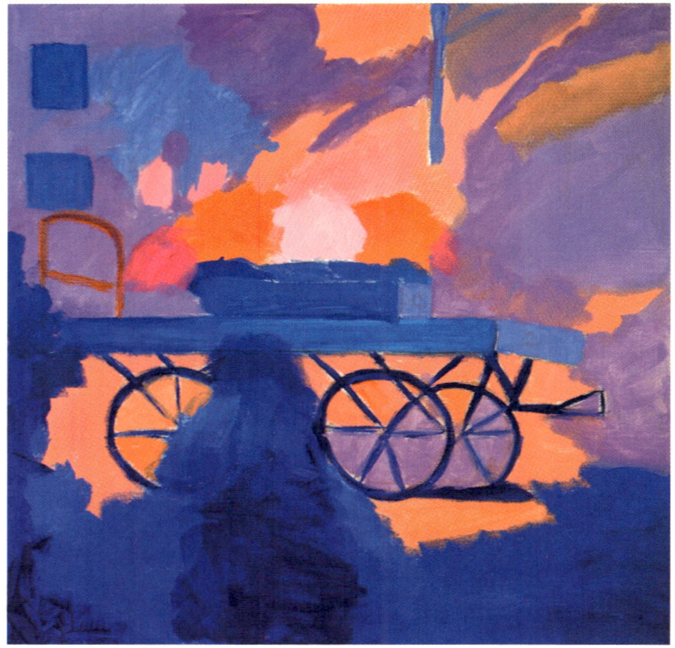

We chose Mary's finished painting to showcase. Remember, Mary has been working in acrylic. This medium is much harder to blend. This is a very complicated subject matter and Mary handled it like a pro. Her colors are magical!

Mary's primary tones.

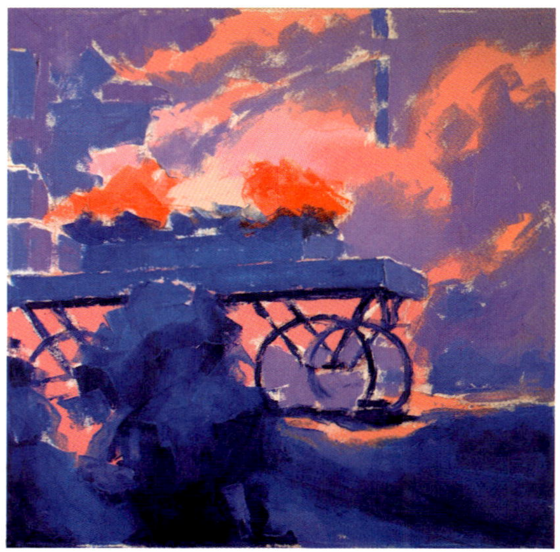

FIGURE 64.
Julie's primary tones.

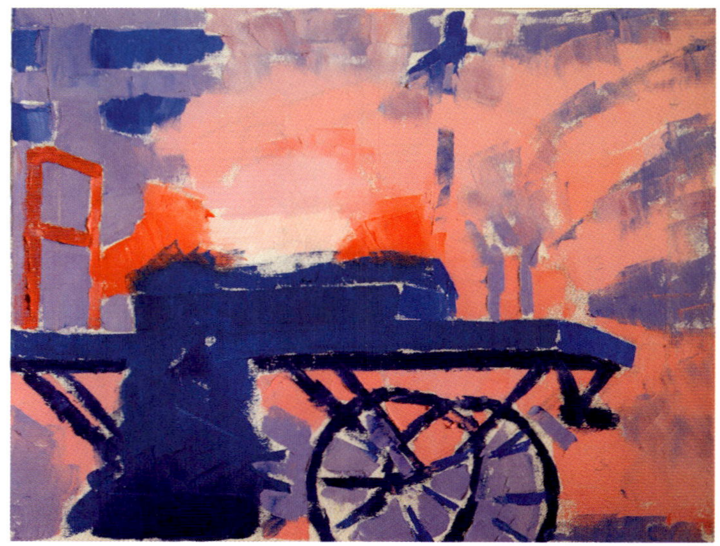

Jim's primary tones.

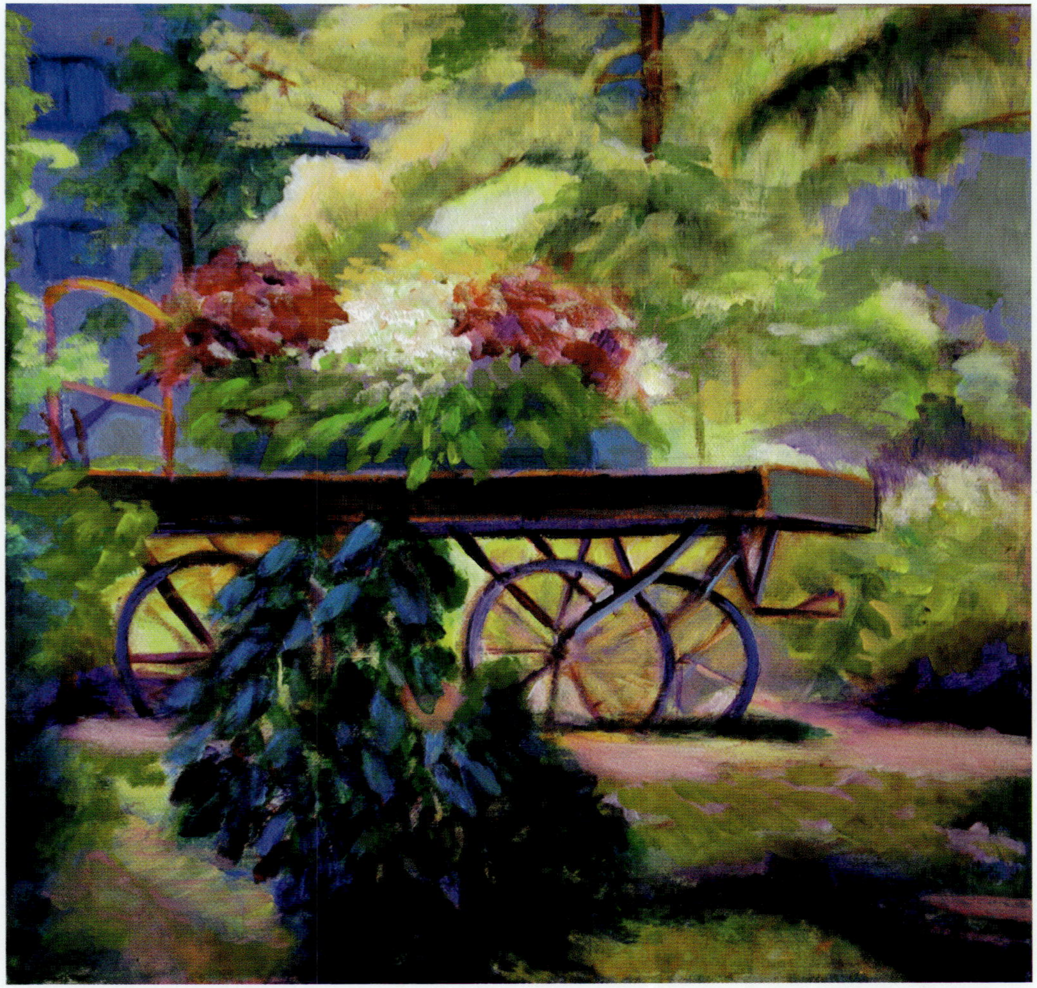

Mary's finished painting.

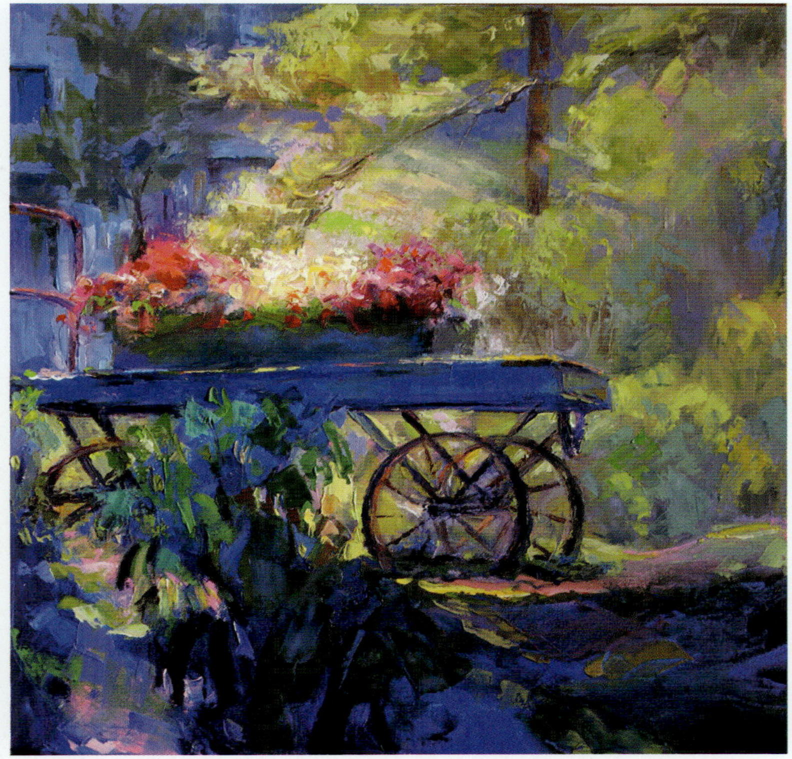

Julie's finished painting.

This one was a joy to paint. I loved it. I guess partly because the background was soft and unimportant. When the light greens and the bits of yellow were added, the painting came alive.

This subject matter has inspired me to do a larger version. The current painting will be treated as a preliminary study for a more detailed painting.

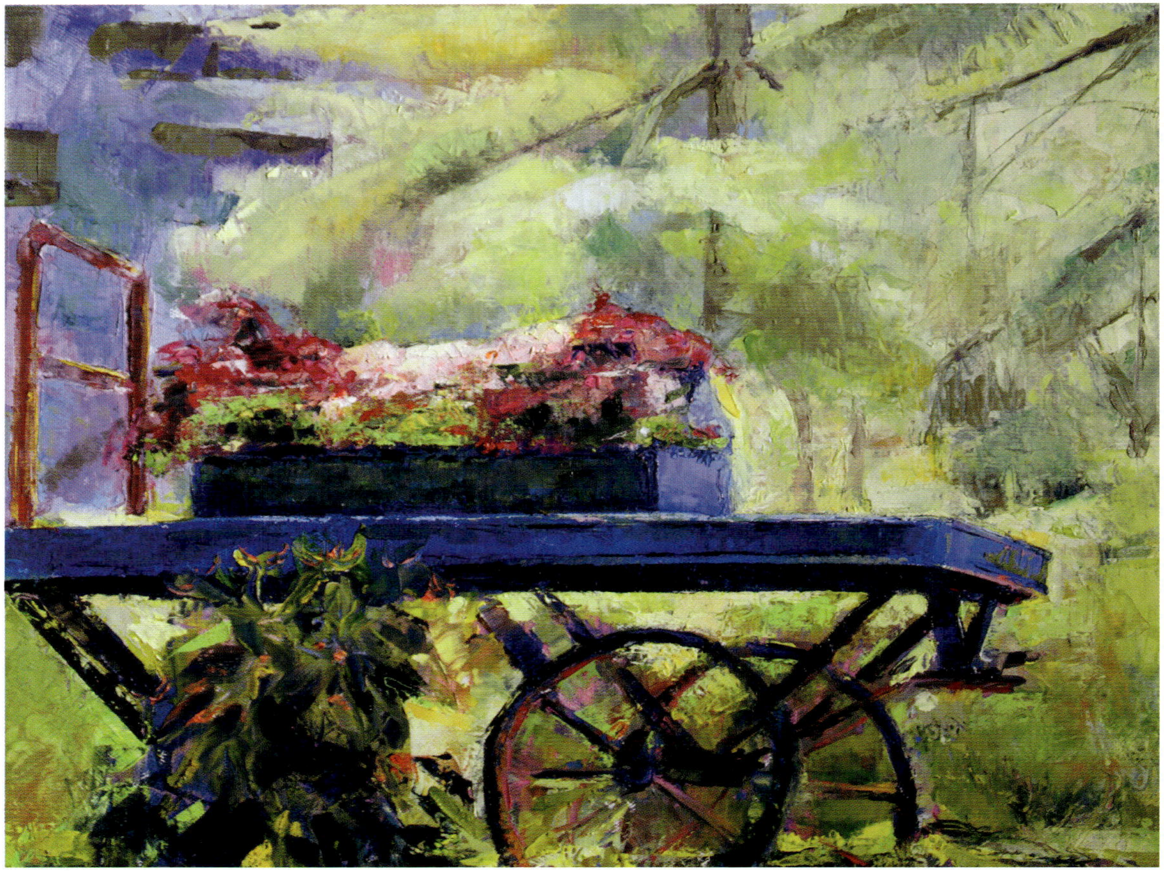

Jim's finished painting.

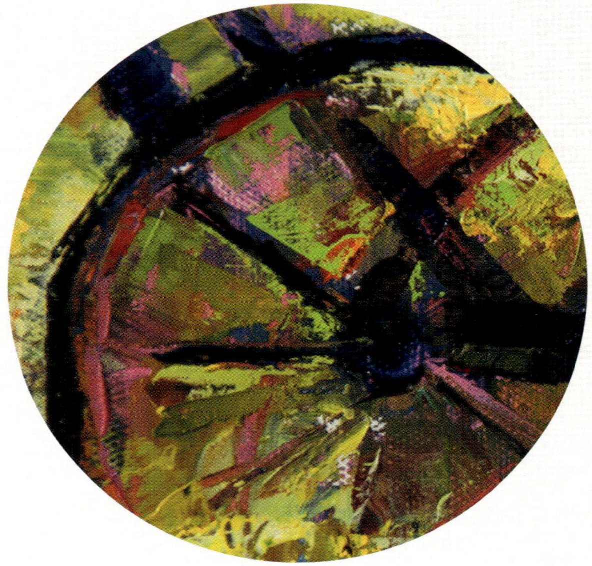

Close-up of Jim's cart.

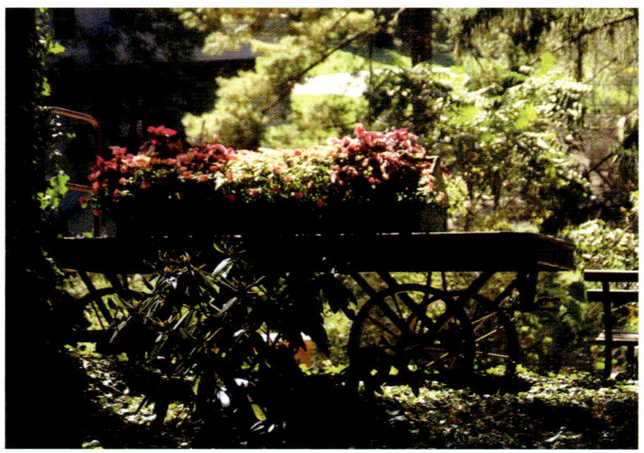

We all struggled with the background. There was so much of it and its use is really just as a background for the flower cart. It needs to be kept less important. Its contribution is to enhance the lighting in this subject. My favorite part of Jim's painting is the foreground. I love his handling of the bush in the bottom left and the incredible mix of reds and greens around the spokes of the wheels.

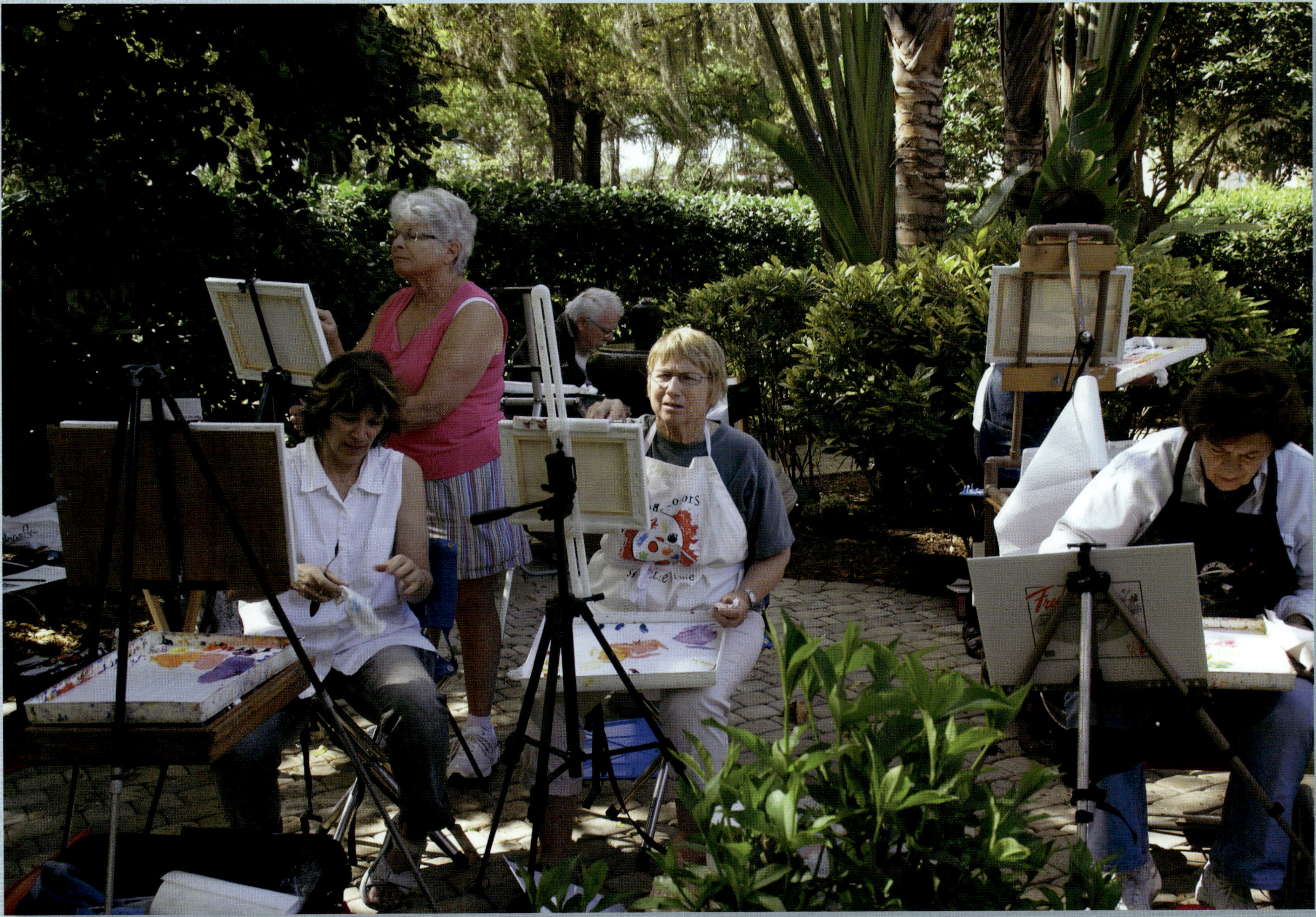

Chapter Ten

Students' Paintings

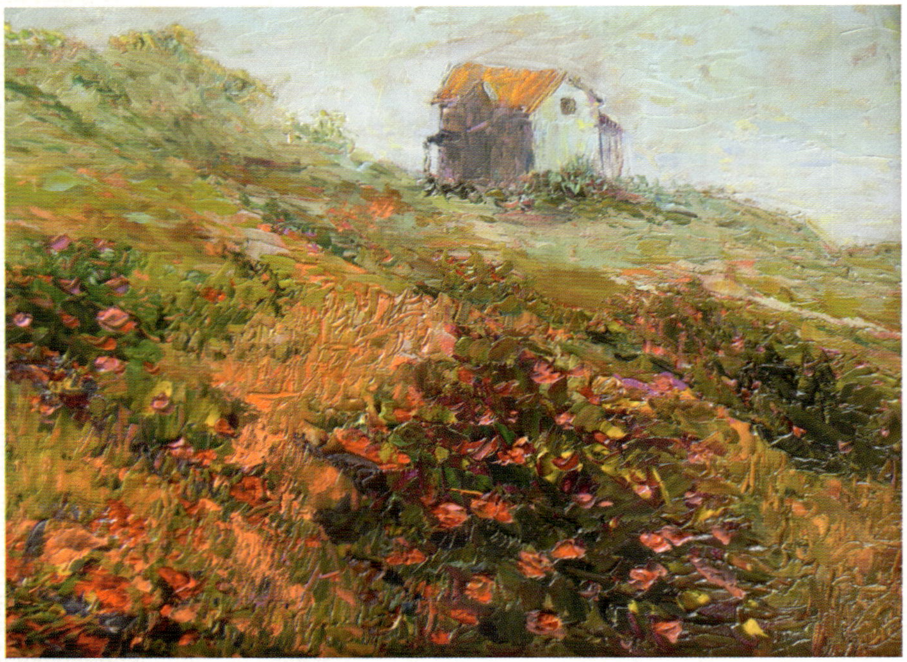

Boothbay Harbor by Karin Billings, 2008. Oil on canvas, 11" × 14".
Courtesy of Karin Billings

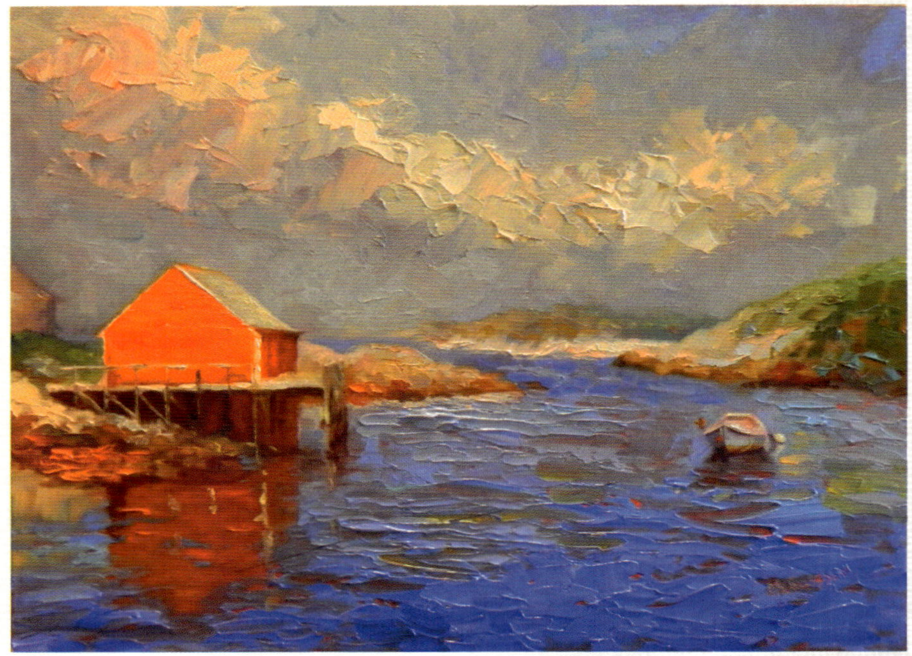

Calm by Maryanne Jacobsen, 2012. Oil on linen, 16" × 20".
Courtesy of Maryanne Jacobsen

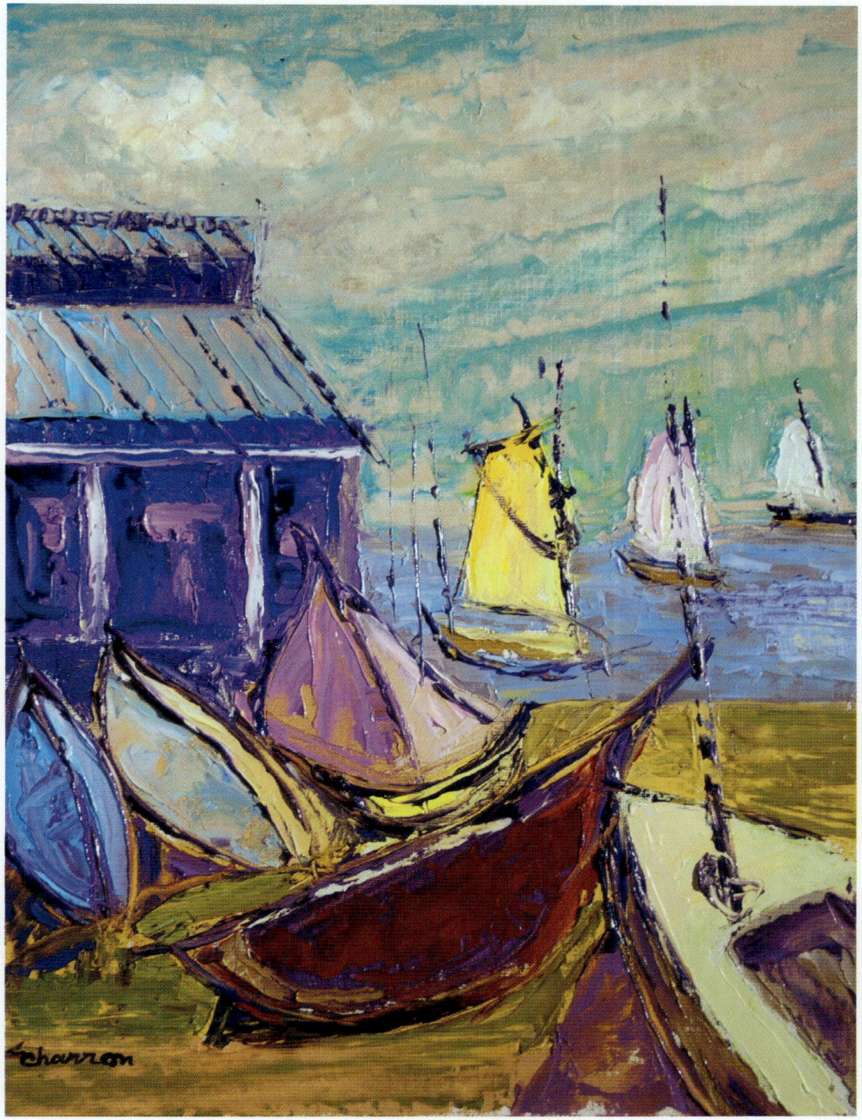

Sarasota Boats by Shirley Charron, 2011. Oil on canvas, 12" × 16".
Courtesy of Shirley Charron

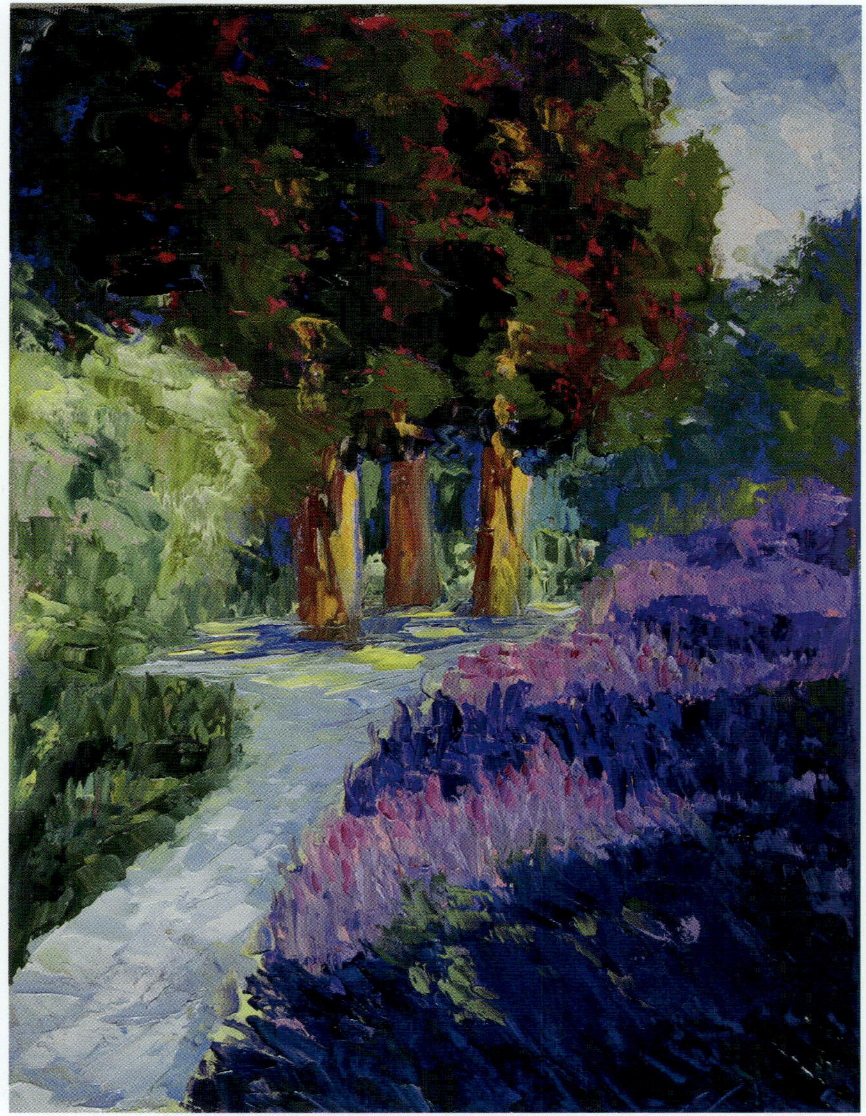

Walk in the Park by Pat Lundy, 2013. Oil on canvas, 12" × 16".
Courtesy of Pat Lundy

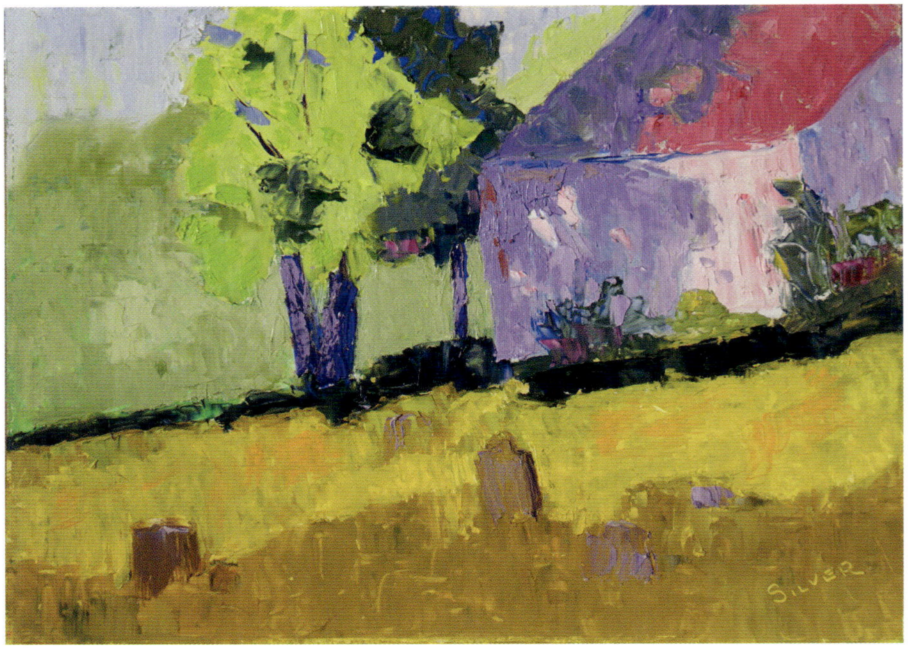

Peaceful by Judy Silver, 2014. Water-soluble oil on panel, 9" × 12".
Courtesy of Judy Silver

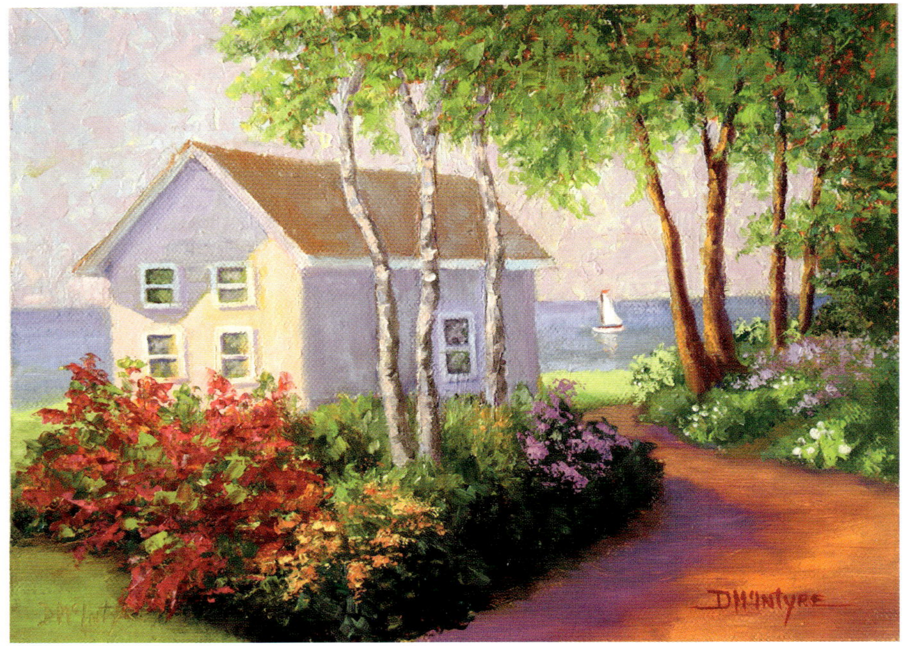

On Sister Bay by Donna McIntyre, 2014. Oil on panel, 9" × 12".
Courtesy of Donna McIntyre

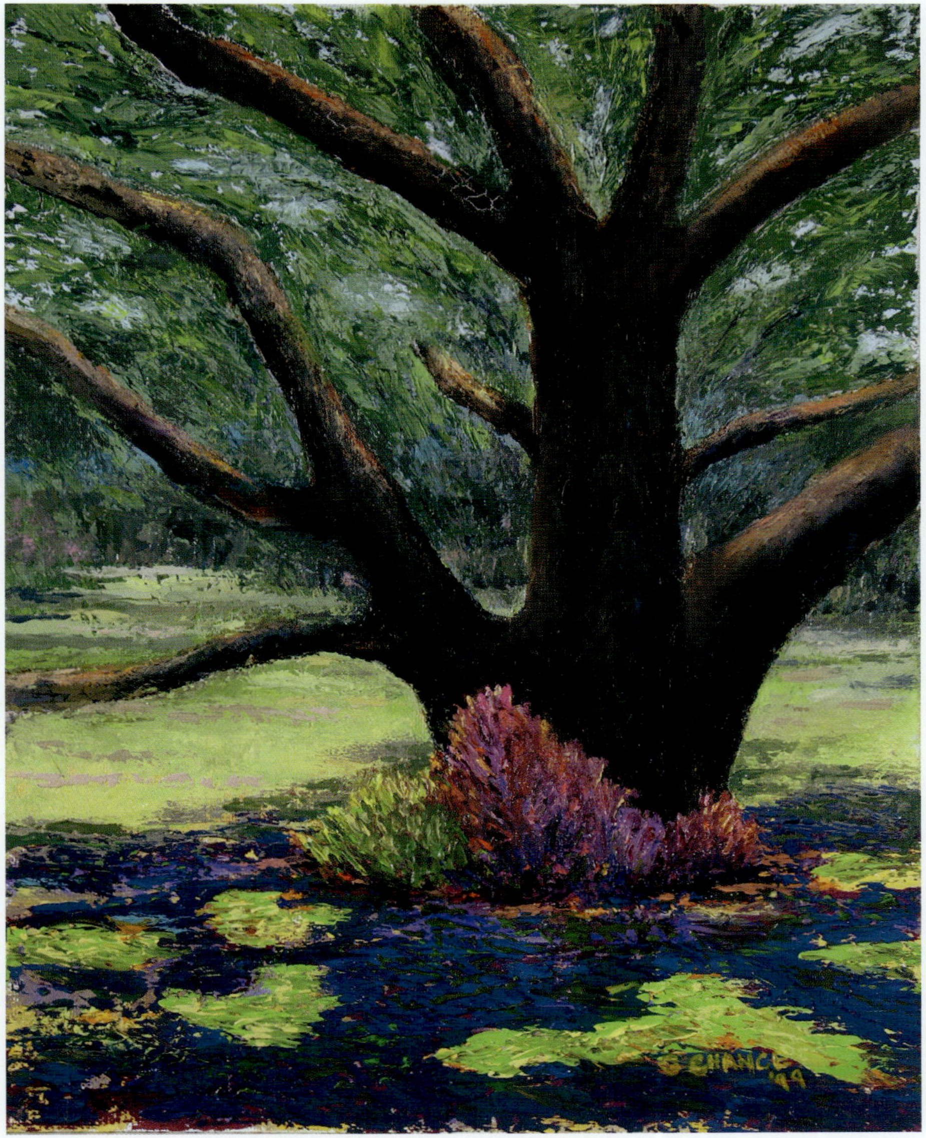

Old Oak by Carol Chance, 1999. Oil on panel, 11" × 14".
Courtesy of Carol Chance

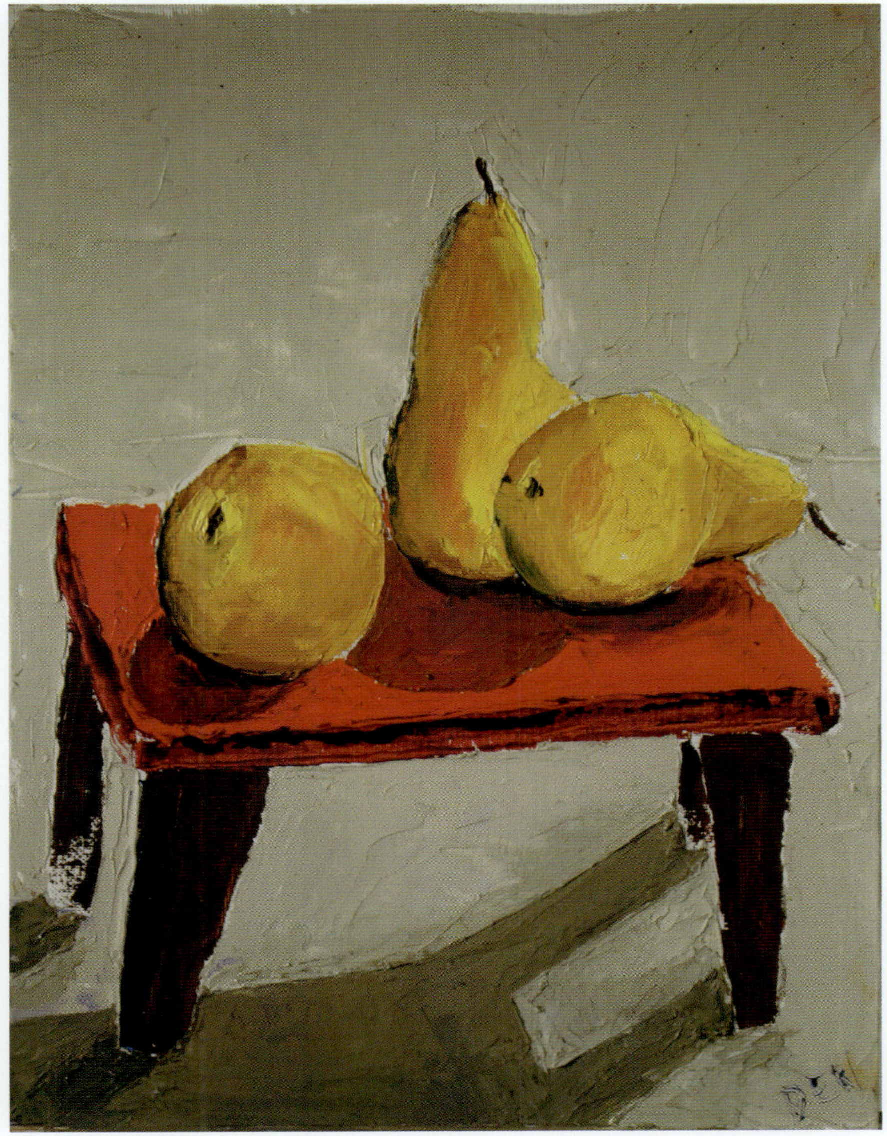

Pears by Dale Wettlaufer, 2014. Oil on panel, 12" × 16".
Courtesy of Dale Wettlaufer

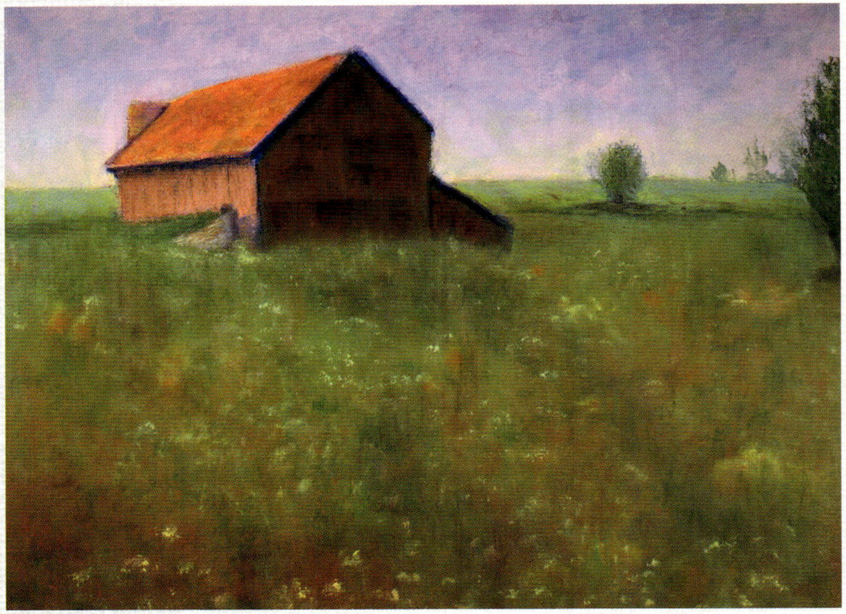

Dawn on the Farm by Sandy Miller, 2013. Oil on canvas, 16" × 20".
Courtesy of Sandy Miller

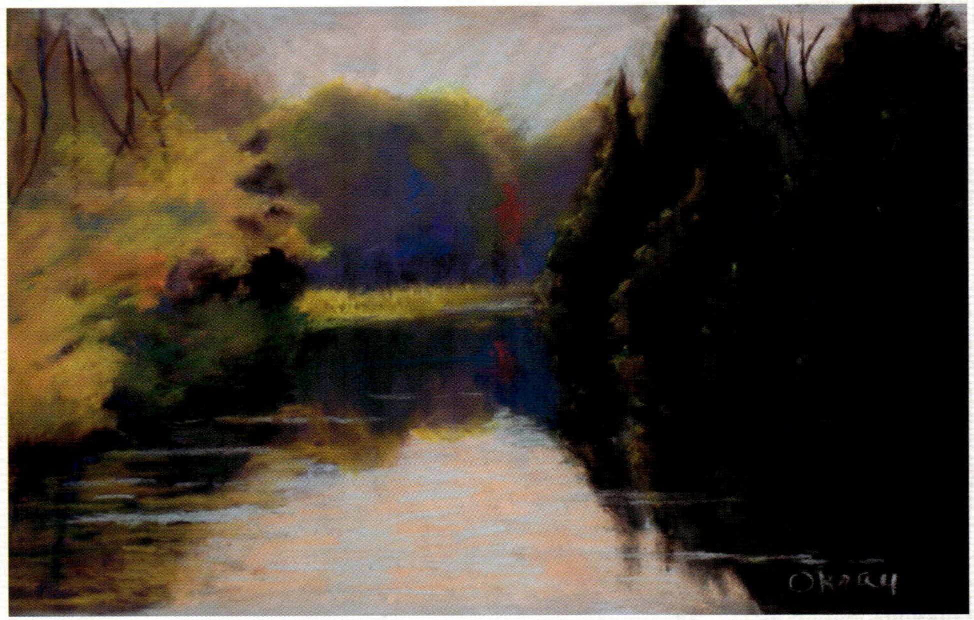

Autumn's Approach by Dorothy Okray, 2013. Pastel, 18" × 12".
Courtesy of Dorothy Okray

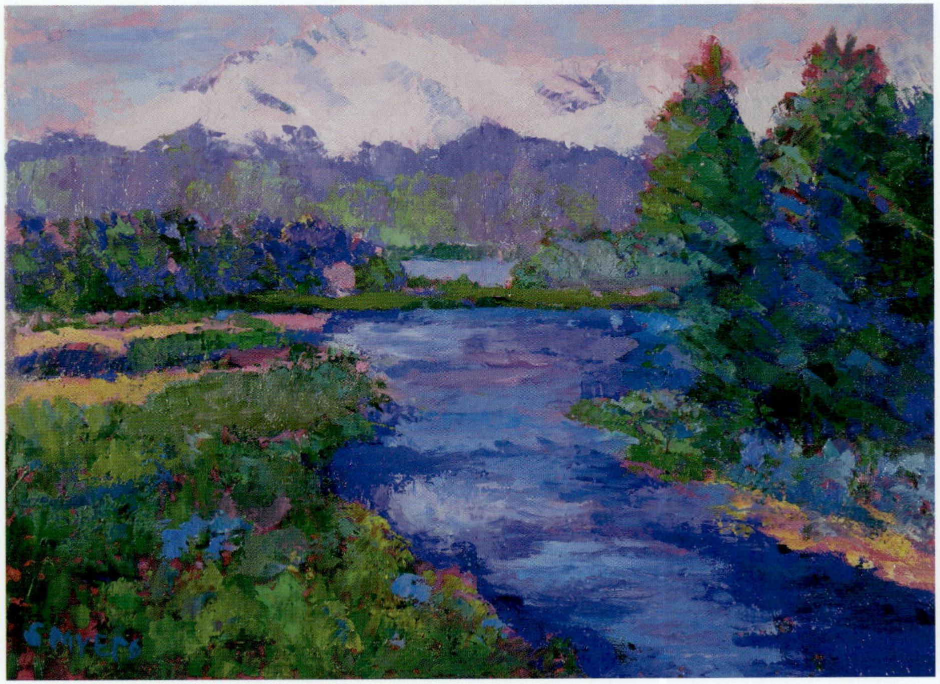

Magnificent Alaska by Sally Myers, 2010. Oil on canvas, 11" × 14".
Courtesy of Sally Myers

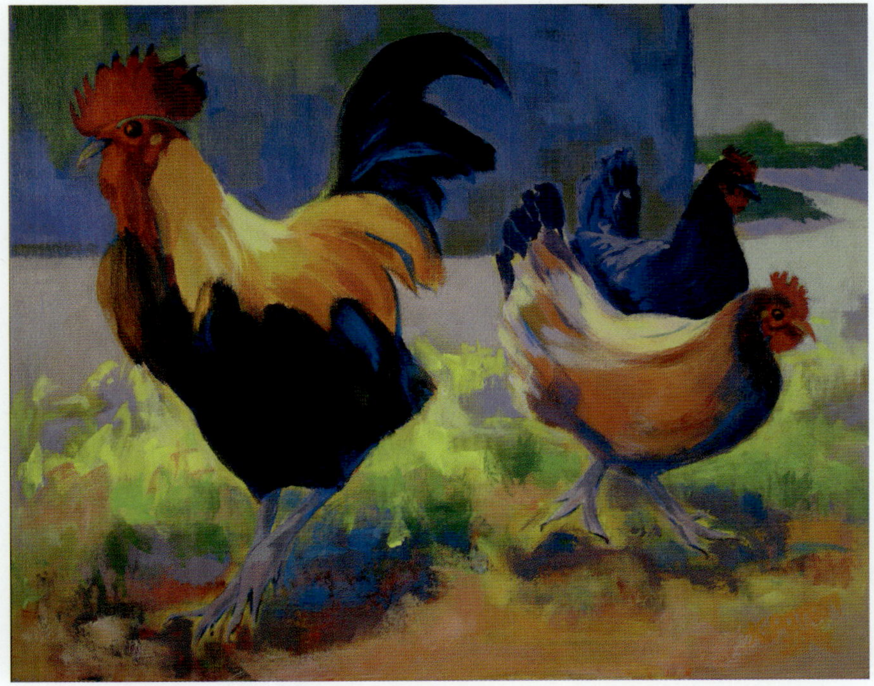

The Farm by Jeanne Guertin-Potoff, 2015. Acrylic, 16" × 20".
Courtesy of Jeanne Guertin-Potoff

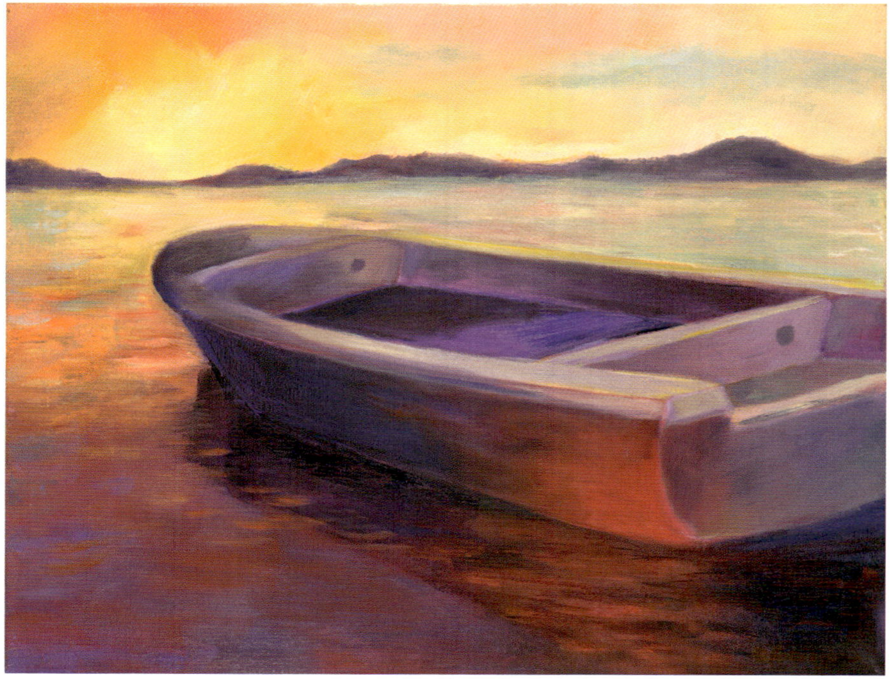

Evening Illumination by Diane Remington, 2012. Oil on canvas, 16" × 20".
Courtesy of Diane Remington

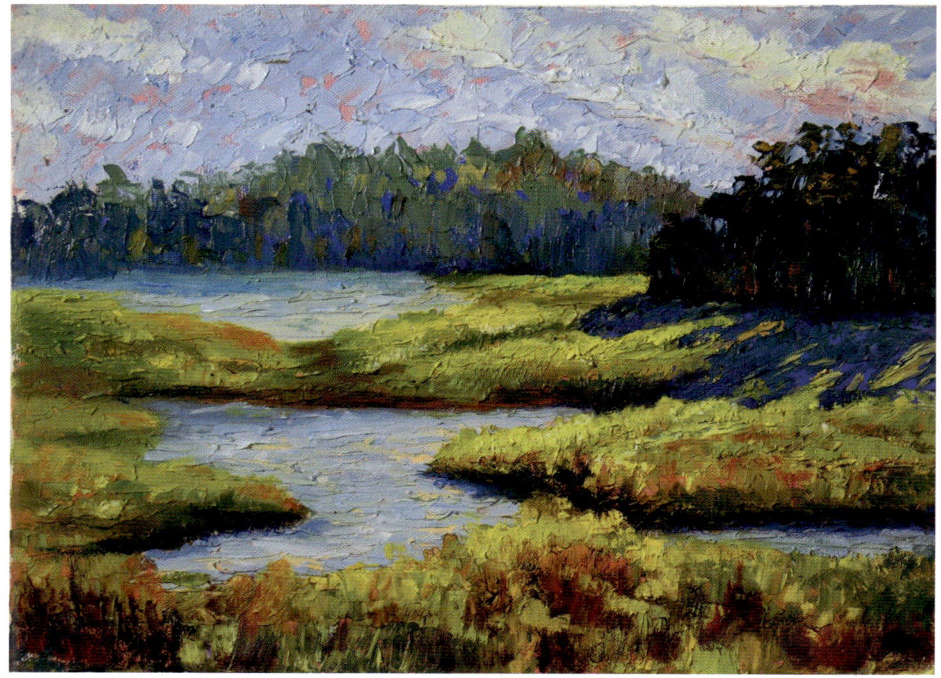

Maine Light by Nancy Donnellan, 2010. Oil on canvas, 8" × 10".
Courtesy of Nancy Donnellan

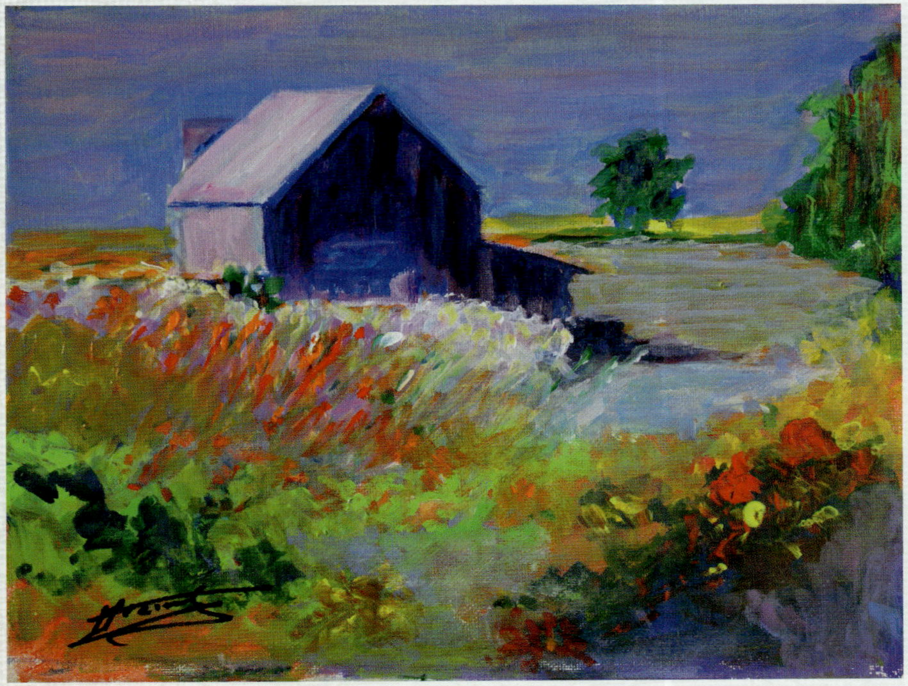

Mon Jardin by Marie-Claire, 2014. Acrylic, 12" × 16".
Courtesy of Marie-Claire

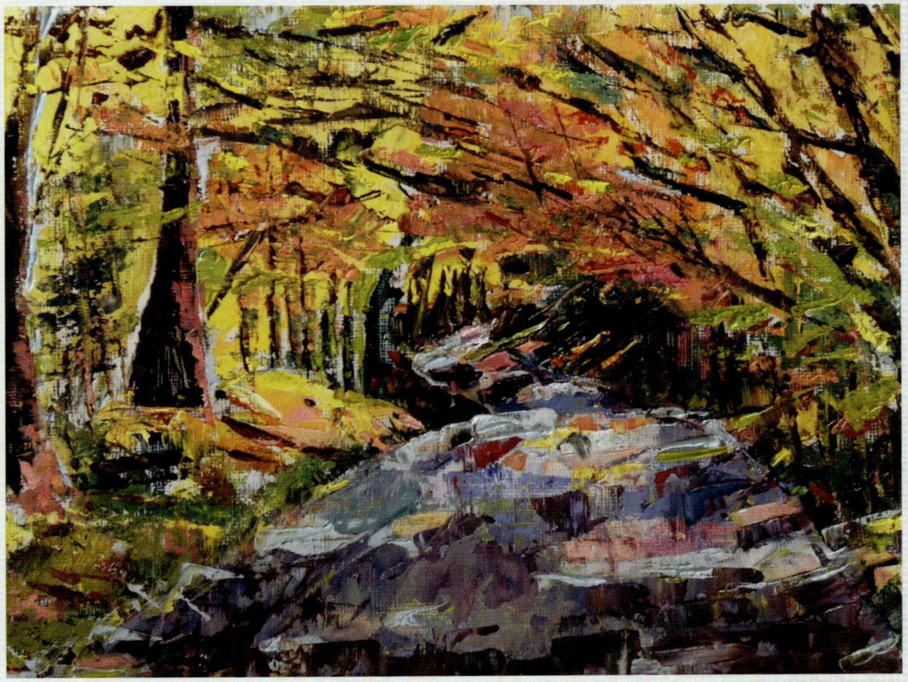

New Road by Elizabeth Ballard, 2016. Oil on canvas, 8.5" × 11".
Courtesy of Elizabeth Ballard

Chapter Eleven

Julie's Paintings

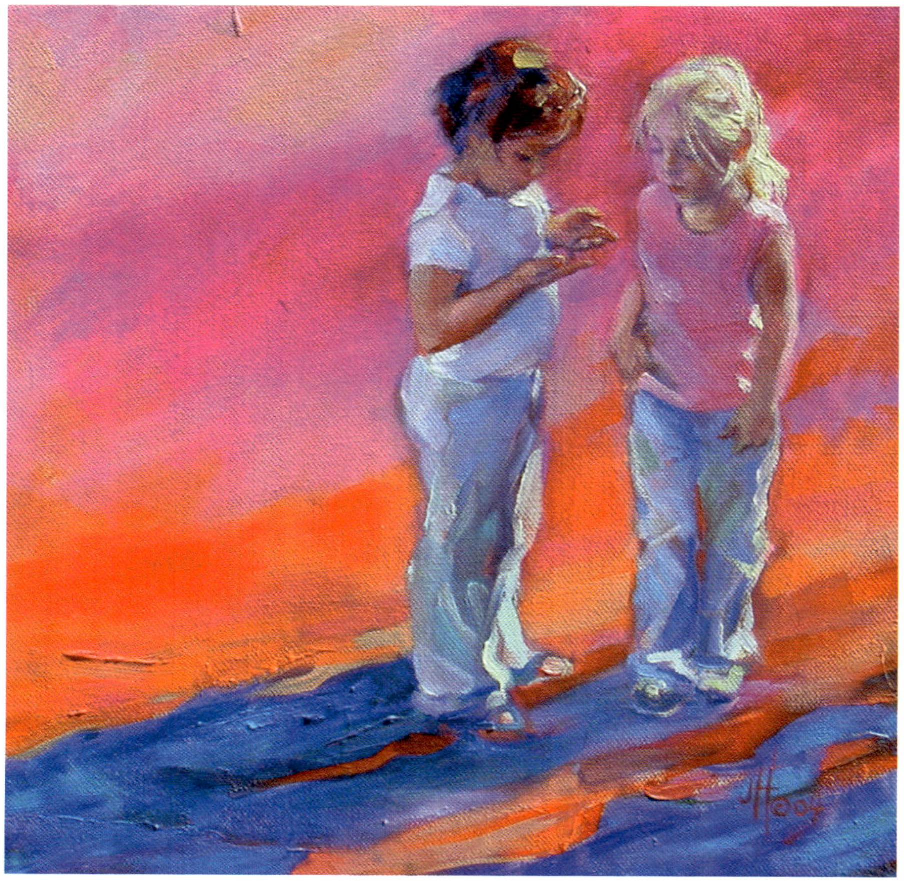

Discovery, 2005. Oil on canvas, 12" × 12".

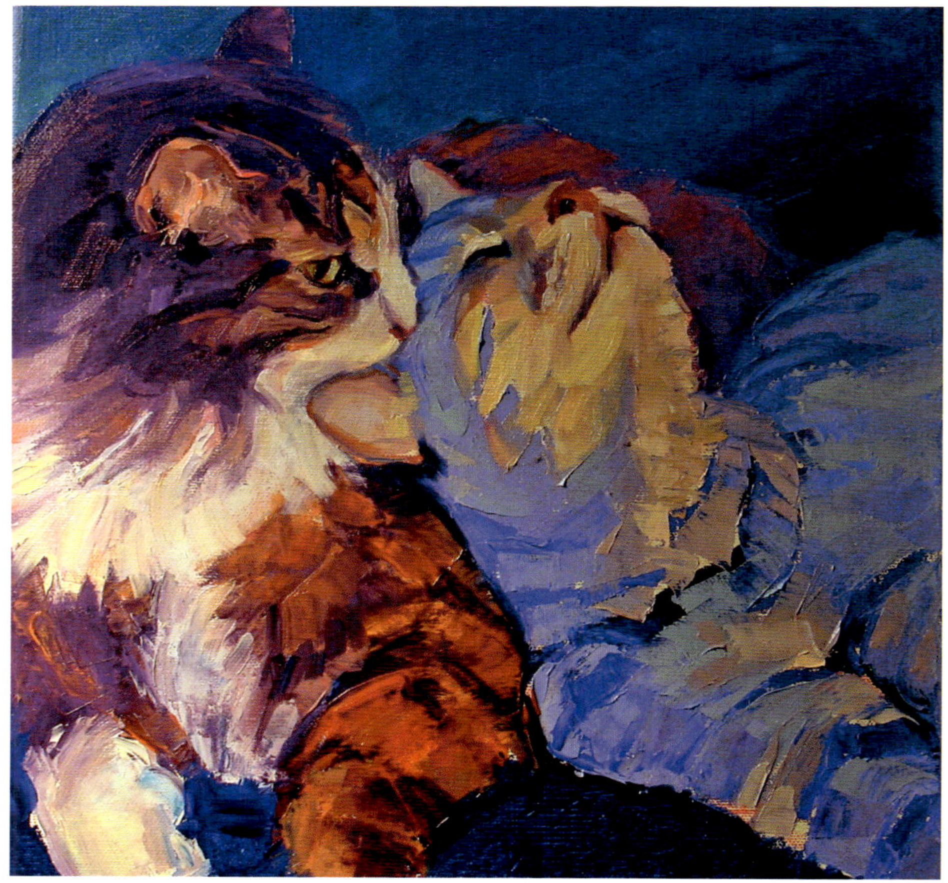

Roxanne and Lulu, 2009. Oil on canvas, 12" × 12".

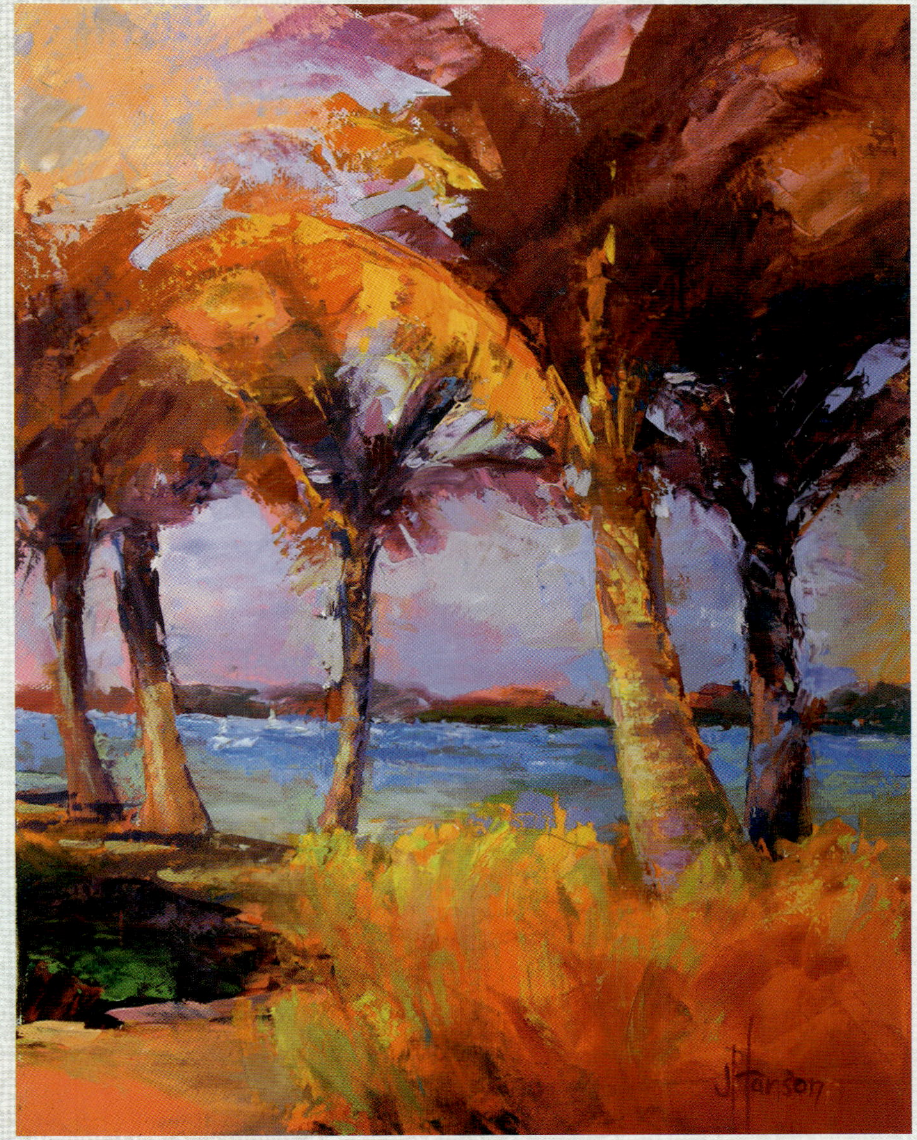

Bird Key Park, 2012. Oil on canvas, 16" × 12".

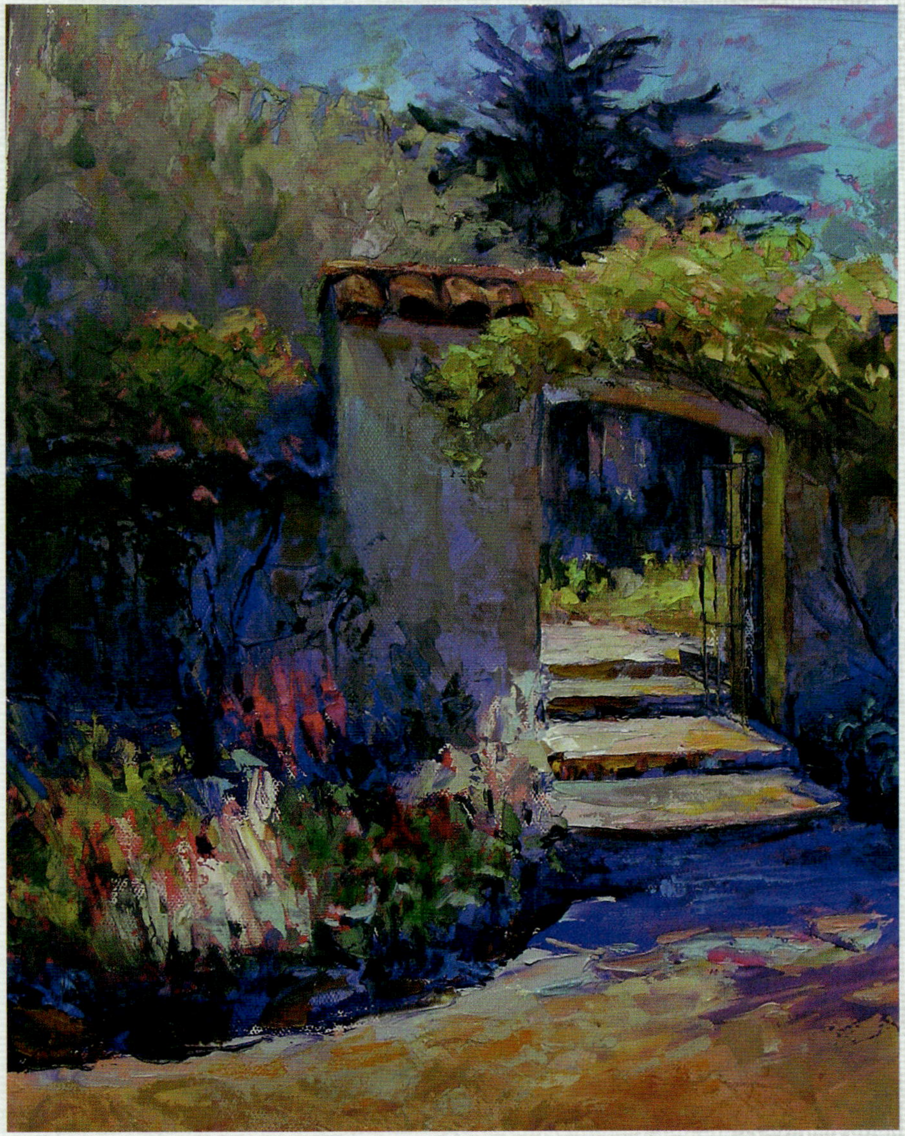

Southwest, 2009. Oil on canvas, 12" × 16".

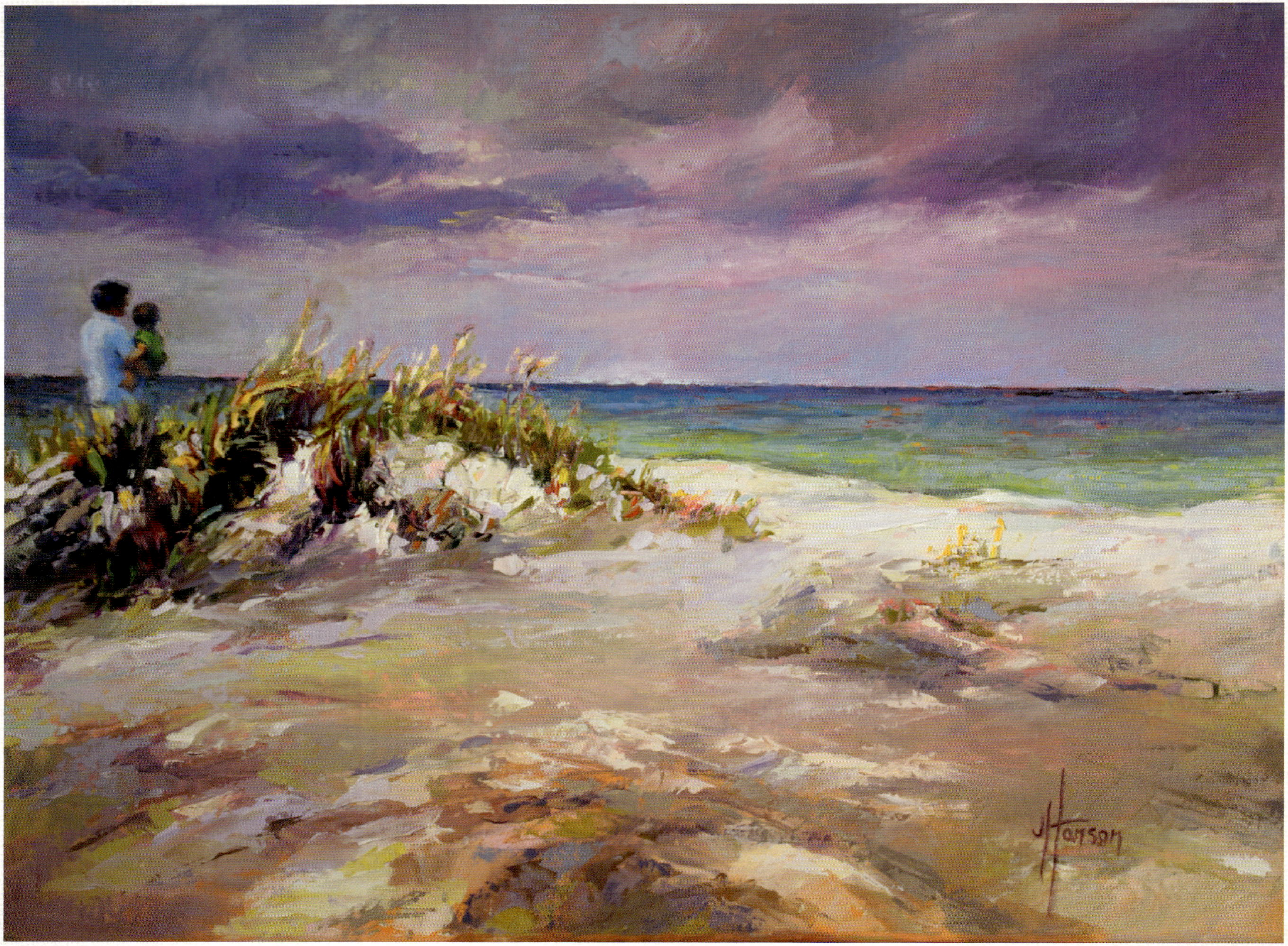

Father and Son, 2011. Oil on canvas, 18" × 24".

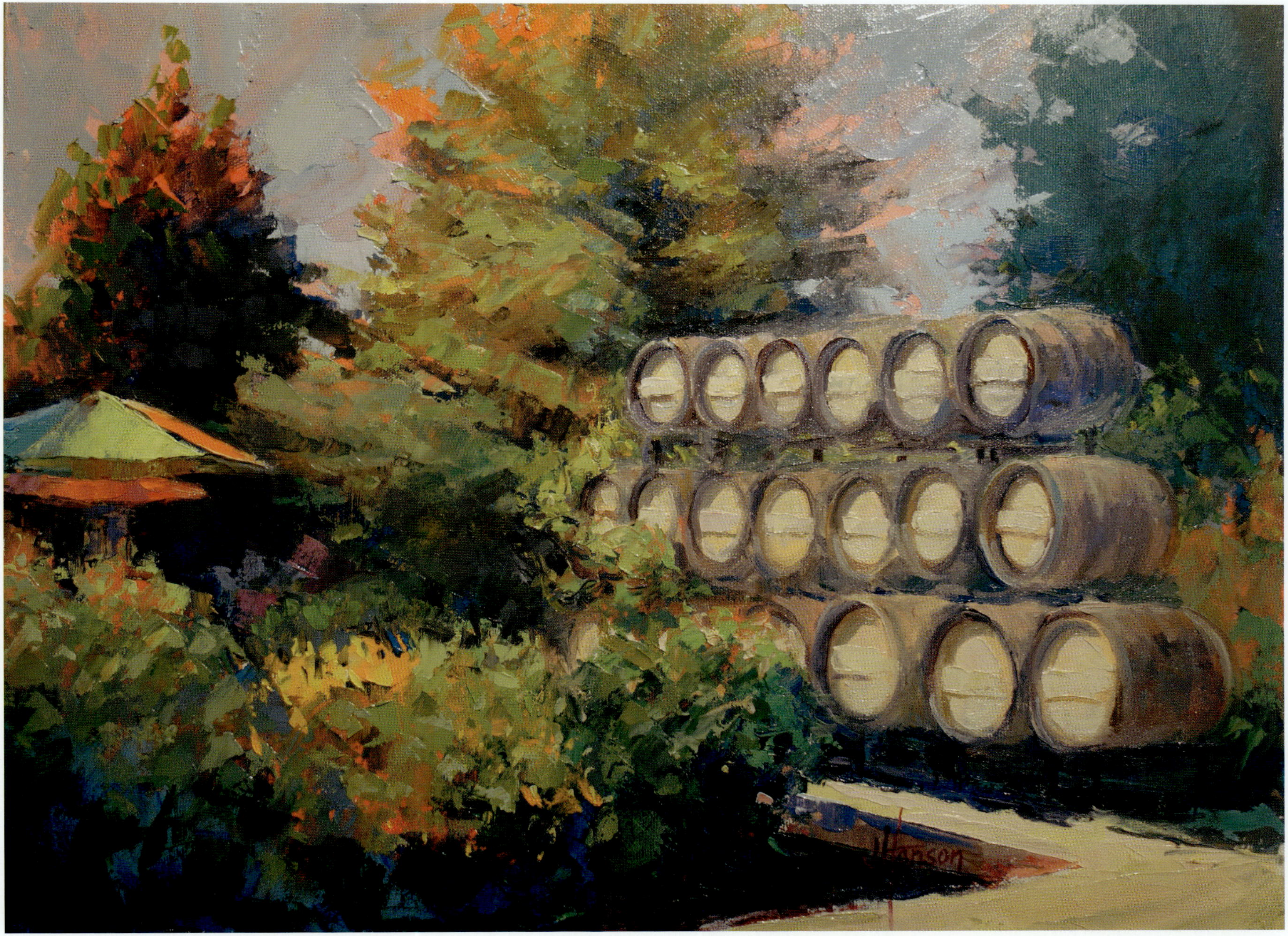

The Winery, 2014. Oil on canvas, 16" × 20".

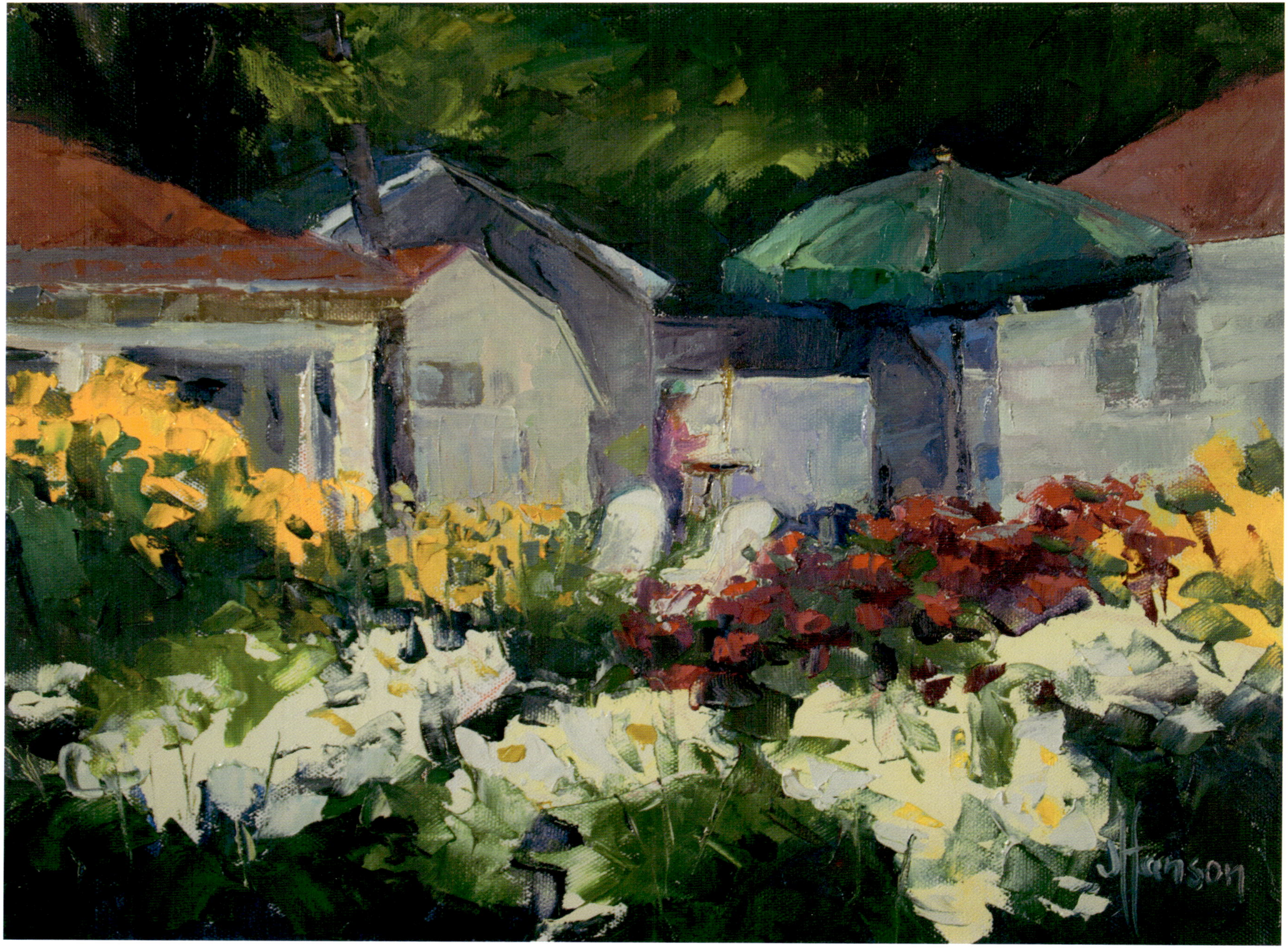

Door County, 2014. Oil on canvas, 12" × 16".

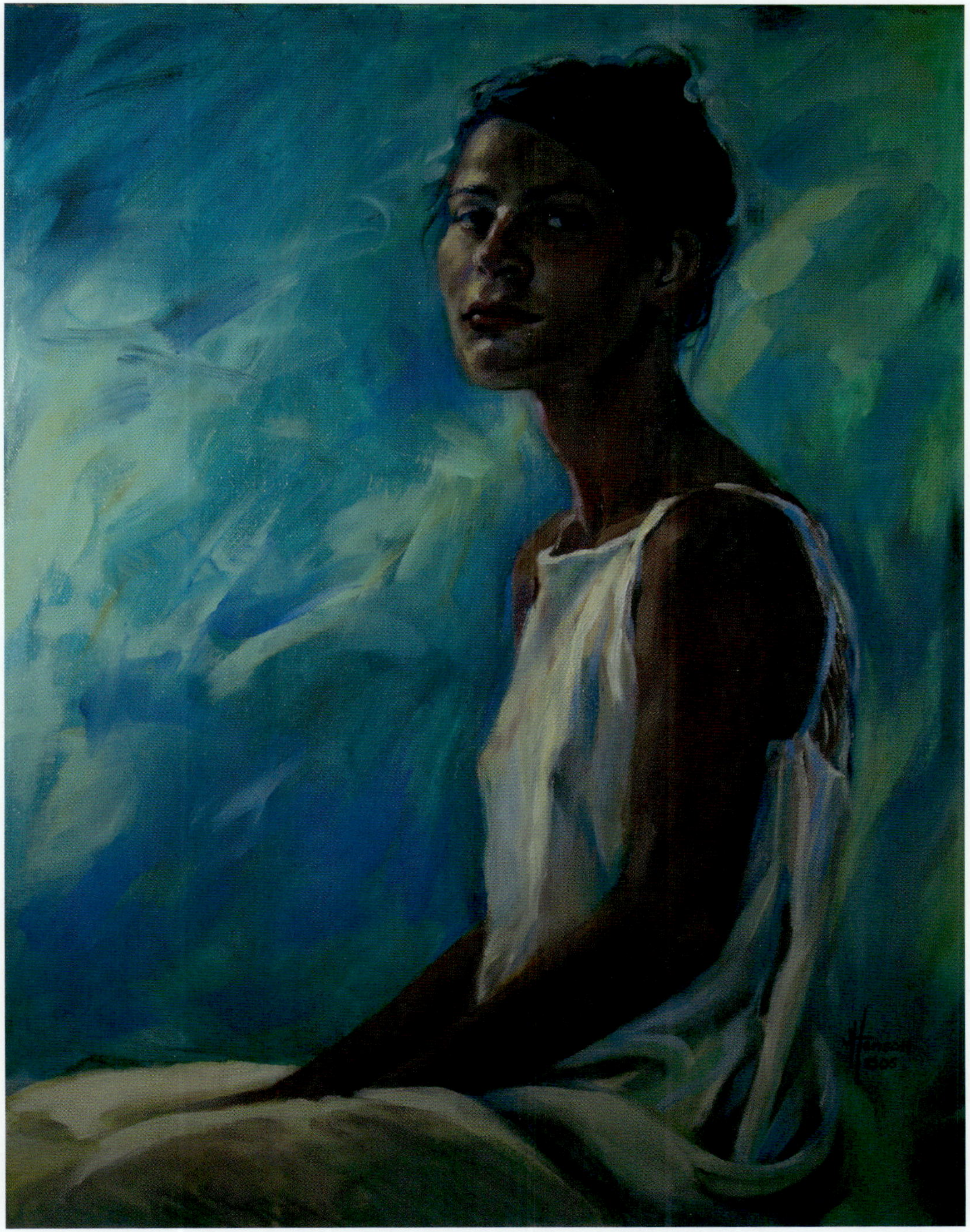

Lady in White, 2005.
Oil on canvas, 18" × 24".

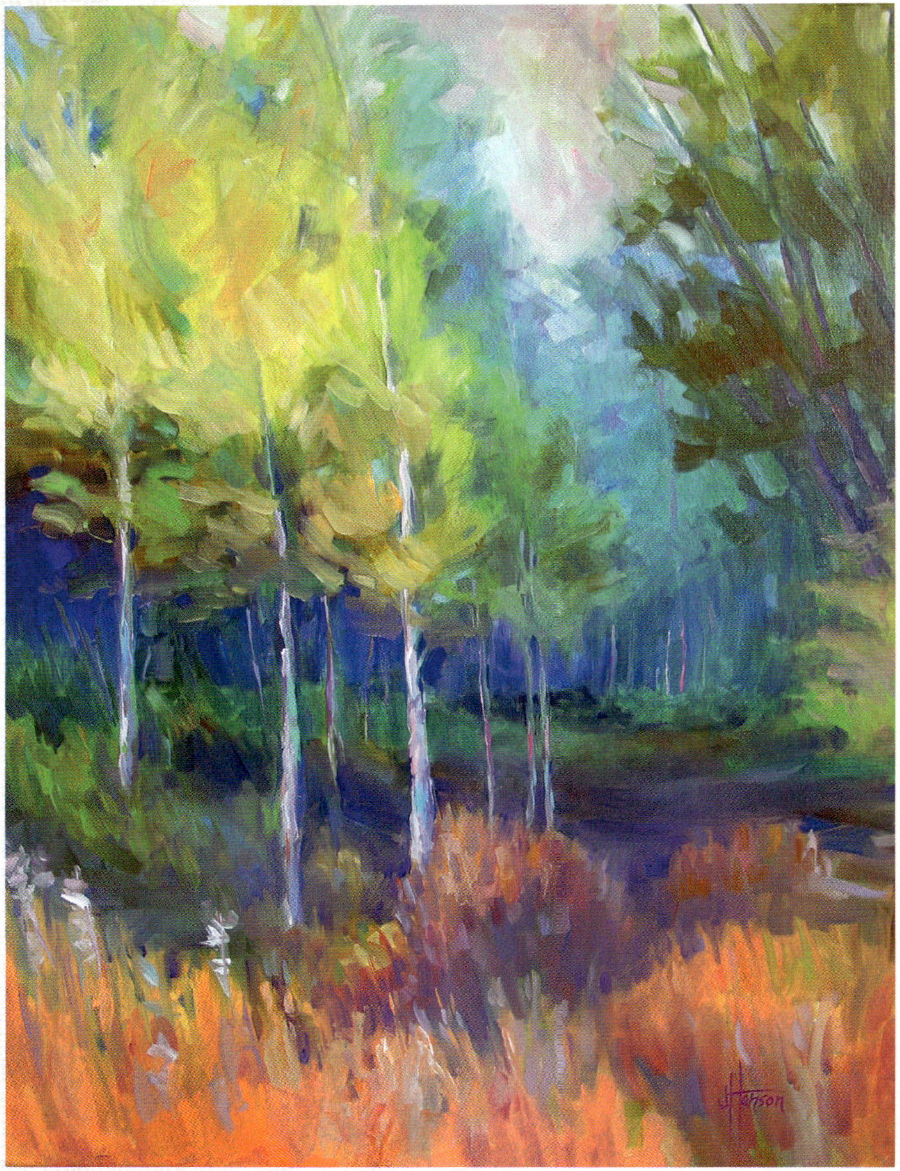

North Shore, 2008. Oil on canvas, 24" × 18".

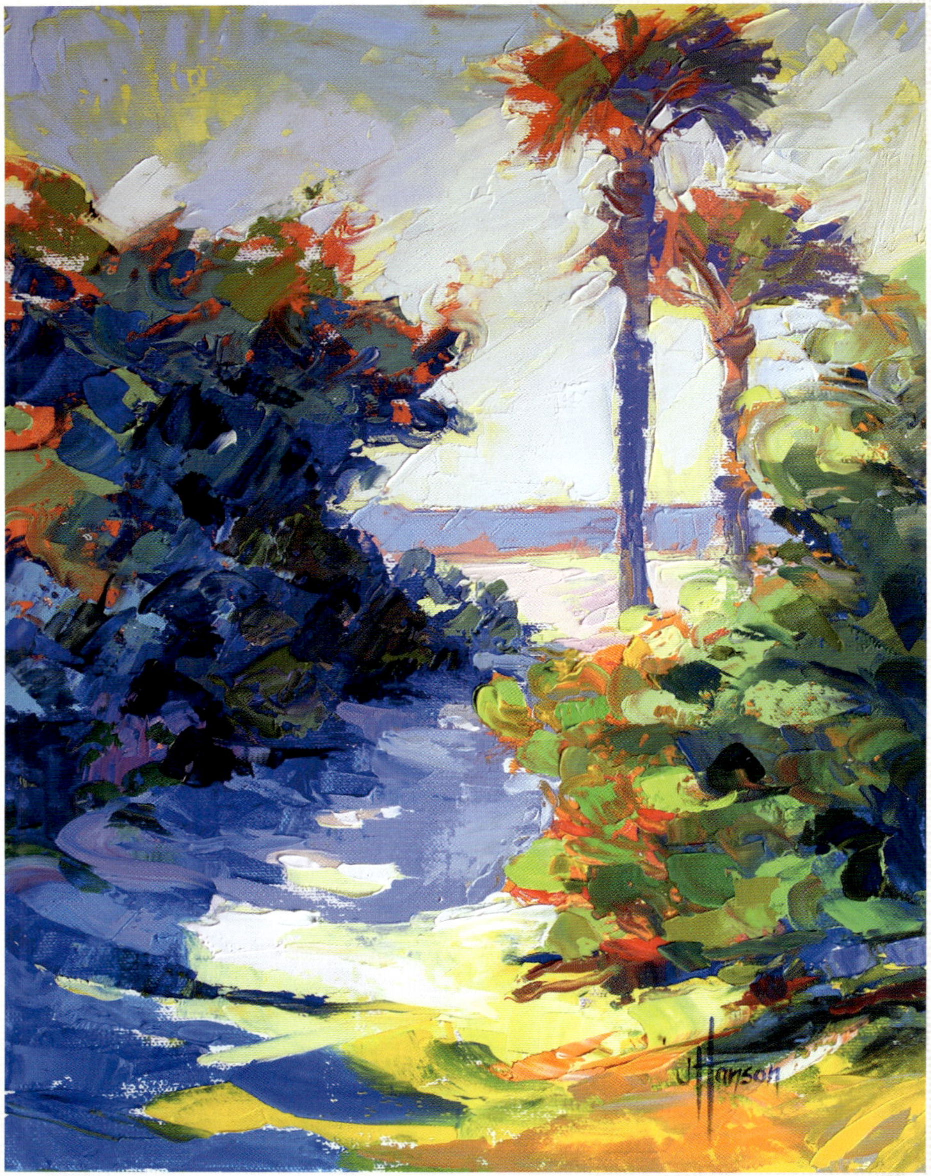

Siesta Key Path, 2006. Oil on canvas, 16" × 12".

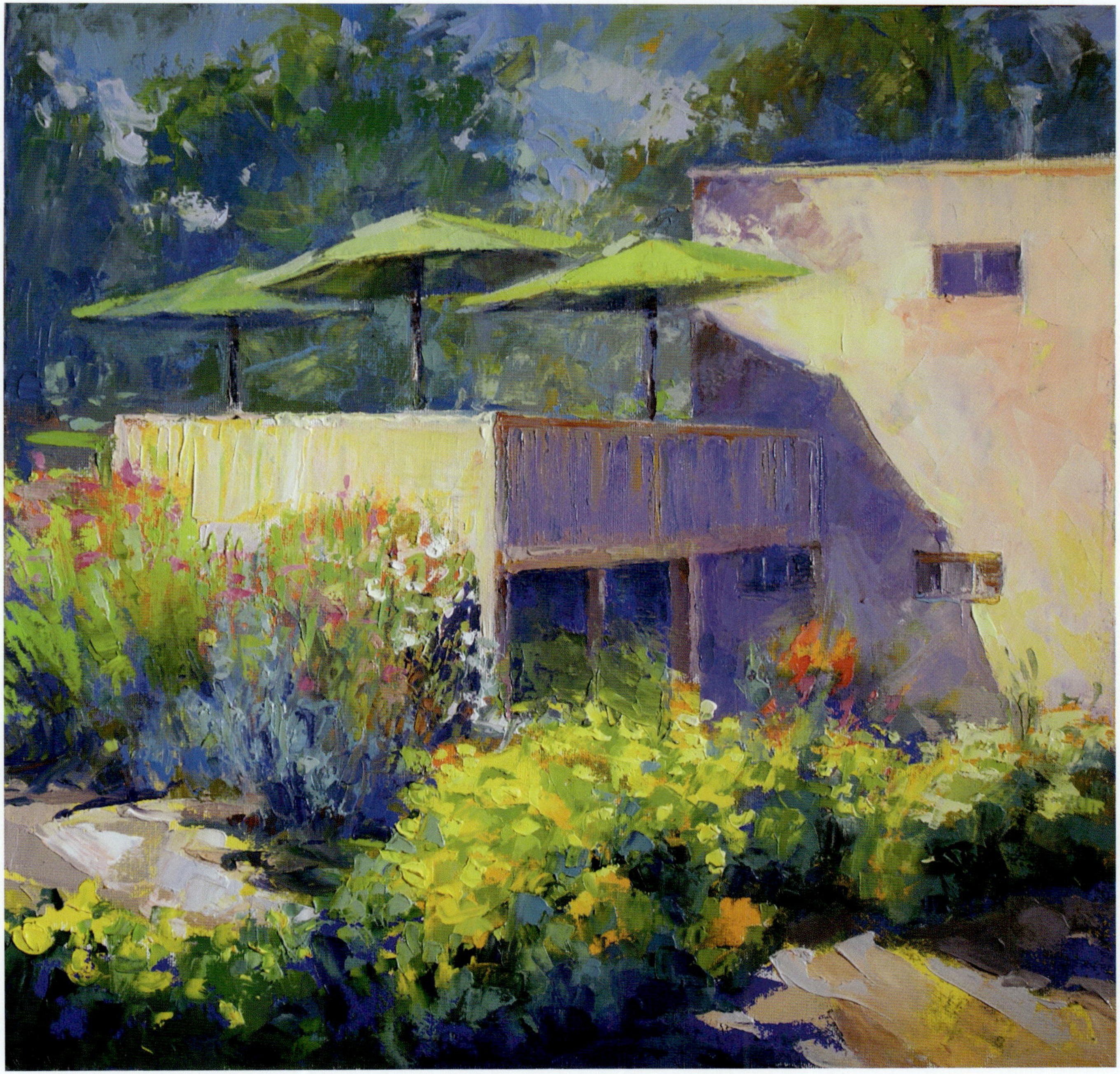

Burnsville Café, 2014. Oil on canvas, 18" × 18".

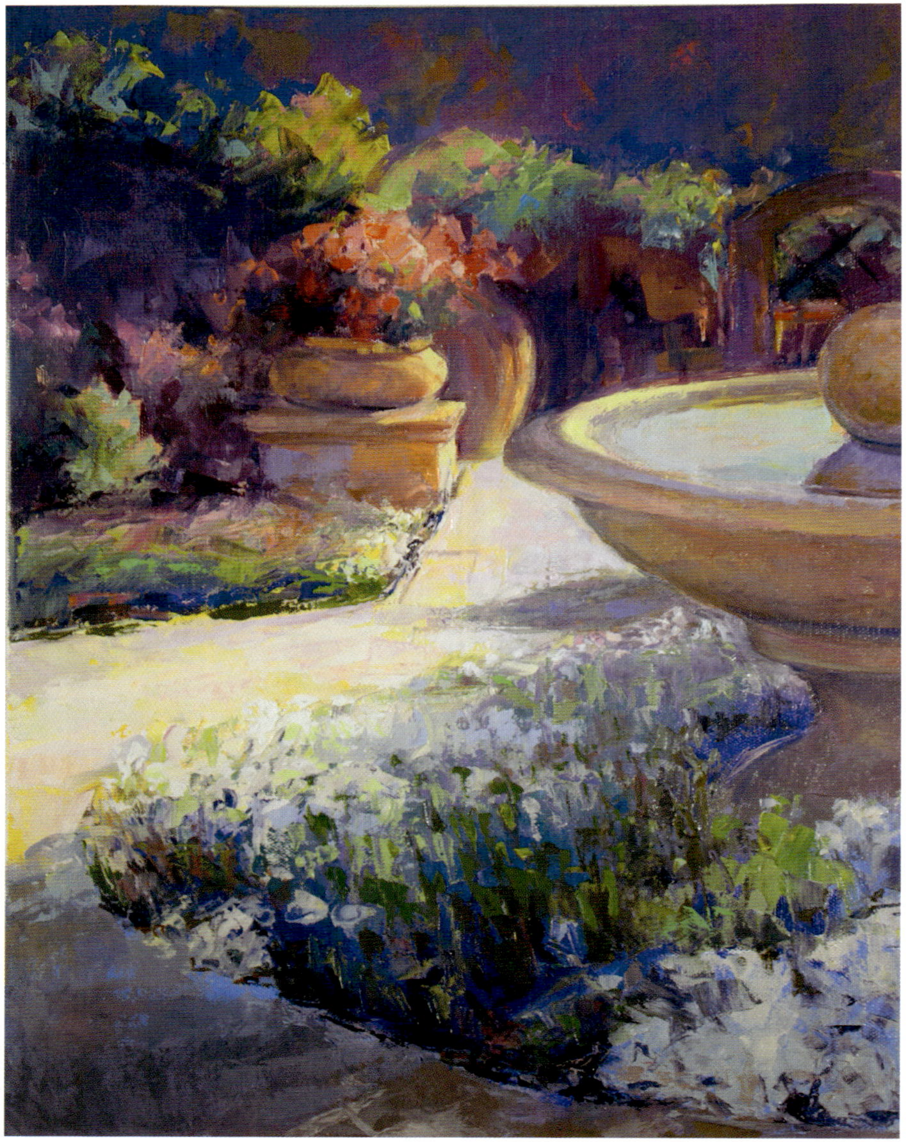

Garden Walk, 2014. Oil on canvas, 18" × 14".

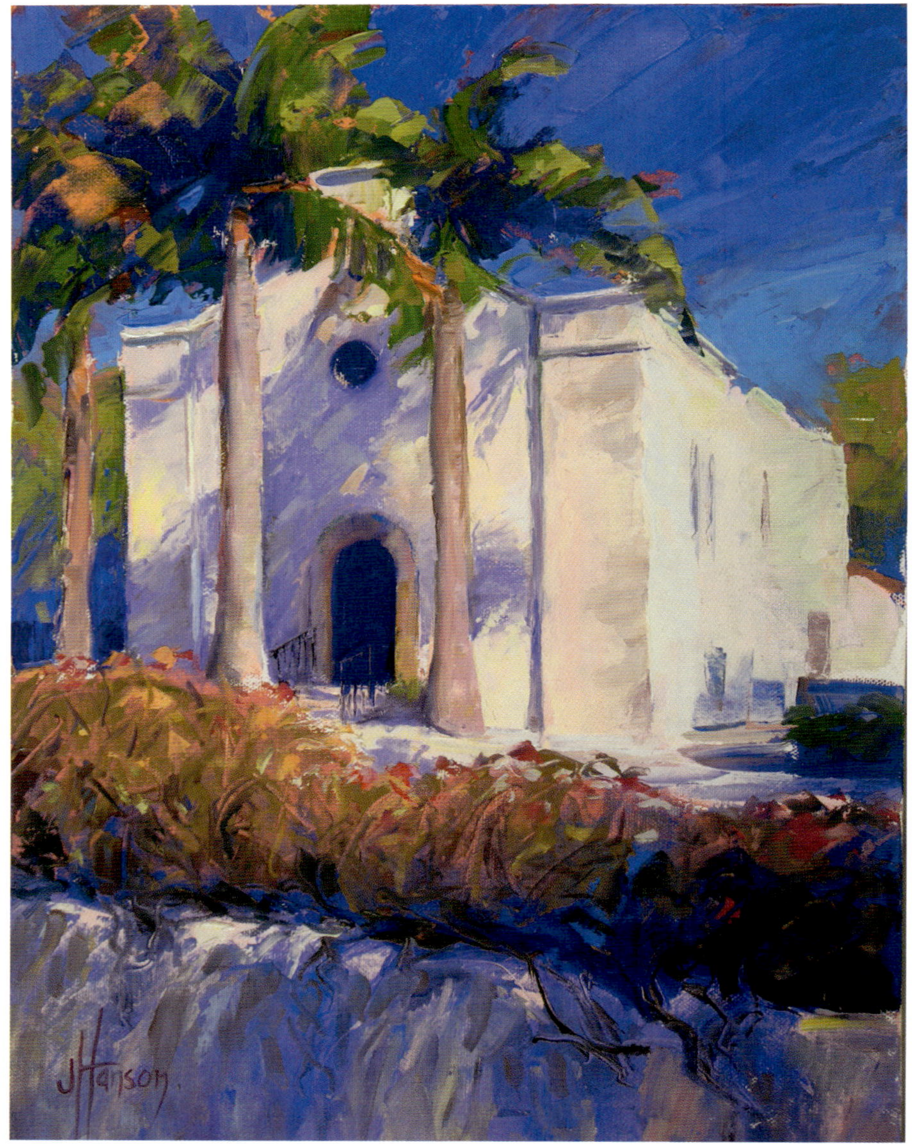

Boca Grande Church, 2012. Oil on canvas, 16" × 12".

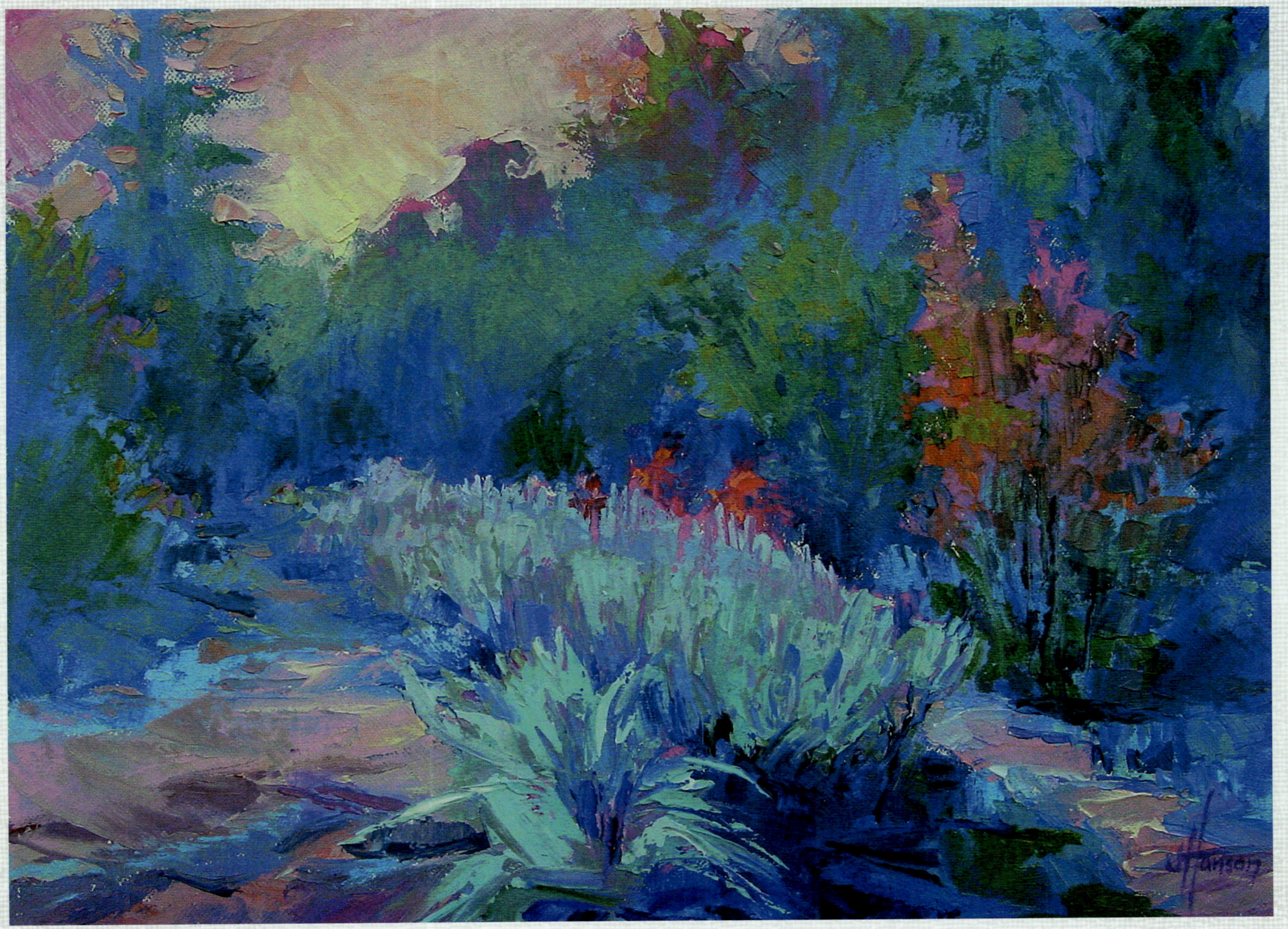

Greens, 2009. Oil on canvas, 12" × 16".

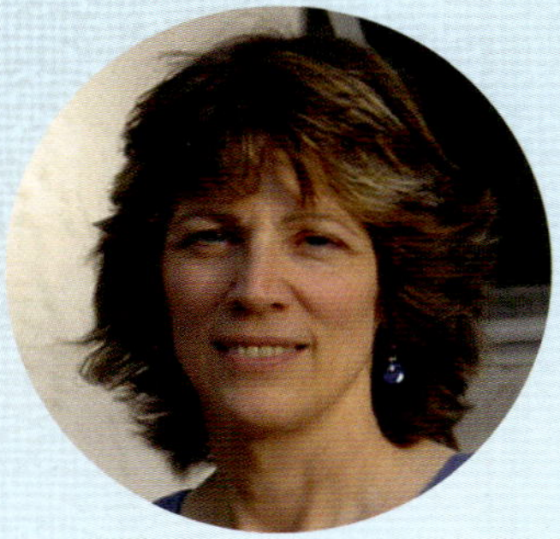

More about the Author

Since Julie was young, she has been drawn to beauty, whether in the natural world, the heavens above, or creatures great and small. This passion led her to art and to this book. But if you asked her what matters, she would tell you that she believes we have a responsibility to show gratitude for all that is good in the world and leave it a better place than we found it. This belief moved Julie to found a nonprofit cat rescue called Be the Change, Inc., and she has contributed most of her art career proceeds to this cause. Over the years, she has found loving homes for hundreds, if not thousands, of cats, kittens, and other animals who were to be euthanized or needed help in some way. She has chosen to act on her belief that we need to "be the change we want to see in the world." Her vision is to continue to support her nonprofit with proceeds from her art.

Be the Change, Inc., is a 501(c)3 cat rescue at 2235 Wason Road, Sarasota, Florida 34231. Donations are tax deductible.

Some of Julie's cat paintings are shown on the following pages.

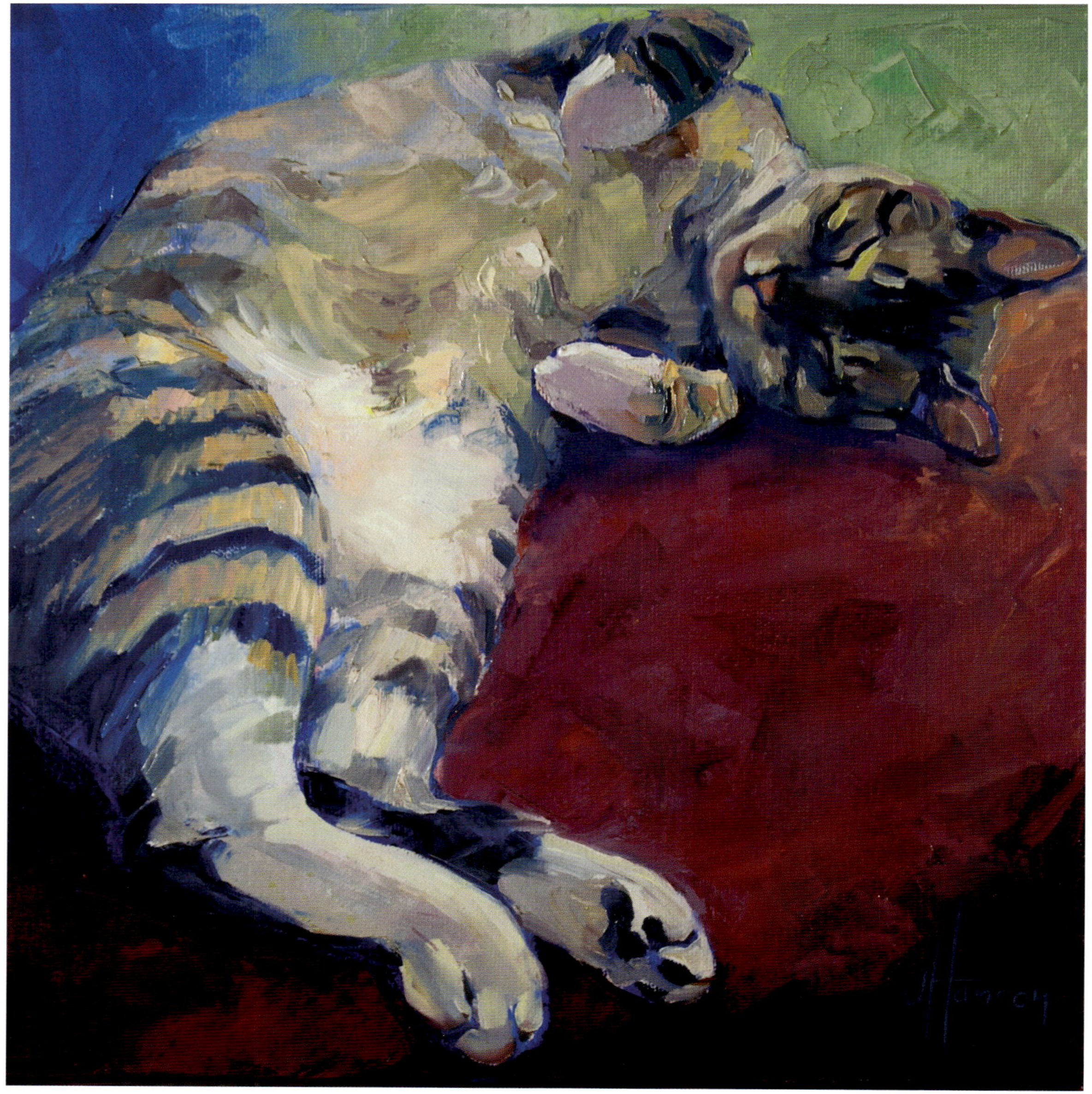

Angel, 2009. Oil on canvas, 12" × 12".

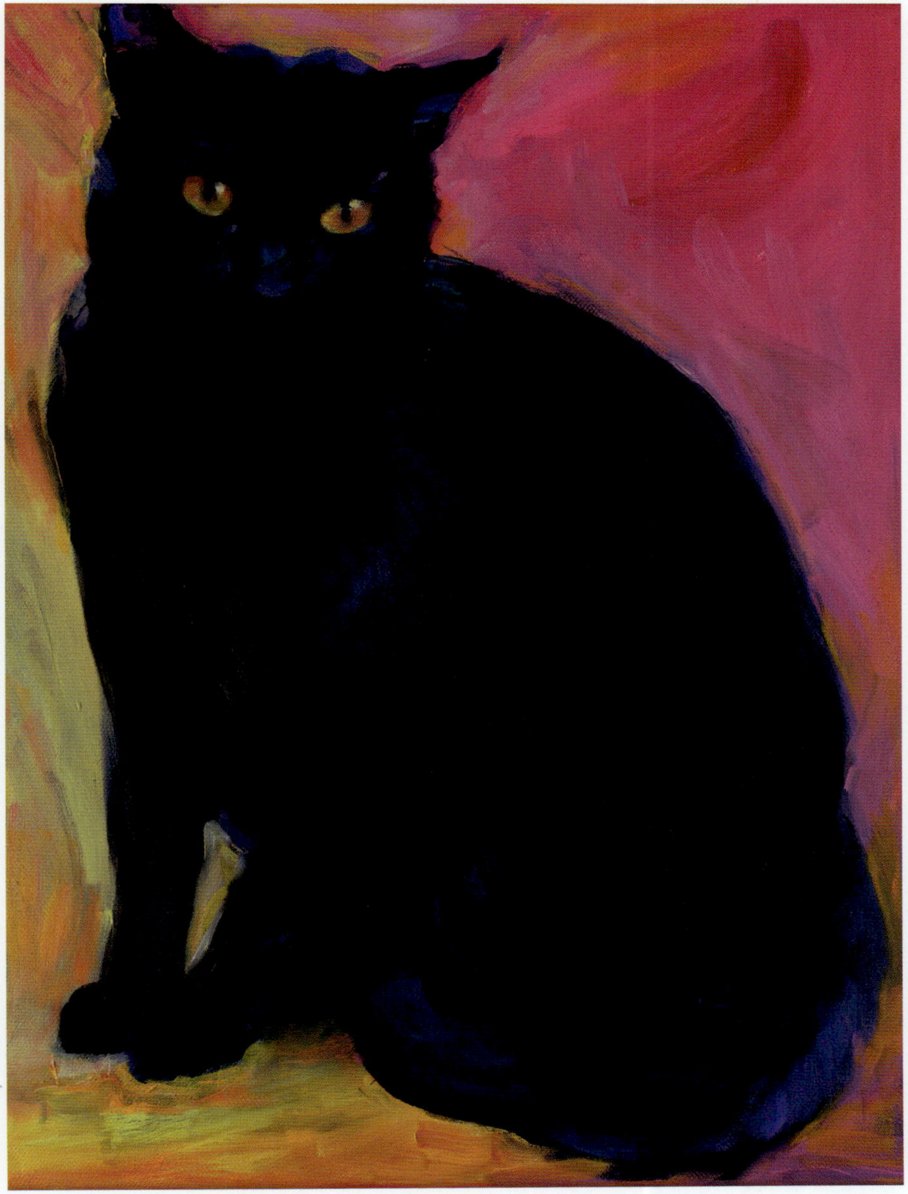

BJ, 2004. Oil on canvas, 9" × 12".

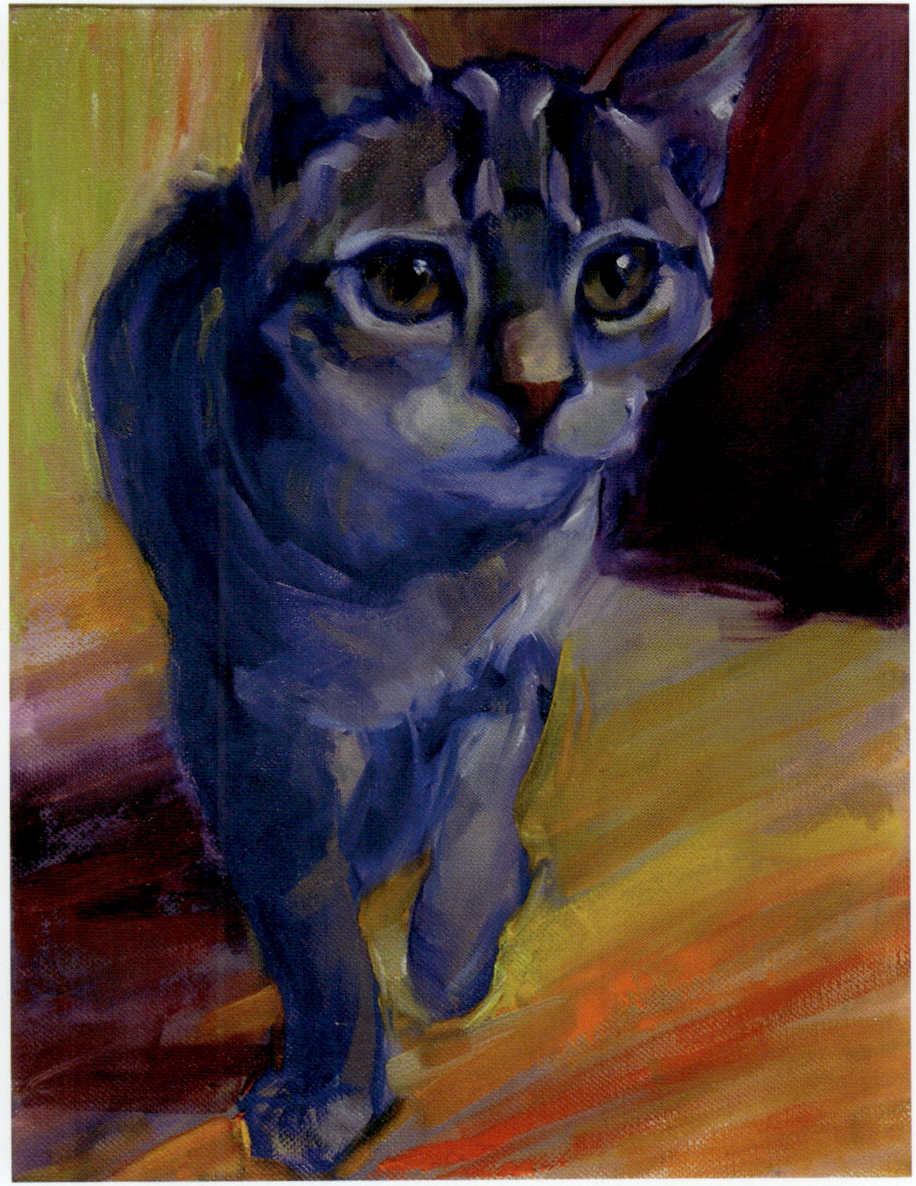

Kat, 2014. Oil on canvas, 12" × 9".

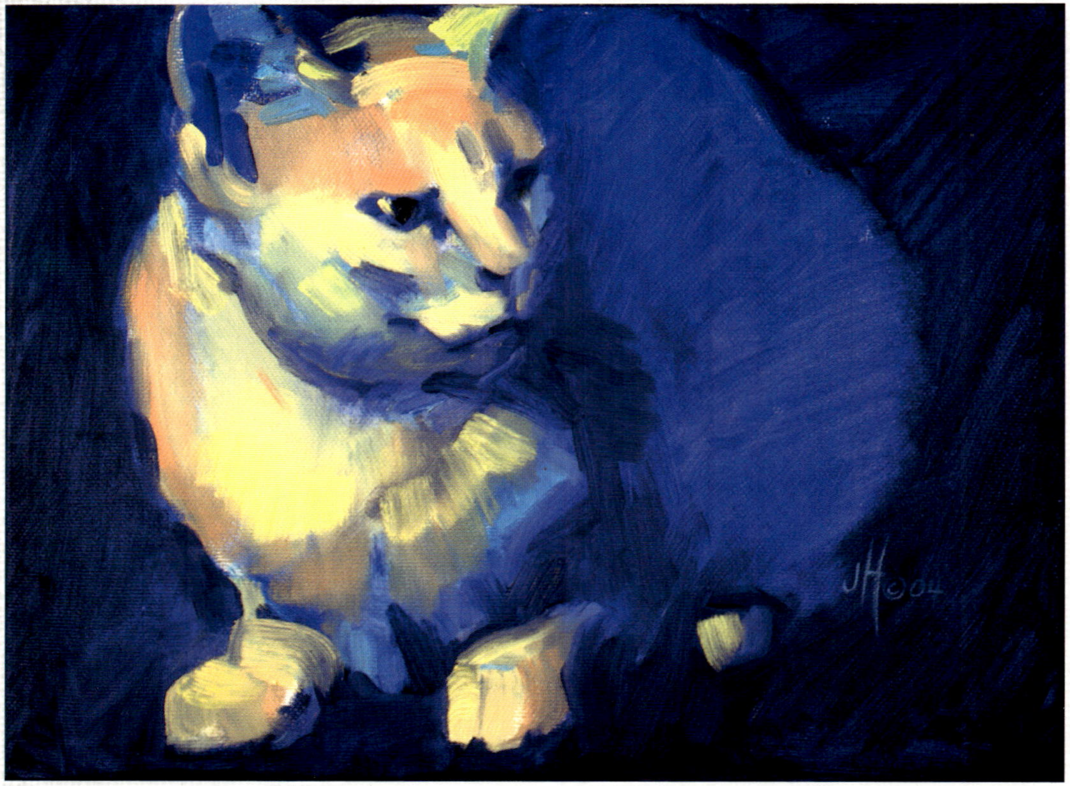

Smudge, 2004. Oil on canvas, 9" × 12".

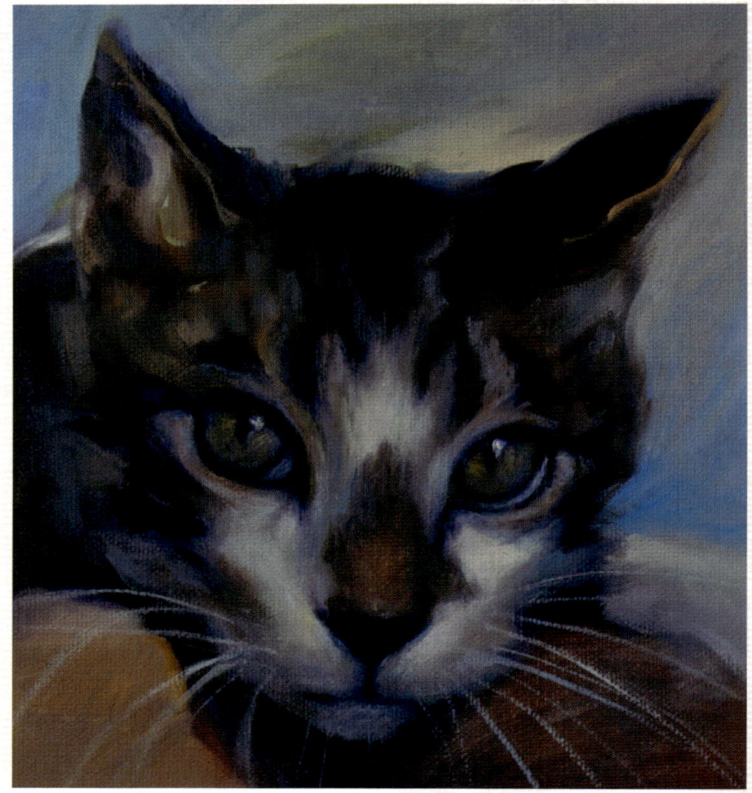

Justin, 2012. Oil on canvas, 12" × 12" (cropped).